The Chil
Spoke With Her Eyes

Erratum: Back cover
teacher should read
teach her

Also by Susan Stern

Rafi Brown and the Candy Floss Kid

The Child Who Spoke With Her Eyes

*A Mother's Spiritual Journey
with Her Disabled Child.*

SUSAN STERN

Red Bank Books

A CIP catalogue record for this book is available from the British Library

ISBN: 978-0-9574948-1-7
E-book ISBN: 978-0-9574948-2-4

Published by Red Bank Books 2018
80 Fog Lane Didsbury M20 6AG

Produced by Biddles Books Ltd, King's Lynn, Norfolk

For my mother, Efra

She told you stories about Georgie, the boy in a picture
pinned to the wall of her tiny kitchen. Fed you scrambled eggs
and rusks and sang nursery rhymes.
The only way you could speak was to shout,
spitting food across the floor
but she laughed, holding you closer,
my handicapped blue-eyed girl
with those extraordinary lashes sweeping your cheeks
and my blue-eyed mother, perhaps from the icebound
edge of Arctic Russia, or from the steppes,
laughing together, singing, each in your own way.

Chapter 1

When I was eleven or twelve, I thought people carried an invisible tower above their heads containing all their life experiences in coloured shapes, one above the other. Later I believed we carried ancestral memories in our souls as well as the past experiences of our parents and grandparents, although nothing in my odd childhood had prepared me for this curious thought. An odd childhood it certainly was: from the age of six I knew that I was Jewish, but with my family's committed socialism and my father's rabid atheism (the original Richard Dawkins), I had no idea what this meant. Not simply left-wingers, we were also vegetarian which in the 1960s made me a crank, an oddity, an outsider. But this was my father's religion and we observed it assiduously.

In 1957, I left home to study French at Leeds University. Over time, I became aware of a kind of emptiness, a void within my heart and began to seek a way, a spiritual path. During one summer vacation, I hitch-hiked with a flatmate to an international vegetarian conference held on the shores of Lake Constance. One broiling afternoon, as we sat with the English contingent in the shade of our tent, noisily debating *the meaning of life*, an older man approached.

'I couldn't help overhearing your discussion,' he said, to much laughter. 'Do you mind if I join you?'

I patted the grass beside me. 'Please do.'

'Have you ever considered reincarnation?' He proceeded to explain his beliefs while everyone sat gripped by his eloquence. Later he handed me a small orange-backed pamphlet he'd published: *The Plurality of Lives.* 'Please accept this.'

I read it, sitting on my sleeping bag, wondering at its simplicity, its profundity. I thought: this is what I believe. This wasn't an intellectual decision, rather recognition of something I felt I had always known. The soul must return and return as it moves towards *wholeness,* was how I explained it to myself.

Five years later I was back in Manchester where I met Sid Stern, the man who would become my husband.

Despite my father's outlandish atheism, he had many Jewish friends. If he had known that an invitation to a wedding would lead me to marrying a Jewish man in a synagogue, would he have gone? Probably, because he was convivial and extrovert, and was soon in conversation with Rachel and Abe Stern who were sitting at the same table. Like my mother, they were Londoners but lived in Didsbury, a leafy suburb of South Manchester where my parents had recently bought a house.

'You must come round for tea,' smiled Rachel, the tiny vibrant woman sitting opposite.

And this is where our story begins.

Sid was playing clarinet with his band in the back room of their house when I first met him. Watching quietly, I thought he was the true jazzman with his black hair, long sideburns, roll-neck black sweater and corduroy waistcoat. And how good-looking he was! He had studied pharmacy in Bradford, where he was captain of tennis and played clarinet in a trad band, progressing to modern jazz when he returned home.

He offered to introduce me to a group of people who met weekly in the apartment of a former girlfriend. But instead of making new friends as he'd suggested, we started going out together – and fell in love.

I was drawn to an unusual gentleness in him, yet he had such a quality of strength. We were two halves of one whole, meant to be together, I thought. Luckily, he felt the same. So we were engaged, and married in March 1965 at the synagogue in South Manchester where his family were members.

Once we were engaged, Sid bought a corner pharmacy in Gorton, East Manchester, and our house was next door. A very respectable working class area with rows of terraced houses, and where stone doorsteps of burnished dark red or yellow ochre were polished sternly by their owners every Friday morning.

Before the previous owners had modernised the house, it had been of the two up, two down variety, but we now possessed a splendid bathroom carved out of one of the back bedrooms. A great boon, since our neighbours were forced to use the outside privy in the stone-flagged yard. The pharmacist and his wife had also extended the house to create a room above the pharmacy, and this became our bedroom. Despite the four doors in the living room: to the dispensary, the kitchen, the tiny front sitting room and the fourth, opening on to a steep, narrow staircase, this had such a sense of dark embrace it reminded me of Lawrence's *Sons and Lovers*, and I would often imagine the women who lived here, mill workers in clogs, hurrying out at six in the morning through smoky, soot-blackened streets.

There was no such thing as central heating – Sid would light the coal fire in its black high grate and sit as close as he could, while I sat at the sturdy wooden table with its wartime utility kite mark we'd inherited with the business.

Most of my friends had married before the cut-off age of twenty-one and already had at least one child, whereas I was twenty-six, for heaven's sake. Yet it took me a year to decide, and even though I discussed every possibility, questions continued to whirl around my mind, and how could I bring a child into the world when I was so anxious, so immature, hardly grown-up? How could I ever become a mother?

One afternoon, watching young women, rollers in their hair half-hidden by a scarf, pushing their shining Silver Cross prams down Gorton Cross Street, smiling and proud as they showed off their new babies, I was filled with the startling desire to have one of my own. I imagined looking down at this little girl or boy, wondering if they would be like me or practical like Sid. Slowly I came to the big decision. On our first wedding anniversary in March 1966, giving Sid a mock terrified look, I said, 'I'm ready, or as ready as I'll ever be.'

After a short sun-lit holiday in Majorca, I was certain I was pregnant.

'I'll wait before going to the doctor,' I said, 'but I'm really dying to know if I am.'

Across the road from our pharmacy lived Dr Burt, the venerable Scottish doctor who came to discuss various medications with Sid. Two weeks later, sitting in his surgery and almost blushing, I said, 'I think I'm pregnant. How can I be sure?'

'You could wait and see if you've missed two periods, or you could take these tablets.' He held up a small white box. 'They're called *Primodos*. Innovative. If you don't bleed, you'll know you're pregnant. Why don't you give them a try?'

Back across Chapman Street, I slipped into the dispensary. 'Look, he's given me these pills.'

'He doles them out all the time.' Sid's gaze was on the tablets he was counting. 'I've dispensed loads.'

I was boiling the kettle on the ancient gas stove, when I heard Sid come through the connecting door into our living room. 'Here's your coffee,' I sang out, and brought in two beakers of Nescafé, handing him one as he opened the sports page of T*he Telegraph.*

Chapter 1

'I've taken the pills,' I told him, shaky but excited.

'Good. Now it's a waiting game.' He grinned, glancing down at the paper and back to me. 'So what are you going to do with yourself today?'

I considered his question. 'Perhaps I'll write about working in France and one of my adventures there.'

'Better show it to me before it's published.'

'If only,' I said wistfully.

'You never know.' Groaning, he rose from the fireside chair. 'Well, back to the grindstone.'

Going to open the window, a question flashed through my mind. Where would I put the baby's pram? It would have to be there, in the backyard. Not too near the dustbins and certainly not by the privy. Nor could it be by the wooden gate opening onto the ginnel, the narrow passage between the terraced houses. It would have to be close to the window where I could always see the baby.

Stop it. You don't know if you're pregnant yet.

What about that story I intended to write? Kneeling in front of the bookcase I had brought with me from Didsbury, I drew out my folder of stories and poems. I'd been moved by a little Algerian girl, whom I had seen begging on the beautiful *Cours Mirabeau* in Aix-en-Provence. I would write about her. Half an hour passed but nothing came. This was no good. I slid the folder back in its place.

Shopping – that's what I'd do. The butcher wouldn't deliver until Thursday, which gave me the excuse to cook something vegetarian. I exhaled; I would never be able to eat meat, even as I was learning to cook it for Sid.

Walking along Gorton's crowded High Street, I thought of what I would be doing right now if it hadn't been for the cuts: teaching English as a Foreign Language in the College of Adult Education. Such a great international atmosphere; the students were my age, and we had invited some of them to our wedding. I stopped in mid step. *What about those pills you've just taken? Something extraordinary might await us.* Smiling to myself, I entered the Maypole Grocery.

'Morning, Mrs Stern, you're looking cheerful.'

'You're right; it's a lovely day despite the cold.'

She nodded. 'And what can I get you?'

'A pound of cheddar, please.'

Laying a sheet of greaseproof paper on the scales, she placed the block of cheese upon it, cutting off a narrow wedge with the wire. 'I'm sorry, it's a little over. Is that all right?'

'That's fine, thank you.'

'There you are. Three shillings and six pence, Mrs Stern.'

That evening we had cheese and potato savoury dotted with slices of tomato and lashings of melted cheese, one of my mother's dishes. We enjoyed it so much, I secretly wondered if it was some kind of mini-celebration.

Days passed after taking the tablets. I waited, and nothing happened. Nothing at all. Trembly with anticipation, with awe, I whispered, 'You're pregnant.' In the bedroom, I took surreptitious looks at my body, stringy thin as ever, but my breasts were rounder, firmer. For once in my life, I was certain.

But then, nine weeks pregnant, I found something in the lavatory bowl. Small, spider-shaped, as though made from transparent skin. *What was it?* Panic stricken, I phoned Doctor Burt who came over at once and told me I had probably miscarried, a common enough event in first pregnancies.

'Take it easy, and try again,' he said.

After he'd gone downstairs, I took a jagged breath and persuaded myself he was right. Mustn't panic. Everything will be okay.

Chapter 1

Within a few weeks, I was definitely pregnant again. This time our doctor referred me to St Mary's Maternity Hospital in the centre of Manchester.

'You'll be having your initial antenatal appointment in the ninth week,' he said. 'They'll write to you.'

A week later I was checking the time of my first ante-natal appointment when a burst of pain seared my body, and doubling over, I cried out.

Sid was drinking his coffee beside the fire. 'What is it?'

'Pain,' I groaned, holding my stomach.

He ran to phone the doctor, returning at once. 'You must go straight to the hospital. '

'Hospital?'

'That's what he said. I'll call a taxi.'

'Can't you take me?'

He hesitated. 'Yes I will, even though it's illegal to leave the pharmacy unattended. Should be only half an hour there and back. '

We flew along Hyde Road, passing London Road Railway Station, and halted at the side entrance of the hospital, a gaunt, soot-blackened Victorian building.

'Phone me as soon as you know anything,' Sid said. Leaning towards me, he gave me a peck on the cheek, and sped away.

It had tall forbidding windows, more like a workhouse than a hospital, I thought, but making my way into the darkened lobby, I pushed through the swing door and gasped. A huge room stretched out before my gaze, with hundreds of pregnant women, their stockings rolled round their ankles, all seated on row after row of wooden benches.

As I stood transfixed, a passing nurse caught hold of me, 'Go and see the midwife in charge.' She indicated a woman wearing a white cap and blue uniform, who was perched at a high raised desk, her eyes scanning the room of women, as though they were her subjects.

I went to her and explained why I had come without an appointment.

'That's all right. They all have problem pregnancies here.' My heart began to pound. 'There's a toilet over there. Take off your suspender belt. Roll down your stockings, and come back. Then we'll sort you out. You see those cubicles down the side?'

I saw a series of white screens, some beneath the tall windows, and others against the wall. Perhaps a dozen in total.

'Is that where I'll see the doctor?'

'That's right. I'll call your name when one is free. A nurse will take your blood pressure and pop you on the scales.'

'Thank you.' I grasped my stomach as the pain intensified, even circling my back.

Taking my place on a bench, I sat, a specimen bottle in one hand, clutching at my stomach with the other, occasionally glancing at my neighbours who continued to face the front in silence. What a strange, horrible antenatal clinic, I thought. We could have been hundreds of naughty girls waiting to see the headmistress. Even the cream and green walls reminded me of my primary school. Finally, it was my turn.

The doctor was Chinese, small, gentle, deft-fingered. Handing her my card, I noticed it stated *Nine weeks pregnant.* Giving it a cursory look, she said, 'Please climb onto the bed and I'll examine you.' She palpated my stomach, took my pulse. 'You can get dressed now, Mrs Stern. Then I'll tell you what I've found.'

As I dressed, I had a dark feeling in the pit of my stomach as I tried to see what she'd written on my card. Her eyes were sombre when she turned to me.

'Mrs Stern, you're twenty weeks pregnant but I'm afraid you're contracting.'

'Twenty weeks?' I froze.

'Yes, and I want you in hospital at once, for observation.'

'Is it serious?' My heart was pounding; there was a pulse in my neck.

'I'm afraid so. Please wait at the central desk while I make the arrangements.'

Finally, the doctor said, 'We're sending you to the new gynaecological hospital on Wilmslow Road as there's no room here.'

'Where can I find a telephone?'

'In the lobby, by the front door.' The midwife sitting at her high desk smiled.

Pressing the pennies into the slot, I dialled our number and waited. At last Sid answered.

'Hello, I've seen the doctor.' I hesitated. 'She wants me to stay in hospital for observation.'

'Why? What has happened?'

'The obstetrician says I'm twenty weeks pregnant, not nine.' I didn't mention the contractions but rushed on. 'They're sending me to the new St Mary's Hospital.'

There was a long silence. 'Don't worry. I'll be fine. They're looking after me.'

I did not miscarry, thank goodness, the thing I most feared. After two weeks I was allowed to go home. With what joy did I climb the steep staircase to the bedroom and sink into our comfortable bed. How peaceful it was, away from the insistent noise of the hospital, the traffic below.

Little by little, my thoughts came to centre and I became aware of my body. *My bump*, as I had learned to call it. I began to notice tiny jumps, occasional fleeting kicks coming more frequently as the days passed. My mother and mother-in-law were reassured.

Nevertheless, something troubled me, something shaming, which I kept to myself. I didn't think I was a pessimist, but I was certainly a worrier and these disturbing events seemed to upset my flimsy confidence. Maybe it was the constant malaise, the pain when I walked, the strangeness of my body. Weird thoughts began to flit around my mind and I was finding it hard to believe in the existence of this baby. I felt as if I'd been invaded by some tiny alien being when I should have been cherishing a new life.

'You're unnatural,' I whispered to myself and told no one, positive that I was the only one in the world to think this way. Who'd have thought that years later, other women would say they felt exactly the same?

One night in December with only a month to go, and heartburn sending its fiery tongues at my throat, I knew I wouldn't sleep. Wandering into the room next door, 'the nursery', I could see the moon shining through the window on the surrounding streets of terraced houses, blinds down, curtains drawn, and everything still, as only busy streets could be at night. People were sleeping in their tightly packed houses, nestling close together.

I felt so frightened about this pregnancy my eyes filled with tears. Sitting down, I wrote in my diary, *I can't believe there's a living baby growing inside me. I'm afraid it will be born dead.* I didn't know where this had come from, didn't dare confide in anyone in case *saying* the very words would make it happen.

The days passed wearily until the twenty-eighth of January when the baby was due.

Chapter 2

On the first of February I had a sign: a small patch of blood. Surprised and thrilled, I telephoned the hospital.

'Come in if you like,' someone said, 'there's no hurry.'

Of course I went, leaning against a radiator in the ward for hours until a nurse found a bed for me, beside the nurses' station.

'You'll be going up soon,' called the women nearby. 'Always keep the bed near the door for those in greatest need.' They seemed to cackle.

Although I had read the family doctor's books about relaxation, and had pored over the strange images they'd used to illustrate the various stages of delivery, I really had no idea about what would happen. Nobody here said a word about the actual birth until that evening, when a nurse gave me a mixture she called *Mother's ruin,* potent and sweet tasting. 'You'll sleep well on that. Happy dreams'

Even though I feared being drowsy and doped, unable to deal with the pain, I swallowed the five millilitres of viscous green liquid, fell back against the pillows, and closed my eyes.

'Good girl,' said the same nurse, next morning, 'you're doing very well. You've been having some lovely contractions in the night. Two fingers dilated. Well on the way.'

Grabbing her hand, I muttered, 'What if I can't push?' This was another of my secret, inexplicable fears. 'What will happen?'

'Of course you can push.' She laughed. 'You'll be fine. We'll look after you.'

In one of the interim rooms, alone, white walls, high hard bed.

Terrified. My nightdress replaced by an open-backed hospital gown, a sheet stretched over my small swollen stomach. Pains spreading over me, down my legs, along my back, coming more frequently, more and more... Desperate, I wanted to escape them. Tearing me apart. I was not me at all. They had given me an injection which submerged me.

I tried to find a bell to call someone, anyone, as pain tore through my body. Black fear ran through my mind.

It was behind me, on the wall above my head. I managed to twist round, reach through the bars of the bed, press it again and again. *Please come, please come, help me.*

Minutes later a midwife walked in.

'The pain,' I groaned, 'it's tearing me apart.'

'I'll get you some gas and air.'

She was just leaving when something weird, totally unexpected happened – everything stopped. 'Nurse, come back. I can't feel anything,' I croaked. 'The pain's gone. All the contractions have disappeared.'

She marched back, frowning. 'Nonsense. I'd better take a look. Goodness, the head's there. You'll have to push. Start pushing now!'

'I can't. I can't. There are no more contractions.'

She ran away. People came, nurses pushed my bed to a delivery room full of light, a doctor spoke. 'We'll have to act at once, Mrs Stern.'

The obstetrician explained he would have to do a small cut so they could use forceps to deliver her. They said she was in distress, and I said, 'Of course,' and lay there calmly enough even though the forceps looked like my grandfather's tailoring scissors, but longer, narrower. The doctor strapped my legs up somehow, and gave me injections, and I felt nothing.

They pulled the baby out, and told me she was a girl, but then they laid her on some kind of table and attached a box to her mouth. I saw she had black hair sticking to her head but that's all I could make out from where I lay on the delivery bed. Above her on the wall was the kind of clock you'd see in railway stations, large, with black figures. It was eleven o'clock when she was born but when they removed the box, it was quarter to twelve.

Then a nurse took her away, and I was taken back to the ward, and I slept.

I remember nothing more about that day except they inserted a catheter, a common occurrence they told me after a forceps delivery, which was excruciating. It acted like a restrainer, fixing me to the bed, but as I was hollowed out from pain and fatigue I had no desire to move, and lay silent and still for hours.

Yet even in my hazy state, I knew something awful was happening. Even though my mind couldn't focus and I needed to shake the thick muzziness out of my head, I longed to ask the nurses where she was, and was she all right. They brought the other babies to the ward and I waited for mine, but no one carried her to me. Eventually, I managed to call to a passing nurse: Where's my baby?

'She's ill,' she said, keeping her eyes averted.

When Sid came in the evening, his face was drawn, trying not to cry. I think he'd seen her for some moments but he was too upset to speak except to say that she was very ill. He sat holding my hand until the bell rang for visitors to leave.

The following day the sister came over. 'Please take these tablets, Mrs Stern.'

'What are they?'

'Stilboestral. They'll stop your milk. And nurse will bind your breasts.'

Stop my milk? While the nurse wrapped a wide crepe bandage around my chest, fixing it with a large safety pin, I muttered, 'Why are you doing this?'

'You know your baby is very ill.'

I lay down again as she left, terror at my throat, wishing they would tell me more, wanting to ask them what was happening. Just tell me something.

A nurse bustled by. 'Have you tried sitting on the ring we gave you yesterday?'

I shook my head,

'Sit on it. Good for circulation. Don't lie down, Mrs Stern.'

So once again, I did as I was told. After ten minutes' wobbling on the ring, I climbed into bed, sliding down carefully, only too conscious of the pain. Forcing myself to be calm, I looked around. I let my gaze follow the beds down this long ward that seemed to stretch away like the steppes. There must have been forty women in this ward, all from the Greater Manchester area, and all, I knew, had difficult gynaecological histories, frequent miscarriages, still births. Closing my eyes, I tried to escape the dark feeling of dread in my heart.

My baby is three days old, I thought, and I *still* haven't seen her. My heartbeat racing, I asked a nurse how she was. She shook her head and told me to be patient. I didn't know what to think any more. I had never imagined how exhausted you could be after giving birth, and if I hadn't felt like a wet dishcloth, I would have gone to look for a phone to speak to Sid, for there was no telephone on the ward. I felt so helpless, so desperate at being kept apart from my baby, weak tears trickled down my cheeks. Nobody would give me an answer and I hadn't the strength to demand it.

'Tell me where she is!' I wanted to cry, but it was only a whisper in my head. 'I want to see her. Let me see my baby!'

This afternoon I watched them bringing the other babies to the ward to be fed. I saw the tiny bottles the nurses carried, putting one on each side cupboard. Once I called to a nurse, and she came to my bedside. 'She's still very ill,' she muttered as though she didn't want anyone to hear.

I turned on my side, trying to sleep.

'Mrs Stern.' I looked up over the bed cover. It was the sister who repeated, 'Mrs Stern, I need to speak to you.'

A nurse was drawing screens around my bed. It grew darker, the ward disappeared.

The sister, slim, dark-haired, her eyes grave, came close to me, and took my hand. Something told me I should be upright to hear what she was about to say. With an effort, I sat up, trying to lift myself to avoid the stitches by pressing my hands down on the bed. The nurse stood near the foot of the bed, her eyes down.

'Mrs Stern, I'm afraid your baby is very ill and we need to baptise her.'

Something like a buzzing of confusion made me close my eyes for a second. Baptise? What did she mean? Yes, I knew the baby was very ill, but baptise… I didn't grasp what this signified. But I found myself saying, 'You can't do that. We're Jewish. You can't baptise my baby.'

The sister turned to the nurse who handed her the notes she was carrying. She looked at the first page, drew a breath. 'Is there anyone we can speak to? A rabbi perhaps?'

'I don't know. I need to talk to my husband. Ask him what to do.'

'Of course.' She touched my hand again. I noticed her watch, pinned to her breast, shining as it moved gently with her breathing, and remembered it was Saturday, the Sabbath.

Although I couldn't tell her that I'd had no rabbi until we'd married in Sid's synagogue two years ago, I knew that a rabbi should not be disturbed until after sunset. Fortunately, it was

February, and the days were short – only a few hours before he could be contacted. When I explained this to her, the sister asked if Sid had visited today. I told her he was a pharmacist and still at work. 'Please give me his phone number,' she said. 'I promise to keep calling until I get through.'

They drew back the screens. I lay in bed, a sheet drawn up until I couldn't see the ward or any of the women – I did the first positive thing I had done in this pregnancy. Over and over again, hour after hour, I whispered, 'Awake, awake, Dvora!'

I had no idea how the words came to me. I didn't know they were from the biblical story of Deborah the prophetess, who'd saved the Jewish people. This was my call to our daughter. To Debra Vanessa, as we'd chosen to name her if we had a girl. Debra after Sid's grandmother, Deborah, and Vanessa, because we thought it was beautiful.

I prayed that my spirit would awaken her to the world.

In a mysterious way, calling to my daughter had drawn me out of the acquiescent, helpless state I had been in since her birth; I began to imagine seeing her and vowed to find where she was, whatever was happening and however I felt. I was still awake around one o'clock on Sunday morning when a little nurse came into the ward, making a beeline for my bed. I saw she was smiling.

'Would you like to see your baby? She's beginning to feed!'

I felt as though the sun was shining.

'Oh, yes.'

Ignoring the stitches, the weakness, the wobbly feeling in my legs, I threw off the heavy yellow bedcover, slid out of bed to the cold floor, and the little nurse helped me put on my dressing gown. My heart racing, I followed her along a corridor into the nursery, where there seemed to be hundreds of identical babies, most of them asleep in rows but with one distinction, their lacy cot blankets were either blue or pink.

She led me to the second cot, and I saw her for the first time, my little Vanessa, covered by a flannelette sheet. I saw her face, her black hair, her amazingly long black eyelashes, and the pink candlewick bedspread tightly tucked in. Tears rolled down my cheeks but elation surged through me. *Love.* I wanted to pick her up, hold her close to me forever. I heard the tiny sighs, snuffles, mews of the babies surrounding us, and here, at last was the one I had carried inside me during those strange, long months. Even the harsh clean smell of the hospital was almost sweet, in here.

The little nurse said, 'Cot-nursed, but she's beginning to thrive.'

'Can I hold her?' I leaned forward, seeing her eyes flicker beneath closed lids, and wondered if she was dreaming at only three days old.

'Not yet. She must be kept especially warm. See, she has two blankets to maintain her body heat while the others have one.' Then I noticed there were indeed two blankets, one folded above the other, not quite aligned with the one below. 'Instead of an incubator,' she continued, but seeing my anxious start when she said the word, she added, 'Now don't worry. She'll be fine.'

I stayed until I began to shiver, and she took my arm, walking me back to bed where at last I slept.

Thank goodness, nobody said any more about baptising our baby. I would slip into the nursery to see her and a nurse would remark, 'She's eating and sleeping now.' I would sit by the cot, watching her breathe, this tiny mysterious being who seemed to have chosen to stay.

She was two weeks old when the paediatrician spoke to me on the ward, 'You can go home,' he smiled. 'Your baby's all right now.' He paused. 'Although I can't predict the future.'

Chapter 3

We drove home through foggy, sombre streets but Vanessa lay warm in my arms, swathed in a shawl my mother had brought. Anxiously watching her face as she slept, I noted every breath, every tiny grimace, then I would glance out of the steamed up window, eager to be safe from the bitter cold.

'I've fixed an electric fire to the wall of her room,' Sid said, when I asked him about the temperature in the house, insisting it must be the same as the hospital. 'There's another one on the floor. And I've banked up the fire in the living room. It'll be roasting.'

I carried Vanessa through the tiny lobby opening directly into the front room, then straight into our living room. An enormous fire blazed in the hearth, filling the room with heat, and I was reassured. Without taking off my coat, I carried Vanessa up to her room, overlooking Highmead Street.

Unwinding the shawl, I draped it over a chair, and placed her carefully in the yellow carrycot, given by a cousin, my fingers awkward, stiff with cold. Thankfully, she continued to sleep, so I went along to our room next door, collapsing on the bed.

'Why don't you get *into* the bed?' Sid had come in with my case.

'She's due for a feed any minute.'

'So put on your dressing gown, it's more relaxing.'

'You're right. I'll get undressed.'

He went back to work, but unable to rest, I kept creeping next door, watching for signs of her waking up, and when she continued to sleep, I would lie down again, but as though on a spring, I'd be back in the nursery, peering into the cot.

And then, just as I was back in my bedroom, I heard it – a kind of whoopy intake of breath, and her cry, which became louder, ever more piercing. Glancing at my watch, I saw it was two hours and a half since the last feed. But they told me every three hours – what should I do? I hovered over her, my heart racing, but now her crying had reached a terrible crescendo. Still shaky, wobbly, I ran downstairs and took one of the eight feeds of half-strength Cow and Gate baby milk lined up in the fridge, that Sid had already prepared.

Back upstairs, I warmed the milk in an electric bottle warmer, easier than using a jug of hot water like most people did, and a benefit of having the pharmacy. All the while she was screaming horribly, and I was shaking with fear. I lifted her from the cot, hesitated. Didn't they say I should change her nappy before feeding her? By now, she had become a demented little elf, her face bright red, her hands clenched in tight fists. Feed her! I'd change her afterwards.

Breathe, I told myself, remember what the midwife had told me when I was taking my first steps in 'how to feed your baby.' Not too much, not too fast. Don't tip the bottle or hold it too high. Above all, stop for wind, or she'll be sick. And so, sitting on the edge of the small leatherette settee I had brought from home, with Vanessa still screaming, I rubbed the teat against the side of her mouth, she turned and, thankfully, began to suck.

There was a knock on the door. Mrs Whiteley, the wonderful lady we'd inherited with the business, was standing there. She came daily to clean the shop and wash medicine bottles and her great dream was to leave her terraced house, two doors away from ours, and be rehoused in a nice area with a garden.

'I don't want to disturb you, Mrs Stern – oh, isn't she beautiful' She advanced two steps round the door. 'But there's a nurse here, come to see the baby.'

A woman wearing a blue uniform marched in. 'I'm the special nurse from the Town Hall,' she announced. 'We visit all babies who've been at risk at birth. I'll be coming every day for a week or two. So let's be seeing her.'

Taken aback, I meekly allowed her to lift Vanessa from my arms.

Holding her up to the window, she remarked, 'Well, little lady, I'm sorry to interrupt your feed but we need to have a good look at you.'

'I've only just got home,' I muttered.

She glanced back at me, her lips pursed. 'No wonder we're run off our feet. They had you down for today. Never mind, I'll finish her feed and then leave you in peace.'

She sat beside me. In the blink of an eye, she'd given the baby the rest of her feed, and brought up the wind. Vanessa lay content in her arms.

'Here you are.' She passed her back to me. 'Do you have any questions?' I shook my head. 'Use your common sense. Takes time to get used to a baby, and for them to get used to you. Don't worry; all new mothers are the same. You'll soon get into the swing of things.' At the door, she pronounced, 'Always put her to sleep on her stomach. Lying on her back she could choke if she brings up any food. With her head on one side, you just wipe it away.'

She was right, and looking after a baby, I soon discovered, was a twenty-four-hour occupation, relieved once a day by the special nurse from the Town Hall who seemed to have uncanny powers of knowing when the baby was satisfied with two and a half ounces of milk, or needed perhaps a little more, And why did she settle and feed in their arms, yet she would hesitate and wriggle in mine? An hour to feed her, half an hour to change her, one hour's break, and we'd start all over again.

As for the night feeds – Sid and I were supposed to take turns for the middle-of-the night feed whenever that might be, (any time between two and four in the morning), but there was some desperate, invisible bond between me and her which caused me to wake even before I heard that strange whooping, piercing cry. I would fall out of bed and warm up the bottle, snatch her up from the carrycot ready for the feed. The following morning Sid would complain he hadn't had his 'turn.'

Nowadays, young fathers talk about: 'When we were pregnant' or, 'I always feed him like this.' In the nineteen sixties, you would never see a man pushing a pram – perish the thought – and it was a rare and precious gift to have a husband who would even think of feeding his baby – and I was very grateful! What is more, with calm chemist's hands, he would make up the eight bottles of half cream Cow and Gate baby milk – formula, as they say nowadays, which is more in keeping with a pharmacist's skills. Eight feeds, one every three hours night and day. When she awoke desperate with hunger after two and a half hours, I still panicked. Should I make her wait or should I feed her at once, and end up with two night feeds instead of one?

I told myself to be calm and decisive – and always failed.

Then there was the bath. What an ordeal. I would get the cotton buds, baby shampoo, talcum powder and two towels, one to cover the changing mat, one to fling around her, then the Halex bath on its stand. But I never knew if it was better to bathe her while she screamed or wait until after her feed because I was so terrified of her losing body heat, which she always did. She hated the bath and by the time this torture was over, she'd fall asleep on my knee without feeding. I wondered if I should bathe her after the feed when she'd be sick.

I cheated, omitting the bath for a couple of days, thinking it crazy to do it. I didn't believe a tiny baby could get so dirty, but it was essential, the nurses told me. More guilt.

After two weeks at home, I made that awful, wrenching transition from living and breathing baby, wearing my dressing gown, to donning a skirt and blouse in order to face the world. We went to the nearby park with my mother-in-law Rachel, who proudly pushed Vanessa in our hand-me-down yellow carrycot, complete with its new transporter wheels. Sid took photographs and we were all enchanted.

My mind had shattered into a myriad of coloured objects, bottles, nappies, and baby paraphernalia. I continued to live and breathe 'baby,' hardly aware of night or day until one morning, as I sat on the leatherette sofa in Vanessa's room, and a weak sun pierced through the leaden sky above the chimney pots, light caught her face as I held her in my arms – and she smiled. I gazed down at her open eyes, which no longer reminded me of those of a three-week-old kitten. Here was a little person beginning to recognise someone else. I shook my head in wonderment, whispering 'Hello, my lovely girl. We'll have to wait to tell your daddy.'

Her tiny mouth curled into a smile again. The nights drifting into days, the constant feeding, the uncertainty – it was all worthwhile now.

When Sid came to eat his sandwiches at one o'clock, sitting in his usual chair by the fire, I couldn't restrain my excitement.

'She smiled! She smiled at me this morning!'

'Sure it wasn't wind?'

'Sure I'm sure. It was different. She really looked at me, and then, she smiled.'

I went to the little bookshelf I'd brought from home, and selected our baby bible, Doctor Benjamin Spock's *Baby and Childcare* in its yellow and black cover. Unlike the theories of

Truby King, followed by my mother, with his rigorous four-hour feeding regime, potty training the baby from a few weeks old, Dr Spock's ideas were radical: it was the mother who had instinctive awareness of her baby's needs. This clearly hadn't filtered through to the medical or nursing professions, and as we felt so ignorant about looking after a tiny baby, we frequently consulted his book.

'See, he says it's definitely around the sixth week. And she was six weeks old yesterday.'

He glanced at it briefly. 'I was joking, didn't you realise?'

I have to admit that I didn't always recognise his jokes – still don't – they were dry, and in those days, I hadn't much of a sense of humour. But that very evening, when he took her up to bed, Vanessa repeated this mini-miracle. 'Wasn't wind,' he acknowledged when he came down to eat.

I wasn't much of a cook. To make the transition into becoming a non-vegetarian cook, my mother had taught me about cooking fish whereas my mother-in-law had instructed me in the arts of koshering and cleaning meat, and how to make chicken soup, which I continued to find disgusting.

'First you sprinkle salt all over it and leave it for an hour, to kosher it. You clean off the salt with plenty of water. Chop up an onion, a couple of carrots, some celery, and season it, then pour boiling water over the fowl. Then you skim the muck off. When the water is clear you leave it to cook for three or four hours.'

'How do I know it's done?'

There were no recipes, it was a pinch of this or a handful of that, and though I knew how to cook simple vegetarian dishes using a recipe or following my mother's instructions, meat was alien territory. I still marvel that presently, half the first world has become vegetarian, if not vegan, which they claim, is the only healthy, honourable way to eat, whereas in those unenlightened days, and to the uninitiated, vegetarian food used to consist of eggs and limp salads.

But over a lamb chop for him and a nut cutlet for me, we sat together at the sturdy dining room table, still with its wartime utility kite mark beneath the flap, and toasted our daughter's first milestone in a drink of orange squash for me and a strong black cup of 'Stern' tea for Sid.

When I remember how frazzled I felt in those early weeks looking after a tiny baby, I think how it is for a young, fledgling mother today. There are midwife groups, the Internet, Facebook I suppose. And kindly unobtrusive grandmothers who understandably, aren't always consulted. In this far-off black-and-white time, if you lived as we did, in a working-class area, young women frequently lived with their families or very close by and their mothers cared for the baby while their daughters worked. Though I sometimes asked my mother her advice, our respective mothers did not interfere and as they lived some distance from our house in Gorton, I couldn't pop round for a chat. On our own, however, we were learning just a little about this tiny person who had clearly chosen to stay.

The only wisdom I had gleaned during my postgraduate certificate of education which I adored, were psychological theories about encouraging children to blossom, from the writings of Maria Montessori and Rudolf Steiner, somewhat useless when it came to looking after a newborn baby.

Then something changed in Vanessa's behaviour.

She developed a fierce reaction to being lifted up when lying on her stomach and would scream hysterically, as though terrified of being moved from a foetal position, where I imagined she must feel safe. If hunger stirred her sufficiently, I hoped that she would open herself up to the world and if I could persuade her to take the bottle for a few moments while I held her with firm determination, she would feel a wall of protection from my arms and body, and relax her guard to take some food.

One afternoon when my parents were due to visit, I had put Vanessa to sleep in her carrycot in the front room with the door open so that I could reach her before the terrible crying began. On this particular Saturday, my mother said something which startled me but which I forgot soon afterwards in the *ongoingness* of life. Dad walked in first, my mother followed carrying her weighty handbag and an assortment of bags in the other hand. My father settled in the easy chair beside the fire, making sure the window to the yard was closed as he disliked draughts, whereas Mother always felt the heat, which I attributed to her Russian ancestry.

'Tell me as soon as she wakes,' I called, stepping into the kitchen to make the tea. Placing all her bags on the table, Mother followed me in. 'I've got something to tell you,' I said, catching her arm. 'She smiled at us yesterday.'

'I'm so pleased. I was wondering when that would happen.'

She carried a cup of tea to my father, who took it without looking up. He was deep in the *Daily Telegraph* Sid read for the sports pages but which my father deplored for its right wing attitudes. At home, we had read the socialist *Daily Herald* until it disappeared, followed by the *News Chronicle*. We frequently bought the communist *Daily Worker*.

Dad folded the newspaper, returning it to the rack, and held up *The New Statesman*, the liberal weekly.

'You should read this,' he urged, waving the newspaper as though to prove something.

'Dad, I barely have time to think.'

'Can't you make a minute?' He frowned and returned to the paper.

Mother pointed to the packages on the table.

'I've finished knitting the suit for the baby. It's blue, but I don't think it matters do you?' I shook my head. 'Here's some fruitcake I baked yesterday.'

Her cake was famous, and I was cutting a slice when I heard the familiar whoopy intake of breath, the cry that grew shriller, ever more piercing. It was time for a feed.

I snatched up the bottle of baby milk and ran into the front room, with Mother close behind me. In the cot, Vanessa's hands were flailing above her head, and as I turned her over, I saw her face screwed up in desperation. I lifted her; she stopped crying for a moment, screamed again. Pressing her body against mine, I managed to get the bottle into her mouth. Mother watched intently with more than a little anxiety in her eyes.

Nothing was said after Vanessa finished the bottle. We ate cake, drank tea and finally it was time for my parents to leave. At the front door, Mother said, 'Has she ever put her hands in her mouth when she's hungry, or sucked her fingers?'

'No I've never seen anything like that. Why?'

'Just wondering.'

Chapter 4

Two weeks later, at about three in the morning, the sound of her shrill crescendo awakened me; I warmed up the bottle and offered it to her. After a few seconds of sucking, she began to scream. I put her back in the cot where she slept for some minutes, then screamed again. I lifted her out of the cot. As I held her in my arms, I felt her back grow rigid until she was actually standing upright, screaming and screaming. How could a baby two months old stand up on her mother's knee?

She was some little alien being standing rigid in my arms with her feet plucking at my nightdress. My heart began to race, I tried various explanations – she didn't like the teat, she couldn't suck it, the milk must be too hot or too cold. But how could that be – it was the right temperature to my hand. I didn't want to wake up Sid, asleep in the other room. Carefully I put the baby onto her stomach which made her feel safe, then with a quick glance at her, I went out and down the dark stairs, into the sitting room, unlocked the door between our house and the dispensary, and crept behind the counter in the darkened shop.

Feverishly I searched through the drawer that held the teat boxes, finding two similar to those she liked. In the early morning light, for now it was about half past four, I blunted a darning needle in the gas flame on the kitchen stove to enlarge the teat hole and ran back up the stairs. But still she refused. I picked out the original teat from the small container of Milton sterilising solution, the one good teat she preferred, engorged like some obscene object, and offered her the bottle. She sucked for a few seconds. Stopped and screamed once more.

Now nothing, none of the methods known to me would silence this desperate sound. Neither patting, nor walking nor sucking made the slightest difference. My last resort was to wake Sid, the thick walls masking the sound of the baby's screams. If he could just feed Vanessa over my shoulder, I thought, it might work.

I put her back in the cot. The screaming stopped. She slept.

It was half past seven. I crept back to the bedroom where we discussed what I should do. I would take Vanessa to the local clinic as soon as we'd had breakfast. Fortunately at this age, I didn't need to dress her. She could stay in the Babygro in her little cot and I would wheel her to the clinic twenty minutes' walk away.

But the clinic doctor told me that I was an anxious mother and the baby simply sensed my anxiety. That's why she wouldn't feed. 'Go home,' he said, 'and try again.'

For three days we continued in this way until afraid and desperate, I returned to the clinic. A social worker weighed the baby and we both saw she had lost weight. 'I'll refer you to the Children's Hospital at St Mary's.'

It was back to the hospital, to the small babies' wing behind the postnatal section. At the reception desk, the sister said, 'Don't worry, Mrs Stern, feeding problems are common to babies who've had a difficult arrival into this world. Just you leave her with us, we'll sort it out.'

The nurses would feed her, she said, and meanwhile she would be under observation. With my woolly, unformed views about the attachment of mothers and babies, I was frightened that a separation from me would cause her some indefinable damage. Naturally I didn't say this to the sister but when I hesitated, she leaned towards me, 'You go home and get some sleep. I bet you haven't had any since she was born.'

I gave the baby to a nurse waiting impatiently behind me, and watched her carry Vanessa away, but I couldn't bear to leave. The sister was flicking through her file, already thick with information. Lifting her head, she said, 'Don't worry, Mrs Stern. You'll be back soon enough. We'll probably ask you to stay for a few days to learn how to feed her again.'

I couldn't keep away and was back next day. In the small ward, a nurse was sitting beside her cot, feeding Vanessa with one of those elongated hospital teats she had persistently refused at home. 'Look, she's taken nearly the whole feed.'

I turned my gaze away, thinking how useless I was. Good thing the nurse couldn't see my face.

Various tests were carried out. The electroencephalogram, used to measure the electrical activity of the brain, showed normal, but they said it was really too soon to show with any accuracy. Over the next couple of days they showed me how they gave her a small sedative before every feed to quieten her alarm, thickening the milk with cereal which they gave her by spoon at every feed. On several dramatic occasions at home, I'd tried giving her baby rice, but it had landed on me, a mess of white globules surrounded by milk.

Worn out by broken nights, the difficult pregnancy, the challenging delivery, I realised I was a nervous wreck and it wasn't surprising she refused to let me feed her. Finally, the sister asked me to come in and stay for a few nights, sleeping in a small bed in a tiny room at the end of the ward. Learning again to feed and burp her; I felt such a fool, so inadequate, under their constant scrutiny I believed, although this was probably my paranoia to think this. But I made a great discovery: stopping to bring up the wind at every half ounce of milk, she would suck, and I smiled to myself – I was making progress.

29

We finally left the hospital when she was nearly three months old. Since Sid was absorbed in modernising the pharmacy, we stayed with his parents in Didsbury. At that time, before I had come to know my mother-in-law Rachel, I would rather have gone to my parents, but they had tenants on the middle floor of their house nearby, and my sister had the top floor bedroom so it was out of the question. But Mother came often to see us and as always, Rachel made her most welcome.

Rachel, whom I always thought of as my 'little mother-in-law,' had travelled with her mother from Warsaw to London, at the age of nine. She'd left school at twelve to become a seamstress, living in the East End of London, surrounded by family and friends. Speaking Yiddish with her mother at home, she was a true Londoner, having a Cockney accent.

Rachel directed the household, maintained the Jewish traditions she knew, lighting the Friday night candles, the *yarzeit* candles to commemorate someone's death. A home-maker and wonderful cook – she made chicken soup, chopped and fried fish balls, fried fish, chopped liver, all the traditional Eastern European food. She loved beautiful things and was always smartly dressed, as they both were.

She cooked, chatted, encouraged, and everything about her was neat, sparkling, ordered. One afternoon, she found me crying at the bottom of the stairs.

Hands on her hips, she faced me, her lips pursed, 'You must talk yourself in.'

Translated from the Yiddish, I guessed this meant: *You must believe in yourself.* I would remember that on many occasions in the future. But in their large, comfortable bedroom at the back of the house, I laboured to feed Vanessa, until I knew we should go back to the hospital. I was in despair. I couldn't even feed my own baby.

Once there, I discovered that a nurse had mistaken the dose of the sedative and I had been giving Vanessa only a quarter of what was prescribed. This time it was a thin bristling woman doctor who saw us. When I told her of my uncertainties in handling the baby, she snapped, 'There's nothing wrong with you. It's the baby who is not normal.'

I recoiled, feeling heat flood my neck, up to my hairline. I held myself in but wanted to shout, 'How dare you say such a thing? Of course it's me. Vanessa is reacting to my anxiety!'

Although I swallowed it, I didn't forget. Here was a woman who was supposed to heal but had a tongue like a blade. Something was taking shape in my mind: the medical hierarchy was becoming my enemy. Doctors saw patients as drones, on the lowest level of the triangle, invisible, unimportant. To be ignored.

We stayed this time for two or three days.

One afternoon I was sitting beside the cot when the ward sister approached, deep in conversation with a short bespectacled man.

'This is Doctor Epstein,' she said when she reached me. 'We've asked him to take a look at Vanessa.'

Nobody had said anything about consulting another doctor, and I frowned.

Doctor Epstein bent to shake my hand. 'Good afternoon, Mrs Stern. Is that all right with you?'

I liked him. He was warm, empathetic.

'Of course,' I murmured.

Vanessa was lying on her back, one hand clutched in a 'left' salute, the other arm stretched out across the mattress. He took the hand and she curled her fingers around his forefinger. He talked to her, she smiled. Placing his hands, one under each of her legs, he moved them gently in a sort of kicking movement.

'At the moment,' he said gravely, turning to me. 'I can't tell you if there's anything wrong with your child. There is something lacking in the muscle tone. Would you like to bring her to my clinic at the Duchess of York Hospital?'

I felt heat rush to my hairline and I nodded.

'I'll arrange an appointment, Mrs Stern.'

He shook my hand and left.

I stared down at Vanessa, his words *anything wrong with her* circling my mind. My heart beat faster; I wondered what on earth this could mean. Moments later the sister returned. 'Lovely man, isn't he?'

'What kind of doctor is he?'

'Oh, he's the world specialist in cerebral palsy.'

A couple of weeks after we had returned to Gorton, the letter with an appointment to see Doctor Epstein arrived. Meanwhile, I rejoiced in watching our baby smiling at everyone and devouring her meals. I would give her four feeds a day when most babies were taking three and she grew chubby and rosy, a relief and a delight for us both.

She was five months now; her black baby hair had disappeared and fine blonde hair had become a golden cap over her head. It contrasted wonderfully with her large blue-green eyes and the long black lashes fringing her cheeks. And that perfect little nose, that delicate bone structure, where had they come from? From the Sterns, I told Sid, although he didn't care which family genes predominated so long as she thrived.

'She's been doing so well.' I handed him the appointment letter. 'I can't believe there's anything wrong. The doctor must have made a mistake. But of course, we have to go.'

The consulting rooms were in a large white Regency house opposite the main hospital. A flight of steps led to the front door; inside rows of seats faced the far wall with their backs to the entrance. There were huge pictures of Minnie Mouse, Mickey

Mouse and Donald Duck on the walls, while nurses in their short blue dresses, watches swinging across their chests, marched to each patient. With Vanessa in my arms I waited for over an hour but retained nothing about the other little patients, who they were or why they might have been there.

'Doctor Epstein is ready to see you in his room.'

I followed the nurse, who led me down a narrow corridor.

He welcomed us in his ringing South African accent but the expression on his face was sad, grave.

'Please undress Vanessa except for the nappy, and place her on this bed.'

At once, she 'startled,' flinging her arms in the air and gasping, as though losing her balance on thin ice.

'A Moro reflex, I'm afraid.' Doctor Epstein made a tutting sound with his tongue and wrote something in the notes.

I didn't know this was the first clue.

He encouraged her to grasp his finger, curling hers around his, which she did fiercely, but unable to let go. This was an accentuated grasp reflex, he said. I glanced at him, bemused. Then followed the usual medical routine: eyes, ears, chest, and reflexes in the knees. He took her legs, now chubby, and pushed them backwards and forwards as though encouraging her to ride a bicycle.

His gaze sombre, he looked up at me, 'You have, I'm afraid, a child who will be profoundly handicapped. How much, I can't say. Look, she already has great spasticity in the legs. There's much resistance when I bend them. And she has all the limited reflexes of the newborn child but to an accentuated degree.'

He clapped his hands. Vanessa jumped, going into the startle reflex again. I rushed forward to prevent her falling off the high bed.

'She hasn't made any of the normal progress expected of a child of five months. I am very sorry to tell you this, Mrs Stern.'

I gazed at him, barely comprehending what he was saying. Finally, I whispered, 'But how did it happen to her?'

'From your notes I see you had a difficult pregnancy.'

I nodded.

'You twice threatened to miscarry. Once at nine weeks, again at twenty weeks. The brain damage could have happened at nine weeks, although we can't be sure. It could have been an accident of birth.'

I closed my eyes. I was dumb. Silenced.

As I lifted Vanessa from the bed and held her in my arms, he said, 'I'll explain how it happens. Children with this kind of handicap retain the primitive reflexes with which we are born. We should outgrow them as long as we follow the normal pattern of development. These children don't pass this initial stage unless we teach them to do so.'

I gazed at him, barely comprehending what he was saying. Finally, I whispered, 'What can I do?'

'Many things. We'll do all we can to help you. There's physiotherapy. The physiotherapy department is over there in a building next to the hospital. Please go there and make an appointment.' I managed to thank him. 'You must also stimulate her in every possible way, with lights, with music, with play. Another thing: I think you should enquire about residential care for her when she reaches the age of two. The Rudolf Steiner schools are wonderful places. Contact them, and find out if you can have a place in two years' time. They have long waiting lists.'

A little bell of recognition rang in my mind – Rudolf Steiner – but I couldn't locate what it meant. He turned to the nurse hovering in the background. 'Will you take Mrs Stern to physiotherapy, please?'

He started to write the notes but stopped and smiled at Vanessa, who smiled widely. 'Thank you, Mrs Stern. Please bring her back in two weeks.' He made a clucking, weary sound as though grievously saddened by what he had told me.

After I had dressed Vanessa, my fingers awkward and fumbling, I returned to my place on a bench in the hall. The nurse said she would be back with me in a moment.

I sat clutching the baby close to me, questions whirling around my mind.

Why had I bought this child into the world? For what? To be profoundly handicapped? The words wouldn't register. I felt only terribly shocked, upset. A vision of the world and me and this poor child rose before my eyes. Dark, a space void of people. Silhouetted from behind, I saw myself standing alone with her in my arms.

And yet strangely, Doctor Epstein, the first doctor who'd showed any kindness, any humanity, did not entirely unnerve me. Deep within myself, almost as though I could see into my soul, I knew that this was inevitable. She was destined to come to me, although I didn't know why. There was nothing abnormal in our daughter. She was a beautiful baby girl. She was Vanessa, and we would learn how to live with her. Glancing down at her sweet face, I thought, I will do everything, everything in my power to teach you, to help you develop. Inhaling deeply, I told myself I could, and would, do this.

The nurse broke into my thoughts. 'Mrs Stern, would you come with me to physiotherapy?'

'Yes, of course.'

I followed her to the physiotherapy department, a single storey prefab-like structure outside, where Miss Burgess, the chief physiotherapist, introduced herself. Grey hair, which must have once been black, pale skin with a scattering of delicate lines mostly around her mouth, she smiled often. This dedicated lady would say as the months passed, 'A handicapped child in the family adds a special quality to life.' I'm sure this philosophy upheld her over the years.

Our first lesson.

Miss Burgess pushed Vanessa's legs up and down just as Doctor Epstein had done, but this time in a regular rhythm.

'She has to do her cycling,' she said. 'We must keep her legs supple.' She took Vanessa's hands as she was lying on her back and stretching them out, grasped them with her own, drawing her up into a sitting position. The baby's head lolled backwards, and then fell forwards onto her chest.

'This will give her the feeling of sitting up.'

She turned Vanessa onto her stomach, which pleased her immensely. With one hand supporting her chin and tummy, she used the other to move Vanessa's arms in a crawling fashion. The baby protested at all this surprising movement, but when she was placed in a sitting position with her legs crossed, and facing one of the long mirrors edging the physiotherapy bench, her face lit up. She managed to lift her head a little to smile, but it went too far, she jerked backwards making her cry out. Miss Burgess prevented her from falling onto the bench by pulling her up with both hands.

Although quite wobbly, Vanessa was now seated again in front of the long mirror. She smiled with delight at the smiling baby in front of her.

Chapter 5

We went home. When Sid came into the living room, I told him everything in a great rush of words – the diagnosis, the physiotherapy treatment and my passionate resolve to help our daughter become everything she could possibly be. Nevertheless, I did watch him anxiously. He sat down and closed his eyes and a great sadness swept his features. But then he looked up at Vanessa, still in my arms, and smiled. Getting up, turning his serious gaze on me, he said, 'Of course we'll do everything we can.'

We had no way of imagining how our tiny daughter might be in the future. I don't remember ever having seen a child with cerebral palsy; people would keep handicapped children hidden away, ashamed, fearful of the stigma on their family.

We were lucky. As soon as we told our parents, they asked us what they could do to help. Even though they might secretly have thought there was something wrong with the baby, they had kept their misgivings to themselves. Far from rejecting her, they smiled when we met, they held her in their arms and talked to her, and behaved just as they would with any grandchild.

As for me, fired with my mission to teach her how to become a 'normal' child, I could think of nothing but her. Her every cry and whimper was mine. I dreamed about her when I could sleep, and my day was hers entirely.

There were her meals, each one taking up to an hour because she had an 'extension reflex,' one of those reflexes that should have disappeared in the first few days, and this affected her entire body, especially her head and tongue. When I put a spoonful of food in her mouth her tongue would thrust it out, which meant I had to scrape the food back again, and again.

Twice a day we did the physiotherapy exercises: after breakfast and again in the afternoon. I would lay her on a blanket on the kitchen table, and taking her arms I'd pull her into a sitting position; I would spread out her fingers, give her things to hold and close her fingers around the tiny wooden train or spoon. After that I would encourage her to straighten her back, all the while saying, 'Come on Vanessa, you can sit up, you can use your hands, you can lift your head.'

For all her fragile appearance, she adored being rolled, shaken, and held in a crawling position while I worked her arms or legs.

Then it was time to have her morning sleep in the gleaming dark blue Silver Cross pram we had bought. Just as I'd imagined that day I had taken the pregnancy test tablets, I would wheel the pram into the backyard to where I could see her beneath the window, but not too close to the dustbins. In those days, everyone put the pram outside whatever the weather, either in the back garden or failing that, by the front door. No one worried about babies disappearing.

While she slept I rushed round, washing clothes and cot sheets in the kitchen sink, tidying up, making lunch, mostly cereal and milk although sometimes jars of ready prepared baby food. In the afternoon, we had another exercise session, this time with her lying on the rug in front of the fire, where I knelt to encourage her to practise the bicycling, sitting up, and crawling, just as we'd done in the morning. Around half past four, when Sid came for a break I would leave her with him and he'd talk to her, or play, 'Peep bo' or 'I see', which she adored. Finally, it was tea and bed. Not quite finally, as I gave her a drink at ten o'clock and inevitably, she woke in the night for yet another one.

Chapter 5

During our first physiotherapy session, Miss Burgess had explained the condition of cerebral palsy; she described different kinds: *spastic, ataxic, athetoid, floppy*. With her wide-mouthed smile, and the way she threw back her head, Vanessa had athetoid characteristics, but she was floppy, her limbs having little tone. Miss Burgess said that it would be good to sit her in a chair like other babies of this age, but how to find the right one? Our cousins had given us a small chair with a plastic blue seat, possibly a potty chair which stood a couple of feet above the ground.

A photograph from our album: Vanessa aged about seven months, falling sideways in the chair. She looks a normal chubby, cheerful baby girl. If you peer closer, you would see that her arms turned backwards and her hands were open like starfish. Her toes curl under with the prehensile grip of the newborn baby, which should have opened into a flat little foot ready to support the baby when it stands and walks.

I remember when my mother asked if she ever put her hands in her mouth and now I understood. All the photos of this period, apart from one, showed grandparents smiling as they talked or held Vanessa. The only person to show his feelings was my father. Such a man of contradictions but he had the softest of hearts when moved. Another photo showed him holding Vanessa in his arms, his left hand cradling her fingers, profound sorrow etched on his face. It was reflected in hers as she looked up at him, her mouth closed, her eyes serious. But he knew intimately about disability. After contracting tuberculosis of the hip when he was five, he lay in a spinal carriage until he was nine, when he learned to walk with crutches. He too was disabled.

During the appointment with Doctor Epstein, he told me that all babies with disabilities were given special hearing tests in the audiology department of Manchester University. Vanessa's appointment took place one Wednesday afternoon, which was half day closing, and I was delighted Sid could go with us.

We found ourselves in a light airy room where the audiologist Doctor Wilson, a tall man with black hair, pale skin and rather sombre eyes, shook our hands. He agreed that I could hold Vanessa while he administered the hearing tests. By her reaction, turning her head in the right direction or opening her eyes wide, we knew she'd heard all the rattles and bells he was using.

Doctor Wilson sat back. 'I have devised an innovative treatment for young handicapped children like Vanessa. This behavioural programme offers the possibility of normalising their primitive reflexes. Would you be interested to know more about this?'

I exchanged a quick glance with Sid.

'Yes, we would.'

Two weeks later, we were back with Doctor Wilson.

Taking Vanessa on his knee, he held her firmly in the crook of his arm and talked softly to her. She smiled. He encouraged her to spread out her hands, to pick up small wooden objects on a tray. When she began to stiffen, to resist the toys, he handed her back to me.

'I suggest you give her toys made from natural materials. Wood and metal have properties within them not found in plastic. Natural materials are more stimulating. Would you like to see where we do the work?'

We couldn't have known that this moment in July 1967 would change our lives for years to come.

Turning to look over his shoulder, he indicated a wooden structure standing in the shadow of the bookcases on the far wall. It turned out to be a chair and table, nothing like any baby chair you've ever seen. Imagine it: four pieces of wood, one for the base, one for the back, two for the arms or rather, side pieces. There are four tiny legs. The wood is raw, there is no padding on the seat, none on the back which is movable and can be slotted in and out of the base. There's a small pommel at the front of the chair, and the whole contraption stands a foot above the ground, compact enough to hold a baby of six to eight months. A circular table with a space cut out for the chair surrounds it.

I had noticed this as we walked in and was puzzled because it looked like a cage.

Doctor Wilson took Vanessa from me, walked across the room and slid her into the chair. She had never managed to sit in the ordinary baby chair, and I gazed, wondering what would happen. I soon found out. She screamed and swung forward, her whole body slumped over the pommel, then she flung herself backward, her head and body straining over the harsh back of the chair.

For long seconds I watched in horror. Like a furious mother lion, I leapt towards her but Doctor Wilson held up his hand. 'She'll learn not to fall backwards. She'll choose to avoid a position which is deliberately uncomfortable and crouch over like a young child of six months or so.'

I could not register his words and devastated by her continuing screams, I ran to drag her out of the chair, where by now the doctor was kneeling beside her and shaking little bells close to her ear.

Without looking up, he said, 'Please try to ignore her crying. Look, she's taking notice of this. ' He blew a penny whistle, and I covered my ears at its shrill, deafening sound. It would have terrified Vanessa.

'Despite herself, she's listening to all the sounds I'm using to attract her attention. Please, Mrs Stern…' he continued.

Tears filled my eyes and I clutched my hands together. I could not sit down.

Doctor Wilson got to his feet.

With his eyes riveted on Vanessa he backed away, all the while playing games with her. 'See, she's watching my hands. I assure you she's been taking notice of all I've been doing even though she's crying.'

At last he lifted her from the 'cage' and put her in my arms. We returned to the area where he'd done the hearing tests.

'How can they get used to it when it hurts so much?' I managed to ask.

'They do. I believe every young handicapped child in essence isn't so different from a normal baby under the age of nine months. The main thing is to persuade the child to move away from its primitive positions dictated by its reflexes, and to substitute new, useful positions, like sitting up. Then she can explore the world using whatever movement she has in order to touch, hold, smell, see and examine things. Like any normal child.' He smiled at us. 'Would you like to see another version of the table?'

I wasn't sure I wanted to see any other version of the table. This one was enough. Sid raised his eyebrows and gave me a meaningful look and we followed the doctor. This other chair was identical to the one he'd used, while the table was square with a chair shaped space cut from one side. Doctor Wilson explained the purpose of the table whatever its shape.

'A child will haphazardly move her arms or hands and knock against some interesting toy you have placed deliberately for her to find. You sit behind on the floor, not as the mother or father, but as an instructor, encouraging her to reach for things and pick them up.'

'This is impossible for Vanessa,' Sid said slowly, 'because she's always on her tummy or her back.'

'Exactly.' Doctor Wilson nodded. 'So, would you like to give this a try?'

We exchanged questioning glances. I took a deep breath.

'Yes,' Sid said. 'I like constructing things. I'll make the chair and table when I have the time.'

Although Sid clearly wanted to do this, long working hours consumed every moment of his time, and to tell the truth, I was secretly relieved. Meanwhile, I added all kinds of new games to the daily physiotherapy exercises. I found our daughter tiny objects made of natural materials as the doctor had suggested. I gave her little wooden toys, sticks to hold and bang and shake, and showed her how to put wooden things in and out of containers, mimicking what a six-month-old baby would do. Doctor Benjamin Spock's *Baby and Childcare* taught us about a child's development, without which we were floundering. How little we knew!

With my help, Vanessa did manage to grasp a brick or a little wooden man, but she couldn't let it go. I had to press the back of her hand with my forefinger since her hand had no natural release mechanism. With her head bent over, a broad smile on her face, she loved every activity, especially sitting on my knee. There was nothing to terrify her here and she got used to the feeling of sitting up, using her eyes to look at things and coordinate them with her hands. It gave me a warm feeling. We were learning something together.

Twice a week we went to the physiotherapy department in the hospital, we did her exercises, I did the new work and talked to her constantly. We sang nursery rhymes, and eventually, I would read her stories. Occasionally I wondered if having a normal child first would have helped. We would have known about babies. It might have been healthier, I couldn't have become so obsessively focused on her and her needs. I rarely wondered why I was consumed with such a desire to help her. It seemed so obvious, she was our daughter and that was enough, but deep in my heart, I knew that my life had prepared me for this. A different, unconventional childhood, a father with a disability, and the belief I'd had when teaching that every child had something precious to give to the world, had come together and banished, almost, my self-doubt, my uncertainty.

One morning something happened that would change our lives for many months: I was giving Vanessa breakfast when she cried out suddenly, her body seemed to jack-knife, her arms and legs drawn together by some powerful invisible thread and she clapped them against each other. Her eyeballs rolled upwards and she lost consciousness. My heart raced as I held her with all my strength, almost squashing her in my anguished arms until she came round. It was only a few seconds before her eyes opened and she began to sob, terrified. I knew this was a kind of epileptic fit. Then the inevitable phone call to Dr Burt, who referred us back to the Duchess of York Baby Hospital.

The paediatric epilepsy specialist diagnosed *petit mal* and prescribed the usual anti-convulsant drugs. It took half an hour to give her these medicines even before I started her meals; once again, feeding became a long, drawn-out ordeal. She didn't respond well, the fits were occurring more and more until they affected her minute by minute, despite the battery of drugs I was administering.

All day, neither awake nor asleep, she existed in a twilight state, although sometimes I could see her cringe as a suppressed spasm rippled through her, or hear a faint cry as the fits disturbed her mind. It was pointless to go on seeing Dr Wilson. What use could it be when she was hardly aware of us, let alone his chair which she so hated?

A week before Christmas 1967, Doctor Epstein examined her.

'I shall stop the medication since it's not working. My only alternative is a course of cortisone treatment but which I'm loath to give her. I think she should come into hospital. We'll reduce the medicines, and observe her meanwhile.'

In the early days when she was refusing to eat I had started writing to Harry Edwards, a famous faith healer, in Surrey. I had an uneasy feeling it might be contrary to Judaism, but we were desperate for help, and I made up my mind and wrote to him. None of his recommendations, the massaging, the hopeful thoughts, made the slightest difference and I was downcast.

We needed something more powerful than helpful words on blue writing paper and I decided to visit Patricia or Paddy as she preferred to be called, an old friend who was a naturopath. In the course of her work she found she had healing hands and had joined a group of spiritual healers led by a gifted Frenchwoman whom I knew only as Simone.

It was a cold damp January afternoon when I took the train to Coventry. Only overnight, I couldn't be away too long.

Knowing little of the theology of religious practice, I was positive that spiritual healing could easily be part of the mysterious, recondite world of religion. Whether it was or not, I didn't care, I had to go. I would do anything; go anywhere, if it would help Vanessa. A pattern was emerging that would stay with me forever.

Paddy met me at the station. A tall slim woman, her dark hair cut short, her hands firm as she drew me to her, and kissed me. Reaching her house, she was showing me my room when she said, 'The meeting will be at Simone's this evening, as we are expecting more people. We'll have dinner and go.'

On the way, Paddy told me about the woman who led the healing circle. 'Simone Grimaldi. She's French. Such a gifted healer, everyone is in awe of her.'

'Does she come from the south of France? Grimaldi is Italian.'

'I don't know,' Paddy answered.

We arrived, and Simone opened the door. I recognised the long, waving black hair, piercing dark eyes and strong straight features I associated with the women I had known in Provence. She was small but held herself with the erect stance taught to all French girls, making her seem taller. Her every movement conveyed authority.

'Welcome, Suzanne,' she said in her rich, slightly nuanced voice of the Midi. Taking my hands in hers, she peered deep into my eyes. 'We are delighted you've come to join our healing circle in Coventry.' To Paddy, she said, 'And you, Patricia, as always, are most welcome.'

A comfortable room with many armchairs, a fire burning brightly in the grate, on the walls, pictures of mountains, waterfalls, the sea. The members of the group, all women, stopped chatting as we came in and smiled, welcoming me again. A woman with fair hair, her face full of laughter lines, about fifty years old, said, 'You know we've been praying for your daughter already? Sending her healing thoughts.'

'Thank you. Paddy told me this in her letters.'

'Ladies,' said Simone, and everyone fell silent. 'There's something I must explain to Suzanne.' Her eyes seeming to probe into my soul, she said, 'Do you know about the power of names?'

'I don't think so.'

'A name is a force unto itself. By calling your daughter Debra Vanessa you have been using the wrong vibration. Her true name is Deborah Claire. This is how we shall address her in healing. This is the right vibration for her. It is good if you too speak to her with this name.'

I waited for a moment. As she didn't explain further, I nodded, 'Yes, of course.' Not only was she a woman of a certain age, but she had personality, charisma, whereas I was young, inexperienced, eager to comply, ready to accept anything if it would help.

'So, we shall begin.'

Standing very straight, her head erect, she lifted her hands and the others rose from their chairs, forming a circle. Paddy drew me in, and they began to pray for Vanessa.

Simone spoke. 'We are sending healing to this child, this soul, Deborah Claire. May she be healed!'

The others, their eyes closed, repeated, 'May she be healed!'

They stood in silence for what seemed to me a very long time, eventually moving on to send healing to others I didn't know.

Before we left, Simone took my hands again. 'Rest assured, we will continue to pray for her as long as we feel it's necessary.'

Driving home, I said to Paddy, 'It was very simple. Just a few words, and then the healing thoughts.'

She smiled. 'You have to attune yourself. It takes a long time to learn. I'm still only a beginner.'

'But then it's simple?'

'Then it's simple. Simone tells me there's still too much ego in my desire to heal. It's difficult…'

Train journeys soothed me, they gave me time to think. Rocked along in this private space, even if there were other passengers, my mind could travel backwards and forwards, sometimes recalling the distant past, sometimes imagining the future. As we approached Manchester, I thought about the healing session and especially, the power of names. I saw myself back in the maternity hospital and the sister telling me they were going to baptise Vanessa. When I refused and after they'd left the ward, I had whispered:

Awake, awake Dvora! A call, my call to the little daughter I had barely seen.

Was that the power of names? Had I chanced on some spiritual awareness I didn't know I had? I took a deep breath.

After some moments I became aware of my shabby seat in the carriage, the train slowing down and that we were approaching Manchester. With my sleeve I wiped the murky window and peered out. My heart was pounding in my chest as we rolled into the station; I went to the door, ready to jump out. I gripped my bag wanting to know if there had been any change after last night's healing session, or would I be disappointed once again.

Sid was waiting, a dark shape on the platform. I ran to him, breathless with anxiety.

'How is she?'

'They think she's improving.'

'Really? What's happened?'

'The fits have stopped.' I was so delighted I gave him a great big hug. 'They don't know how or why. Even Doctor Epstein is astonished.' We got into the car. 'The good thing is she won't have the course of cortisone treatment.'

'Maybe it is because of the healing.' I said softly.

'Maybe it's because they've treated the urine infection they found when she went in,' he retorted with a grin.

Vanessa celebrated her first birthday in hospital. The day she left, nurses and doctors crowded round to say good-bye, and she responded with her all-embracing smile.

It was a turning point, and she began to live, to make a little progress.

Chapter 6

Twice a week an ambulance would transport us to physiotherapy sessions, taking more than an hour to pick up various people en route. It was only a short journey from our house and one afternoon, I'd had enough.

'I am fed up to the teeth with this ambulance malarkey,' I told Sid.

'Then pass your driving test.'

'But how? I've failed three times already.'

'You could get lessons, and come out with me. Then you'll pass.'

I failed again.

My sister's wedding in March became an unexpected stepping stone on my journey to independence. I wanted it to be the most wonderful day for Barbara, to enjoy it with her and the whole family. I also had to admit this would have been impossible if we'd taken Vanessa, yet what could I do? Doctor Epstein had the answer, he suggested we leave her on the ward for a night and I would be free to enjoy the wedding. This was so successful that as we drove home Sid took me by surprise, 'It's about time we had a holiday! Couldn't your mother look after her?'

She was delighted, Vanessa was happy and we dared to do this amazing thing. We would go away for a week to Scotland, its wildness, its grandeur so appreciated by Sid. He took photos of me standing at Gretna Green, Scotland's white flag billowing in the breeze from the roof. Another one of the narrow Gorge of Glencoe, its steep jagged mountains evoking the awful massacre.

We went to the wondrous, fascinating Isle of Skye. Up and down those narrow paths, stopping at lay-bys, marvelling at the beauty of valleys and mountains, I finally learned to drive.

Returning home, Sid said, 'I'm sure you'll pass your driving test now.'

Full of confidence, I took more lessons and passed. From then on, Vanessa and I would drive to the physiotherapy appointments in style, and I always believed she'd given me the courage to carry on.

A typical physio day went something like this: I would carry Vanessa into the waiting room, and greet the other mothers and children. We formed a group, a world, there were four of us: May, a slim bright woman, her light brown hair tied back with a green ribbon, would be sitting holding Tommy, who was very much like Vanessa. One afternoon, I drove to her home in Newton Heath, a downtrodden area of Manchester, where we talked about our lives while drinking tea, and Tommy and Vanessa lay on the floor, arms stretched out, touching each other by chance, moments of awareness as their eyes met or a hand brushed against the other's body.

And she told me her story: 'The day my husband left,' she said, tears in her eyes, 'he said he hadn't got a wife any more. There was only Tommy. But I knew the real reason.' She wiped her eyes with the back of her hand. 'He couldn't bear a son who'd probably never walk, play football, be like other boys.'

Then there was Gemma, from Wythenshawe, with short bleach blonde hair, she would sit silently in the corner holding her beautiful baby boy, Jamie. He had the face of an angel in a Renaissance painting, but he was blind. She wasn't married though one day she opened up, telling me she lived with her father who was crippled with rheumatism, never leaving the house. Unmarried mothers were still being banished to mental hospitals by families, to hide their shame, and I wondered how her father treated her and the baby.

'Jamie's dad is a soldier serving in Germany. He said he'd marry me when he comes back.'

'That will be wonderful for Jamie,' I smiled. Would her soldier lover marry her when he saw how disabled Jamie was? I thought how fortunate I was, surrounded by the love and support of the whole family. Over the years I would hear about men who couldn't bear to have a handicapped child, especially a son, and they'd walk away. But Sid was Vanessa's father just as I was her mother. We were a team.

But one morning in July, exactly a year after we had received the diagnosis, I was feeling very low as we drove to the session. Despite all the physiotherapy, all the hours of exercising, encouragement and carrying her correctly, her head was as floppy as ever, she hadn't acquired any skill in picking up toys or releasing them, she continued to push her food out of her mouth and I was still scraping it up. Because she thrust herself backwards despite herself, my arms had developed strong muscles to hold and carry her.

I was thinking about this when we walked into the tiny waiting room of the Portakabin, and sat down on one of the hard backed chairs. I said hello to the other mothers whom by now I had got to know quite well and held Vanessa on my knee, my head bent. Peter Smith, the only child who could walk, was marching heavily around the room when he stopped in front of us and waved and zoomed a wooden plane in the air, almost catching Vanessa's eyes.

'Be careful, Peter,' admonished his mother Barbara, 'you nearly hit Vanessa. Stand further away, please.'

He moved away. 'Mamma,' he bawled, waving the plane under her chin.

Enunciating every word, her eyebrows raised, she said, 'Say what you want, Peter.'

'*Bisky!*' he yelled.

Vanessa's eyes widened in alarm but fascinated by Peter, she stared at him.

'Biscuit?'

'*Bisky!*'

'Here you are.' She handed him a digestive biscuit.

'*Thank.*' He devoured it.

'It's repetition,' Barbara said, turning to me, 'simple instructions. Reinforcement. Peter gets a reward if he's right.

She was ever optimistic, always positive, always energetic: a woman with pale ginger hair and wearing round, black-rimmed glasses, she had worked with disabled children and was headmistress of a special school before her son was born. Her husband lectured about disability at Stockport College. They were entirely original, handling Peter with determination and knowledge, using behavioural techniques similar to Doctor Wilson's. When I first met Peter I couldn't believe he had been as handicapped as Vanessa, or so Barbara said.

We aren't like you, I would think, almost bitter. We make our discoveries willy-nilly, with only the tiniest of results or worse, none at all. If only I had known how to approach Vanessa in a scientific fashion, with rigour and persistence like Barbara, but against all parental instinct, those primitive reflexes that ruled over her every movement might have been overcome...

I looked down at my daughter who was waiting for her turn with Miss Burgess. You couldn't see any kind of disability, only her body told the story. She had become very pretty, her hair pale gold in colour, her face open and intelligent. I thought about the games we played, how she knew the little objects by name. Words like telephone, drink, dinner, kitchen. She even knew where her grandparents lived and as we approached their house or even their road, she began to shout and smile, kicking her legs as though trying to walk. Arriving at the front door, she gave them that great wide smile, and they were delighted.

But it wasn't enough.

I turned my gaze to the floor. There was a curdling sensation in my stomach and I shifted in my chair. What was it? Envy? It was *envy* of the Smiths and all they had achieved. I closed my eyes but the words were still there: *Their handicapped child is doing better than mine.* I was crazy, it was ludicrous, and I felt ashamed of myself.

Luckily, Miss Burgess came for Vanessa; I asked if I could come and speak to her when they'd finished.

'I must find something different to help Vanessa make progress,' I told her.

'How about this?'

She passed me *Handling the Young Cerebral Palsied Child at Home,* a new paperback with a golden-brown cover, its lower half showing a series of mini-illustrations, almost cartoons of tiny disabled children.

'It's from the Western Cerebral Palsy Centre in Finchley, known as the Bobath Centre.'

Two refugees from Nazi Europe, Doctor Karel Bobath and Berta Busse, gymnast and dancer, had set up the centre, she said, and it was becoming world-renowned for dealing with children and adults with cerebral palsy.

She flicked through the pages, showing me how I could reinforce the work we were doing already. I usually carried Vanessa straddled over my hip, supported by my shoulder to prevent her head flopping back. But there was a diagram demonstrating how to carry a child with her back and head against the mother's stomach, the mother's hands a sling beneath the child's bottom. This would stop her thrusting herself out of someone's arms, keep her spine straight.

'I'll try that,' I smiled.

Turning the pages, I found one showing a variety of chairs, modified to suit the child's needs. 'This is brilliant. We've tried mini deckchairs for babies, one of the round blow-up chairs, but they're useless. She slips out or pulls the chair on top of her.'

'You could adapt something. Lots of suggestions here.'

We ordered the book and I was full of hope; I tied a towel around Vanessa's shoulders to bring her arms forward, forcing her to stop pushing herself away, but it had little effect. Despite the diagrams of different chairs or adapting a baby chair, we never managed to create the right one, and again, I despaired. She'd sit lopsidedly in the potty chair for perhaps twenty minutes, then fall sideways, or slide forwards, frequently pushing the chair back with her body and head, dragging it on top of her. Only on someone's knee was she happy and relaxed.

Still, I found original strategies to help her use her hands: I would fold the fingers of her left hand around a wooden spoon, guiding it to her mouth from the plate while she sat on my knee with her right hand wrapped under my arm. I bought pieces of green foam in rolls or triangles from the market, making them into wedges like those at physiotherapy, where she'd lie over a wedge, raising her head for a few moments to see the world.

I read about a questionable way to encourage a sense of balance: placing the child on a pile of cushions, you let them fall.

'Isn't this dangerous?' I asked Miss Burgess at the next physiotherapy session.

'Not at all. Perch her on a thick pile of cushions. She'll fall sideways or forwards but it will encourage her to feel the difference between sitting, falling and lying.'

'Surely she'll hurt herself?'

'Just make sure you have plenty of cushions around her and she'll be fine. She may even enjoy it, so turn it into a game.'

Miss Burgess was right. She loved it.

I added to the exercise routine, practising crawling, rolling her over, stretching her body into all sorts of positions. We'd place an old mirror against the wall, or on top of the table. Her greatest delight was to 'crawl' forwards and smile at the 'baby.' On the floor she could manage a semblance of crawling with her legs while I moved her arms. Alone, she'd move round in a circle, and once she moved halfway across the dining room floor to Sid, whom she adored.

Lying on her tummy was how they'd advise all athetoid children to be placed, to relieve the pressure at the top of spine, the cause of them pushing away and arching their back.

I would say, 'You stay on your tummy, you can see Mummy like that.'

Minutes later, I would hear her weeping furiously; she was on her back, the position in which she always cried.

'Over you go, Vanessa,' I would say, and again she'd roll onto her back, and cry. Did she do this to get my attention? Her constant crying when she wasn't on someone's knee was dreadful. Instinctively we would move to prevent it. Still teaching her we would lift her up despite ourselves.

Something we both loved: playing with dried rice, beans, macaroni, when I'd swirl her fingers through them and she'd laugh. Or dipping her fingers in bowls of water, splashing her a little, which delighted her. I carried her to feel the heat of the gas, spread her hands out over the fire guard before the fire, all the time describing what we were doing or feeling. I put salt and sugar on her fingers, brushing them against her lips. At least I was doing something.

If she couldn't go out to the world, we would bring the world to her.

Since buying the pharmacy, Sid had been at the beck and call of customers, thanks to the precedent set by the previous owners

– open all hours. People would ring the doorbell on Saturday night, 'Can you let us have a packet of hair rollers / cough medicine/setting lotion?'

We didn't mind the baby food or emergency medicine, but hair rollers or make up, that was too much. One evening after three requests for Maybelline mascara, Sid said: 'It's time to move.'

I agreed, and every Sunday afternoon for months, we'd search in the suburbs of South Manchester until we found the very house. An almost new, detached house in Gatley, it had playing fields beyond the garden, which recalled my childhood home in Amersham. We agreed the purchase in November. But getting a mortgage in 1968 was almost impossible; the winter was bitter, pipes in the new house burst, and we didn't say goodbye to our Gorton terraced house, with its tight Victorian embrace, until March 1969.

'Look, Vanessa,' I said on the day we arrived. 'Look at those beautiful oak banisters. Can you see the light shining through the landing window down into the hall? That's what made me and Daddy choose this house.' Gazing up the stairs, she smiled broadly. 'Let's go to your new bedroom. We'll see Daddy in a minute.'

Upstairs we went into a tiny room overlooking Silverdale Road. 'There's your cot with its padding to stop you banging your elbows and knees when you wriggle on your bottom.' She gave a great shout. 'And this is the new wardrobe with a mirror Daddy made for you. I bet you'll like that.' I pressed her spatulate hands against the whiteboard and she smiled earnestly at her reflection. Then she grinned, causing herself to jerk backwards and her body to spasm, but I knew this trick. Heaving her close with my shoulder, catching her with my forearm, I straightened her up, and we went to the windowsill where I showed her the gardens along the road. 'Look, my darling, look at all those beautiful daffodils. And those small houses are called bungalows. This is our new house. Shall we say hello to Gatley?' I smiled and she beamed. 'Now, let's find Daddy.'

There were no carpets, floor boards were bare, but passing the sitting room, resplendent with the orange suite we'd brought from Gorton, and the dining room, empty because we'd left the utility furniture at Highmead Street where it belonged, we went into a small kitchen, just big enough for me to sit with Vanessa for her meals.

'We've got a surprise for you. Let's go through this door. Look, this is your new playroom.'

A powerful reason for buying this house was a former garage, used as a room for an older person, where now we'd have ample space for Vanessa's equipment – her new red wheelchair, a desk for doing hand play, foam wedges, playpen but used only as a receptacle for toys.

'Hello Vanessa.' Sid was unpacking boxes by the window. 'Sue, I checked the boiler in this cupboard, and everything's okay.'

'Good. It's lovely and warm in here.' I carried her round. 'We'll have a wonderful time in this new house, and do lots of work, won't we?'

Chapter 7

What a change in our lives! Sid would drive off in the morning and come home at night, able to leave work behind him while for me it was my first experience of being alone without the intermittent company of my husband, and I felt strange, missing the shop and the warm atmosphere of Gorton. But not for long, as family and friends soon arrived and created a brightly-hued tapestry to enhance our life.

Sid's parents lived in Didsbury, ten minutes' drive away, and on Saturdays when he was working I would take Vanessa to see them; as we approached the leafy corner of their road, she would shout in recognition and kick her legs. Meanwhile, mine would drive over from North Manchester, often on Sunday. Mother would bring me newspaper cuttings she thought would be useful, even a copy of the Reader's Digest she had snaffled from the hairdressers or the chiropodist, her only criminal acts in a lifetime of absolute honesty.

As for relaxing a little in the evening, for Sid it was sport, either taking part, reading about it or watching on television. Captain of tennis when he'd studied in Bradford, then back in Manchester he had joined a badminton class at the College of Adult Education and it was there he met Philip Gabbie, soon to be his closest friend. Always joking, Phil worked assiduously to become an accountant, working by day in an office, then studying in the evenings. While we lived in Gorton, he'd brought his fiancée Paula to meet us. Tall and slim, with shiny black hair and delicate features, she had read law at Leeds University, and was working in a solicitor's office in Manchester.

The swinging 60s had not yet reached Manchester when I married in 1965. It was still the era of *A Taste of Honey, Cathy Come Home*, of the kitchen sink dramas of the fifties, but we were starting to wear miniskirts (extremely so) and the boys were growing their hair. It was the time of The Beatles' famous song, *All You Need is Love,* which they sang on the first satellite television programme *Our World*. We watched it together with the Gabbies on our small black and white television in Gorton. As I fed Vanessa, scraping up the food and encouraging her to swallow, Paula said, 'How on earth can I have any children when I couldn't stand the dirty nappies? I can't even take the rubbish out of the sink.'

They married and eventually bought a house literally round the corner from us in Gatley. Who'd have thought they would soon have three little children of their own, Vanessa's earliest friends. Through Phil, who'd grown up among a close Jewish community in North Manchester where he knew everyone, we made even more friends, something that delighted me.

Estates of new houses had been built locally, or were springing up for the upwardly mobile, working and middle-class families. So many young women pushing their babies in prams, their toddlers hanging on to the pram handle. I'd meet them outside neighbourhood shops and they would invite us for coffee. Because Vanessa loved being with other people I occasionally accepted, although anxious that I wasn't sticking to our routine.

We had acquired an Andrews McLaren baby buggy, specifically designed for children with cerebral palsy. It had a light tubular frame and a seat like a deckchair, softly shaping to the child's body. We had bought ours from the Spastics Society, and despite its flexible contours, Vanessa managed to arch her back and push until her legs trailed along the ground; I would have to drag her up and out before she became entangled with the wheels.

'You're wearing your mummy out,' a shop assistant would say, and she would smile charmingly at them. Thanks to Vanessa's love of being with people, we made friends with other young women shopping like us and with anyone she could charm with her disarming smile.

One of these was Judith: the day after we'd moved in, there was a knock at the front door, followed by loud banging. With Vanessa in my arms, I went to open it. A young woman stood there, in her hands a bunch of flowers, a lively little boy of three or four, jumping up and down beside her, the one who'd done the banging.

'Welcome to Gatley,' she smiled. 'We live just a few minutes' walk away from you.' Although she has forgotten this kindness, it has stayed with me.

A few days later our new house was full of life with the arrival of visitors. They were friends from France, who lived in the tiny village of Herbault, near Blois in the Château Country. Michèle was my first pen friend; we'd been writing to each other since we were thirteen. Who'd have thought we would continue writing for more than sixty years?

So the Viau family had an adventure, coming with their three little girls, Christine, Sophie and baby Laure, born only a few weeks after Vanessa. They'd travelled in a Citroen Deux Chevaux, a tiny but sturdy car with a rolled back roof. The only time they would ever leave France. How did we organise bedrooms? Perhaps they came with camping gear or put-up beds, because there was still only a double bed and Vanessa's cot in the new house.

Since Phil and Paula had holidayed with us the previous year, visiting Michèle and André in Herbault, following which we'd journeyed to Aix and the Midi, so our French friends returned the visit. We still have photographs of them in Phil and Paula's garden, and in our newly furnished dining room, with Michèle already something of the matriarch, carrying plates of food to the table, while I sit with Vanessa and the others. They knew about Vanessa; the children accepted her without a thought.

After they had gone, it was time to work. We had the lovely playroom, Vanessa was happy, her health was stable at last, and I resolved to contact Dr Wilson once more. We'd stopped seeing him when she was so ill with petit mal. Now he told me that I should bring Vanessa to his home in Wilmslow, where he would provide me with a detailed outline of his work.

At our first visit, she screamed and fell back in the chair, just as she'd done before and I wanted to drag her out and drive away from Wilmslow, never coming back.

'She's certainly taking notice of all the toys I'm showing her,' he insisted.

It didn't reassure me but knowing I had to swallow my anguish if she was to make any progress, I took the blueprint and Sid set to work making the table and chair needed for the programme. Very soon it was ready, dominating the playroom. I pored over the plan we had to follow, getting to grips with the behavioural theory underlying this work and how to put it into practice. It was similar to what the Smiths had been doing so successfully with Peter, whom we still met at physiotherapy.

With my heart in my mouth I began to carry this out at home. Vanessa loathed every second of it. The chair was unpadded, its back and sides about nine inches deep reached to her waist, its movable sides were slotted into the bare wooden base. With the pommel between her legs to stop her from falling, her feet couldn't touch the floor. Enclosed by the table-top, a wooden area where her hands could rest, she was supposed to swipe haphazardly at the various objects suggested by Doctor Wilson.

When we went to Wilmslow, the doctor said, 'You must persevere, Mrs Stern.' Seeing my expression, he'd add, 'I think it would be better if you went out so she won't see how worried you are.'

Every week, I left her screaming hysterically while I trudged blindly round until it was over, whereas at home, I couldn't escape. First the traditional physiotherapy exercises for half an hour, then we moved to the chair. After thirty minutes of her screaming, falling backwards and forwards, bruising her back, her fine skin marked with weals where the wood had cut into her, I could bear it no longer. I lifted her out and continued the work at the table. She loved this, sitting playing on my knee but I knew I had sabotaged the whole endeavour and felt dreadful.

Sometimes, as she lay on the floor I caught her gazing at her hands, probably like a young baby discovering its fingers. But her small hands were often closed; open, they hardly moved and I believed she had little sense of feeling in them. So I worked on each hand, picking up various wooden bricks, cotton reels, any tiny shape small enough to fit in her palm. Then we banged sticks on the table, on drums, on empty coffee containers. Her brain, her hands had to learn what it meant to *hold* something.

The entire wooden chair system depended on understanding my role: I was impersonal, no longer Mummy but the instigator of her progress. I gave her orders which she must learn to obey. No conversation about the objects, no encouragement, only terse comments if she achieved anything: *Well done. Good girl!*

The commands were simple: *Pick up the brick, Vanessa. Put it in the box. Put it on the table. Give it to Mummy. To Teddy* perched nearby. She had to learn to differentiate words by name: *round, square, or oblong containers*, to drop objects in the appropriate one. But once in her hands, she couldn't let them go, so I would press down with my forefinger on the back of her hand. And she released whatever it was. We also had an assortment of wooden rings on sticks to be dismantled and built up again.

As I understood the theory, her initial motivation would be to please me, the mother, and eventually she would enjoy the work itself. That was why it was preferable for the child to work with their parents rather than with strangers. Above all, she had to learn that sitting at the table meant *work*. She found it easier sitting on my knee but this wasn't the point, even though here she did learn to reach out very slowly, pick things up and hold them for some seconds.

Why the chair? The primitive pattern in her brain of the *extensor* reflex, which usually disappeared soon after birth, only remaining to us if we lost our balance, dictated all her movements. If she could overcome this, sitting up and leaning forward, she would learn to do what was impossible for her when lying down. Sitting crouched over like a six-month-old baby she would learn to use her hands and eyes in coordination. And her brain would develop.

But she didn't, and wouldn't sit in the chair, screaming, and falling backwards and forwards, and it broke my heart. For weeks I went through the pantomime of putting her there for half an hour but nothing changed. Worn down by her desperation, and mine, I would lift her out. One day, furious we were getting nowhere, I left her sitting in the hall, and went up to hoover the bedrooms hoping the noise would drown out her hysterical crying. I did this for a week, all the while praying she wouldn't injure herself.

The crying stopped. What had happened? Heart pounding, expecting to find her unconscious or worse, I raced down the stairs. She was sitting slumped forwards, her head touching the table, her fingers scratching at some small object I had covered with silver foil. She even smiled at me from under her bent over head, too heavy for her to lift.

How wonderful! How amazing! We had done it at last.

Soon she could sit in the chair for up to an hour, watching me as I cooked or talked to her. After the morning's work, I would make her some lunch, strain it through a Mouli-sieve and spend the next hour feeding her. At half-past one she slept for an hour, and exhausted already, so did I. Then I'd make dinner, and after her drink, we would go to the shops or for a walk, and back for more exercises, and tea. Our days were full. My every moment was hers.

One night soon after our arrival I heard her screaming from her room. Scrambling out of bed I threw open the door. She lay with her head caught between the bars of the cot, her legs twisted through those on the opposite side. I had to wake Sid up to help me extricate her.

As we tried to go back to sleep, he said, 'Surprising it hasn't happened before.'

'It has. But not like that.'

'Now that's she's two,' he continued sleepily, 'shouldn't she have her own bed?'

'She's more likely to fall out of that.'

'True. Better get some sleep.'

The following night around half past eleven when I was already asleep, he climbed into bed saying, 'Got it.'

'What?' I groaned.

'How to stop Vanessa getting trapped in the cot.' As I didn't answer, he went on, 'You know I get my best ideas in the bath?'

'Oh Sid, I'm asleep already.'

'Listen, this is what we'll do. I'll build her a bed wider than a usual single bed. With low wooden sides so we can lift her out but high enough so she won't fall on the floor.'

I woke up. 'Really? That's brilliant.'

'Simple when you know how.'

'All right, clever clogs. Could she scrabble round on her tummy without hurting herself?'

'We can pad the wooden sides with some soft material.'

'Good,' I said, and fell back asleep.

That is how we, or rather Sid, solved another problem.

Doctor Epstein had recently asked me to talk to undergraduate medical students about my experience of raising a disabled child. He would conclude saying, 'Listen to the mother. She knows best.'

How rare that was. The world expert on cerebral palsy, he had progressive ideas about the doctor-patient relationship: that all mothers had an instinctive, exact understanding of the needs of their baby or child. He'd practised this in South Africa which he left because of apartheid. During a routine appointment, he surprised me. 'You're looking very drawn, Mrs Stern. Do you need a break?'

'I thought I was hiding it quite well.'

'There's a nursery across the road, set up by the Spastics Society. Called Rodney House Nursery Clinic. It's supported by the hospital. Now that she's two, your daughter can go there twice a week. Socialise with other children.'

That evening Sid and I mulled this over.

'But I'm making such progress with her in the chair,' I wailed. 'How can she go now?'

'Why shouldn't she have one day a week somewhere else?' Sid levelled his gaze at me. 'Surely it's better for you both?'

'I've worked so hard to get to this point. She *sits* in the chair. She's leaning forward, looking at her hands. She knows where the bricks are, she's really making progress. She'll lose it if we stop, even for a couple of days a week.'

'Just give it a try.'

'All right. But if she goes back to hating the chair, promise me I can take her away and you won't object.'

'I'm not promising anything. I think we should give it a go.'

My heartbeat racing, I took Vanessa for her first day at Rodney House Nursery Clinic. It was a low building set back in its own grounds, and as we went through the swing doors into a broad entrance hall, I gazed round at a huge assortment of toys, bicycles, cars, rocking horses, all clustered around a solid wooden slide on the parquet floor.

Old-fashioned roomy prams and traditional nursery chairs jostled for place with wheelchairs, foam wedges and low wooden corner chairs.

I put Vanessa into the waiting arms of the nursery assistant and ran, with her howling in my ears. I spent her first day of school in the traditional state of anxiety. Would she cry all day? Supposing they couldn't feed her? Would I have to spend two hours when she came home filling up a starving, frantic child? Those early days were not so far away that I could forget the horrors of feeding a demented being.

Of course, she settled down; she loved the attention, and watched the more mobile ones moving across the floor on their backs, their bottoms, even their tummies. Physiotherapy sessions continued while at the nursery, and on other days as well. An optician prescribed her glasses for a very slight squint in her right eye, but she rarely wore them.

Although she'd actually learned to sit in the small chair for her meals, her very first step in independence, now she'd sit on a helper's knee. I knew she was difficult to feed and understood their predicament, but whenever I went to collect her, I had to bite my lip as I watched one of the helpers carry her like a baby.

I couldn't contain my impatience. 'Sid,' I said one evening, 'I'm taking the wooden chair to the nursery tomorrow. I'll explain how to use it and ask them not to take her out even when she cries.'

He raised his eyebrows. 'You can if you want, but they're not set up for that kind of thing, I am certain.'

Nevertheless, I took the whole contraption to the nursery, showed them how she'd sit with her head bowed over the table, and explained about the progress she'd made. But what a disaster! When I went for her that afternoon, the matron ran out. 'Please don't bring it again. It has upset everyone.'

'Why? What on earth happened?'

'She almost pulled the chair and table over herself, she was screaming so much.'

Was she exaggerating? I knew my daughter's crying was wrenching, but she had actually upended herself?

'Did they sit her at the table so that it was enclosing her?'

'I'm not sure.' She called to a passing assistant. 'What happened with Vanessa?'

The assistant stopped in her tracks. 'I think she toppled backwards when they put her in a corner. You know they like her to sit in one of the corner chairs.'

'Without the table?' I asked, a dog pursuing a rabbit.

'I don't know. Just what I heard.'

They'd evidently been talking about it. The headmistress averted her gaze, probably thinking I had caused enough upset with my horrible contraption. 'Please don't bring it again. You must realise that every one of the children needs attention during the day.'

Duly chastised, I knew I was expecting too much, but couldn't they understand that this was vital to Vanessa's development? Surely everyone had the same aim: to enable her to leave her dependent state and become a little girl? I thought they were intransigent.

When I poured out my woes to a physiotherapist, she said, 'Your determination to help your daughter is admirable. But those are revolutionary methods. It's taking them all their time to learn the basics of handling these children, whatever their age. Babies. That's how they see them.'

I got the message. 'I'll just have to do it at home. It's true the first time we saw her in the chair I was as frantic as she was. I wanted to yank her out, stop her dreadful screaming.'

But hadn't I told Sid I would keep her at home, if it interfered with our work? I would talk it over that night.

'I won't let her go.' I glared at him. 'Then all our work won't be… flushed down the toilet.'

He gave me an angry look. 'It's far better for her to be there. It would create some kind of normality in our lives. You could do something different, something you enjoy.'

He was right, but I wasn't going to tell him that.

I was driving to pick up our daughter from the nursery a few weeks later when a thought struck me: how uncertain I had been before her birth, how fearful of confrontation, never able to make a decision. Then Vanessa arrived and I discovered a strength I never believed I had. She had given me purpose, a mission to help her progress, and hadn't I passed the driving test because of her?

So in September, when Vanessa was two and a half, we took a holiday in Bournemouth with Sid's parents, and overcoming my fear of water became my next challenge. I had attended course after course of swimming lessons, often in grubby and foul smelling public facilities, but never managed to swim more than a breadth. The first morning of our holiday I was pushing Vanessa in the new red wheelchair we'd acquired through the physiotherapy department when we passed a local swimming pool and I stopped to read a notice: Swimming lessons for adults.

'You know how Vanessa loves being in the bath, how she twists round to look at the taps. If I could really swim, I would take her to the baby pool at the baths.'

Trembling, I enrolled for six lessons, but the dark water at the end of the pool still filled me with terror. I swam no further than a breadth. Even for Vanessa, I couldn't squash the fear and knew I had failed her, for water gave her a freedom she rarely experienced, and she loved it.

Still, Bournemouth with its beautiful gardens, the magnificent pier and the balmy air, was a delight. We have photographs of Abe, Vanessa's grandfather, sitting on a red and white striped deckchair in front of the row of green or yellow changing booths with Vanessa on his knee. She has on a blue and white checked dress and a soft pink jacket; her bare legs look strong and straight. In another photo of our trip to Tucton Lake, I am holding Vanessa up to see the water, the trees and the flowers. Everyone is smiling. She would smile enormously when Sid folded her hand around the club so she could join in a game of pitch and putt.

Chapter 8

'Sid,' I said, full of excitement one evening, 'I met someone at the shops I knew years ago.'

'Chatting away while I was working hard earning a living?' He gave me a mock disapproving look.

I raised my eyebrows. 'She's called Elsa, the prettiest girl in the school they used to say. Her husband's a pharmacist, and would you believe it, they have a little girl like Vanessa. She's disabled, but older.'

He turned his gaze from the television. 'In what way disabled?'

'Autistic. Maybe after an infection when she was three.' I paused. I had something else to say.

'Is she at home?'

'No, and that's what's so interesting. She is resident in a Rudolf Steiner school in Aberdeen.'

'Didn't Doctor Epstein say something about Steiner schools?'

'Yes, he said we should put Vanessa's name down early for a place when she was two. But with all the awful things in her first year, I completely forgot. She is over two already. I'm wondering if we could go with Elsa and her husband to visit the school one day.' He nodded slowly. 'I could ask them round for coffee, and we can talk.'

We met them on several occasions, and arranged to go in September when they were visiting their daughter. As we drove up to Aberdeen, Elsa told us how the disabled children lived in family groups with house parents and their own children. They

70

followed the Steiner ethos based on the principles of rebirth and reincarnation. No payment was involved.

'They are truly wonderful,' she added.

Once there, we were overwhelmed by the beauty of the school's position and surroundings, the countryside outside Aberdeen high, clear and healthy. A perfect place to heal disturbed minds, to care for twisted bodies. Walking round the complex, we could see that children with different kinds of disabilities lived together in order to act therapeutically upon each other. There was such peace and harmony, the spiritual principle of service carried out with so many smiles, such cheerfulness.

Surely they could enhance Vanessa's life far beyond that which I could give her at home? Such a hard decision but the tranquil ambience of the school had affected me profoundly. We decided to apply for a place in one of their schools. But first there would be an interview.

It took place a weekday in November; Sid was working, but my mother was delighted to come along. A train from Manchester to Euston, then a taxi to a quiet house in Hampstead. I held Vanessa all the way, she was so miserable in the pushchair, while my mother carried the food we needed for the journey.

We reached the house and were greeted warmly.

'My daughter's in the school in Aberdeen,' said the kindly woman who invited us in. 'She's so much like your little girl but older.' She touched Vanessa's hand, and naturally, Vanessa beamed.

'She's the only one,' she continued, 'with such a physical handicap but she evokes the most gentle and protective feelings in the more aggressive children.'

She dropped her gaze, and I asked her if she was happy with her daughter being there.

'I'm delighted. They're the most wonderful people. Because I'm a social worker I've worked for years with the Steiner schools to repay my debt to them.' We were sitting by the table, our bags strewn around our feet. With kindly eyes, she looked at us. 'Please don't raise your hopes. The schools rarely take children with severe physical disabilities, who need nursing care.'

'But then who do they take?'

'Children with no place in the state system. The autistic, the psychotic, and we're having such good results with them. But you never know.'

The interview was with the dignified gentle doctor, who told us the waiting list was very long, but we'd hear from them in due course.

Back home, recounting our day to Sid, I was downcast. 'Not sure if they'll have her.'

The letter came the following week: They believed that our daughter was too physically handicapped, and needed more care than they could provide. They couldn't offer her a place.

Mother was quiet when I told her.

Carefully, she said, 'You know I try never to interfere or tell you what to do.'

'I do know. You're wonderful that way.'

'She's so tiny, and I kept wondering if you'd be able to send her four hundred miles away, if the time came.'

'I thought it would be good for her.' I swallowed.

'She's so happy now,' she broke in, 'we all love her. She thrives on love, all you do for her. Perhaps it's for the best.'

My mother had a rare, unwavering belief that children needed love more than discipline.

Later I telephoned Rachel.

'It wasn't *beshert*,' she said.

'*Beshert*?'

'Meant to be. Not that I believe in that kind of thing,' she added firmly. 'She's doing really well now. Understands everything you say to her. Something else will crop up I'm certain.' She changed the subject. 'Will we see you tomorrow?'

'Sid's working but I'll be there with Vanessa.'

'Don't forget to light the candles. Only joking.'

'Of course I will.'

Recently they had given us a pair of beautiful silver candlesticks, intricately carved with grapes and leaves, miniscule handles at the cornices.

'Can't tell you how many hours I spent cleaning those when I was small,' Sid groaned when he saw them. 'With a dead matchstick, a cloth and silver polish. She always found something I'd missed.'

'Take no notice of him,' Rachel said. 'They were my mother's. When I was nine, we brought them from Warsaw, then to Buenos Aires to see my married sister and they ended up in London.'

'What a fantastic journey.'

'My mother was a strong woman. Good looking. We even went up to the captain's table from steerage. Anyway, you hadn't any candlesticks and we thought you'd like these.'

I was moved by their gift; she treated me as the daughter she never had. When she phoned and Sid answered, she would say, 'I don't want to speak to you. I want to talk to Susan!'

I was giving Vanessa her bath one Friday evening. 'Don't twist round to look at the taps,' I said, after I'd soaped her and she'd almost slipped from my grasp.' What's so fascinating? Is it how they shine?'

Lifting her out, wrapping the bath towel around her, I dried her pale gold hair. Her legs had grown straight and sturdy although her arms were ever more rigid, pressing backwards of their own accord. I reflected on how it would be if she went to live somewhere else. Like tearing out part of me, I realised with a start. I took a deep breath. 'I couldn't,' I whispered to her, 'unless it was the best place in the world for you. Now, madam, are you going to help me light the candles?'

Her eyes sparkled; she thrust back her head and wriggled her legs.

'Okay, you can sit in the wheelchair and watch.'

She adored candle-lighting. Often, seeing her ecstatic little face, I wondered if from somewhere in the depths of her soul, she recognised what it meant.

I lit the candles and Vanessa shouted with joy.

In the few months since our arrival in Gatley, almost by osmosis, I had taken on something of a Jewish lifestyle. Through Rachel, I learned about a kosher kitchen, how to light candles, and like many young Jewish couples, we had joined a new local synagogue, Yeshurun Hebrew Congregation, fifteen minutes' walk from us. It was a beautiful modern building with magnificent embroidered wall hangings representing the twelve tribes of Israel. I was relieved that I already knew several members: Judith who'd brought the flowers; our friends Phil and Paula living nearby; women we'd met by the shops together with their children, even others from my teenage years.

The service in classical Hebrew was opaque to me, even reading the English gave me little clarity but I could slip into the women's section carrying Vanessa and leave when I wanted. Sid worked on Saturdays, so we rarely went together. Not understanding the Sabbath service, I couldn't equate it with my search for a spiritual path but I was developing a sense of identity, a feeling of belonging. Something I'd been seeking since adolescence because my father's precepts made me feel like an outsider. For me, being Jewish was complex. I gradually came to understand that Judaism wasn't simply a religion but a way of being, feeling, and thinking. A people, a culture.

Then there were candles on birthday cakes. Vanessa was invited to parties like any two or three-year-old. While mothers welcomed her the children saw her as a baby, but there was no rejection, no distinction. Our circle of friends was growing, excellent, supportive friends who we could rely on over the years. For me, there were also kindred spirits, an expression I first discovered when I read Anne of Green Gables at the age of ten. I understood this to mean someone with whom you shared a special affinity, the same passions, a close connection and an instinctive understanding. By great good fortune, I've made friends at different stages in my life I would call kindred spirits. Friends forever. One of these was Jessica, tall, blonde and good-looking, whom I met at a children's party. I couldn't have known as I sat feeding Vanessa scrambled eggs and cereal while the other children were snatching up chocolate biscuits, that she would have a significant influence on my life in years to come.

She was also what Rachel would call *balabatishe,* a wonderfully creative housekeeper and cook. She loved to make original dishes from simple ingredients, to bake and sew. The house was always tidy, the greens and subtle tones of its decoration creating a sense of harmony. Modigliani prints on the walls spoke of her love of rich colours, while her daughters were always beautifully dressed.

She reminded me of my French friend, Michèle, whose little girls were brought up in a similar way, knowing at a young age how to do things in the house, disciplined, upright.

One evening she called me, 'We're starting a book club. Would you like to come?'

I was thrilled. I'd spent my childhood and early teens lost in a book.

'I'd love to,' I said. 'Where are you meeting?'

'In each other's houses.'

There were twelve members of the club. Not everybody's idea of a night out but we were at home with tiny children, our brains becoming as soggy as their nappies.

A highlight of the month: for those few hours, we were not someone's wife or mum, but ourselves. Nowadays, book clubs are a tool in the publishing trade where celebrity personalities like Richard and Judy run their own, promoting books they have been asked to promote. Contemporary paperbacks contain convenient sets of questions that anyone can use to lead a discussion, nothing wrong with that. But in 1970, we didn't think we were pioneers. Meeting in suburban houses in a pleasant part of south Manchester, our only desire was to escape domesticity for a few hours, share thoughts, ideas, even arguments. Be ourselves.

I was deeply imbued with my parents' beliefs in making the world a better place, of caring for those who needed help. My mother would read to people who were blind, or work with the WVS serving refreshments in the Eye Hospital, while my father would collect the pensions of friends who were housebound, or give lifts to those without a car, and both were deeply committed socialists. So when Judith (who had first welcomed us to Gatley) invited me to join the League of Jewish Women, I was delighted. They did, and continue to do voluntary work of every kind in the wider community, and I joined. Going to their meetings I met other socially aware young women.

For my 'rota' I offered to serve bedtime drinks in a local hospital with another member of the organisation. As we were serving hot chocolate to a friendly old gentleman sitting in an armchair, she asked me about my family and of course, I didn't hesitate.

She stared at me. Then she stated: 'I think children like that should be put down at birth.'

I recoiled.

I wanted to snap back: 'Stupid, prejudiced woman. You don't know what you're talking about.'

At home, I called the chair person and told her I would never again work with this woman. I knew, of course I knew, that probably the majority of people thought like her. Another time, as I wheeled Vanessa to the synagogue, a young woman crossed the road away from us – did she also feel disgust?

Still, I volunteered for the 'Housebound Library' and really looked forward to taking books to people who couldn't get out, chatting about our favourites, and exchanging the names of authors we recommended to each other. Much more my kind of thing.

In early 1970, when Vanessa was three, Mother brought a newspaper cutting which described an innovative treatment for handicapped children: the American Dolman-Delacarta Method. The article related how a local woman had removed her disabled child from the English medical system and organised the family's life around this rigorous physical system which was unknown here. The newspaper put me in touch with the family. In her compact, neat little bungalow, the mother had gathered a huge group of volunteers essential for this work, telling us with pride she was seeing positive results.

It depended on a theory of the evolutionary development of *crawling*, postulating that human beings developed like animals, crawling before they walked. It claimed that teaching the child to crawl would correct malfunctioning and 'normalise' any child with mental retardation or physical disability. *Patterning* in which the child lay on his stomach while four people worked his arms and legs rhythmically 'teaching' his brain the crawling mechanism. They repeated this procedure many times a day, every day. Another intervention was to place a mask over the child's face so that he inhaled his own carbon dioxide, increasing oxygen to the brain, so they claimed.

'I've got a team of one hundred and forty-four people who work in turn,' she said.

'How could you continue this work if you had other children? Wouldn't they be ignored or even neglected, while you're so occupied with your handicapped child?'

'I suppose they'd just fit in.' She laughed.

We didn't do this. We wouldn't take our daughter away from Doctor Epstein or our Doctor Griffiths, our general practitioner in Cheadle. The founders of *The Institute of Human Potential* demanded that families sever connections with all medical services in the United Kingdom. Plus several thousand dollars to register for the scheme.

Did we make the right decision? I worried we'd been too timid to try something away from the common path. What a relief to read years later, that the American medical authorities judged this to be a scam, with no evidence of improving the life of any disabled child. Still, I thought sadly, we would do anything if we believed it would help.

Chapter 9

A curious feeling began to flutter in my heart. From a feeling, it became a longing, even a yearning. I didn't know how this occurred. Perhaps it was meeting all those young families in their homes or at the shops, maybe it was little hints from our parents. Or perhaps it was some instinctive need just waiting for the right moment.

A baby … I want another baby.

Little by little, we came to this scary decision, although it was fraught with uncertainty and made my heart thrum whenever I thought about it.

'I'd better find out if anything could happen again,' I said to Sid after we'd discussed it for the umpteenth time.

Our general practitioner Doctor Griffiths was Welsh, with the characteristic Celtic colouring, black hair, pale skin, a former rugby player. He was an excellent diagnostician but lacked any bedside manner. He agreed that we didn't want a repeat of our situation and told us to see a geneticist at the Infirmary.

After listening to our story, the geneticist said that since our ancestors came from Eastern Europe, from behind the Iron Curtain, it was impossible to look at family documents. 'Go ahead anyway. Your chances of having another disabled child would be the same as any other woman's. I wish you the best of luck.'

We did, weeks passed and nothing happened. Everyone I knew was having a second, third or even a fourth child. I went back to see our local doctor and he referred me to a gynaecologist, David Warrell.

'Is he at Saint Mary's?' I asked, dreadful memories clouding my mind.

'See him in his rooms.'

He was dignified, reassuring, the most gentle of men. At my second visit, he initiated me into the arts of temperature taking, explaining the steps we'd follow if we were unable to have a child. It was a new, painful world, giving me insight into other women's problems. I was coming to know the dark state of mind of those who couldn't have children, their desperation and despair.

I began to wonder about some kind of spiritual answer. It came to me one Friday evening out of the blue. I was reading the *hatch, match and dispatch* columns in a local paper. Tucked away was a small advertisement: Do you need help and support? Please contact *The Jewish Marriage Education Council*. There was a North Manchester phone number to call.

Despite Sid's warning look, I decided to telephone. Unlike me, he would always seek to solve his own problems. Religion, spirituality, held no attraction for him. Nevertheless, on Sunday morning I made the call, and a Mrs Gruber answered. She had a light intonation, a swift manner of speaking. She told me they helped to supply food and clothing to poor people, which made me interrupt, embarrassed, saying I seemed to have misunderstood the advertisement. She paused. And then she asked softly if I wanted to learn about *Yiddishkeit*, about Orthodox Judaism. This was also their work.

I had been searching all these years. Perhaps I had found the answer.

'I would like to,' I said, and she sounded so delighted when she said we should meet and talk. I explained about Vanessa being handicapped, that it was difficult to come, except on nursery days but at this point I didn't mention anything about pregnancy. She offered to come to us the following Sunday. Her husband would bring her since she didn't drive, and with a mixture of apprehension and excitement, I agreed.

Such a pretty woman, small, with dark hair, and wearing a long skirted flowery dress with sleeves to her wrists; she greeted me as I opened the front door. Her husband who wore a large black hat and suit, a white shirt and no tie, nodded soberly, then turning to touch the mezuzah, the tiny tube enclosing a scroll on our front door, he kissed his fingertips. I stepped back and gripped my hands together tightly. Already I was feeling quite uncomfortable in his presence.

'Please come in. My husband is with Vanessa in the lounge.'

Mrs Gruber went at once to take Vanessa's hand, to exchange smiles. For a moment I wondered if I should give them separate chairs, but she sat next to her husband on the orange sofa. Although she wore no make-up, her skin was beautifully clear, making it impossible to know her age, I guessed she was in her early thirties. Straight-backed, her hands folded in her lap, and she had a sense of brightness about her, eagerness.

There was a long silence. Thankfully Vanessa, who was sitting on Sid's knee, began to make a shouting noise.

'We've been doing unusual work with her,' I gabbled, 'with a doctor at the university.'

Mrs Gruber asked lots of questions, directing them first at me, then at Sid, and we talked for some time about Vanessa, our work with her, while her husband kept his eyes lowered. I offered them tea or coffee but Mrs Gruber, smiling gently, said that they were fine. She bent her head, and I realised that her beautiful wavy brown hair was a *sheitel,* a wig.

There was an awkward pause and I needed to keep the conversation going; timidly I said, 'How do you help people learn about Jewish life, Mrs Gruber?'

She asked me if I knew what *mitzvahs* were.

'Commandments,' I think.

She smiled then she asked if I knew that there were special mitzvahs only for women, and I shook my head.

'Like lighting the candles.'

'I do that,' I said with relief.

'Or having a kosher kitchen with separate dishes and pans for meat and milk.'

'I do that too.' Thank goodness, I thought.

She beamed.

'So much to learn about being an Orthodox Jewish person. If you like, you could come over one day and we could talk about whatever you want. Is that possible?' She glanced at Vanessa.

'She goes to nursery two days a week. I could come then.' My heart was beating faster. It felt as if I was about to do something both terrifying and wonderful.

The following week I drove north through the centre of Manchester, turning into Cheetham Hill Road. I crossed the railway bridge, the boundary, passing Red Bank where my great-grandparents in the 1880s had settled with their brood of children. Then, through Cheetham Village into Leicester Road – and I gasped.

I might have been in a stetl, the 19th-century village of my Russian grandfather in the Pale of Settlement: men with beards, all wearing black garb, running to study houses; women with *sheitels,* wigs sleek as bowls and wearing long dark skirts to the ankle. No wonder Mr Gruber had looked askance at my legs. And children, crowds of tiny children walking as in a daisy chain, hand in hand, until the smallest held onto the pram beside their mother.

The Grubers' house had a very large mezuzah on the door lintel but no bell, so I knocked. At once, as though she was hovering behind, Mrs Gruber opened the door. 'Hello, Mrs Stern, how nice to see you. Please come in.'

We passed through the hall to a small square kitchen, the table close to the window.

'Would you like some tea or maybe coffee?'

'Tea would be lovely, please.'

Mrs Gruber disappeared into the back kitchen, returning at once with a tray. Shyly, a little silent, we both drank the tea then Mrs Gruber said, 'Now tell me, Mrs Stern…'

'Susan or Sue,' I broke in.

'And please call me Hetty.' We began to feel more comfortable with each other. 'So what would you like to know about Yiddishkeit? About Orthodox Judaism?'

'Over the years, I've been searching for a way.'

'A belief. Is that what you mean?'

'I think so.'

'Judaism is a practical religion. When we received the Ten Commandments at Mount Sinai… You do know about the Ten Commandments?' I nodded.

'We believe that the entire Jewish nation was there. And everyone said: *We will do and we will obey.* They said: *do*, so we, as observant Jews, are expected to fulfil all the six hundred and thirteen commandments that were given at this time to get closer to Hashem.'

'Hashem?'

'We're not allowed to say God's name, we say Hashem, which means The Name or the Holy One, Blessed Be He.'

'Did you say six hundred and thirteen?'

'Many of them are connected with the Temple, and we don't have to carry those out.'

Perhaps I should remind her about Sunday. 'You said you would tell me what women have to do.'

'Because of our role in the family, we don't have to pray three times a day. We pray in the morning.'

I frowned. 'Why don't women do the same as the men?'

'Who could run out to the synagogue in the middle of feeding a baby? It's not possible. We look after our families. So we're exempt because of our role in the home, which is also holy. Many of us work as well.'

'On Sunday you talked about candle lighting and having a kosher kitchen, and I think you were going to say something else when Sid interrupted?'

Two bright spots of colour appeared on her pale cheeks, as though she'd banished some thought that had come unbidden.

She inhaled, 'It was better he did. I wanted to tell you about the Mikveh. It's easier when men aren't around. But would you like more tea?'

I hadn't mentioned the real reason for my phone call to the council. With a fresh pot of tea on the table, now was my opportunity

'It wasn't because of Vanessa that I phoned the Council.' I turned my gaze to the hand-sewn mat on the floor.

'I guessed there was something else,' she said softly.

'Some months ago we decided it would be good to have another child. But I can't get pregnant. Your advertisement made me wonder if you could help. Not sure how though.' I gave her a bemused smile.

She became very still.

Locking her eyes with mine, she murmured, 'I understand.' Her voice was full of compassion, and as she spoke I felt that she was choosing every word. 'I suspect you won't know that for us, it's a great mitzvah to have many children.' She averted her gaze. 'But we have only one, our son, Menachem, who is twelve.'

We were both silent. I took a deep breath, wondering what to say. Finally, I touched her arm. 'I'm very sorry.'

'But we must never despair. Despair is a great sin. It cuts you off from Hashem. When the time is right,' she glanced upwards. 'When He wants it, we'll have another child.'

That kind of faith was beyond me. 'I wish I could think like you,' I muttered.

She leaned towards me, her eyes lit up. 'Now I can tell you about the Mikveh, the special commandment for women.'

'The Mikveh?'

'You observe it for yourself and your family.' She paused, 'You did go to the Mikveh before your wedding?'

'I've never heard of it.'

I told her about my father's atheism, that even though my mother was Jewish, she'd been fostered by a Christian family when her own mother had died in childbirth. That my wedding day was perhaps the fourth time I had been in a synagogue.

Her eyes widened.

'Then let's talk about the Mikveh. It's called *Taharat le Mishpacah*: in English, the laws of family purity. The mikveh is a kind of well of living water. A woman goes there for ablution after her period. She counts five days for menstruation followed by another seven days, when she's 'unclean.' Of course, not in a real sense.' She laughed. 'We all shower or take a bath. No, this is a *spiritual* uncleanness. On the twelfth day, after nightfall, she submerges herself in the mikveh three times, followed by the appropriate blessing. There's a woman we call the mikveh lady. She's a saintly woman, who checks everything, really an expert.' She smiled. 'After it's finished, the woman carrying out the mitzvah can cohabit with her husband. But during the twelve previous days they must be apart. We have separate beds, and avoid any physical contact with each other. Until the right time. It's a beautiful, powerful mitzvah. The children born of this union are kosher.'

'Without this, they aren't?' I gaped at Hetty. Was this why Vanessa was disabled?

She must have guessed what I was thinking because she said, 'We learn this when we're young. But I assure you, you feel so uplifted, so glorious, when you come out of the Mikveh, you feel pure.'

'For twelve days, you can't have intercourse? Then you can?'

'Not only you can, but you must!' She smiled.

Spiritually pure? I knew religions used water as purification, but that it was fundamental to Judaism made me open my eyes wide in astonishment. And what about a baby being kosher, or the opposite, whatever that meant.

'Would you like to experience this?' Hetty interrupted my thoughts. 'You'll find it's wonderful.'

'I can't swim very much.'

She burst out laughing. 'It's only a small cubicle of water: you step down two steps, you turn, and step down two more. The walls rise up around you. And the water only reaches your chest.' She pointed to beneath her arms. 'Then you draw yourself down until it covers your hair. Three times. It's so easy.'

'Could this be the right time now that I'm trying to get pregnant?' I whispered

'I think it could.'

'What should I do if I decide to go?'

'Count the days of your period. Then count seven days, making sure there's no spot of blood, and if there is, you start counting again until you've had seven 'clean' days. I tell you what, phone me around the time, and I'll help you decide.'

'You will come with me?'

'Of course.' She beamed.

I glanced at my watch. 'Goodness, look at the time. You've given me a lot to think about, Hetty. Thank you so much.'

'It's been a pleasure. Let me know if you'd like to go one evening.'

I felt such a connection with her. Both wanting a child, and in her case, children; neither of us achieving it.

'I do hope we meet again,' she said. 'Ask me anything about being Jewish, and I'll help you.'

Driving home, I felt I wanted go to the Mikveh, at least once. Later I told Sid. 'It might help me get pregnant.'

He raised his eyebrows.

The rabbi of the synagogue we'd joined the year before but rarely attended, paid us an unexpected visit to 'make himself known.' When we told him about Vanessa, he asked us why we weren't having more children.

I felt quite embarrassed when I said it wasn't happening. He replied that I should speak to his wife, she knew about these things. She'd even tell us how to have a boy or girl. Listening to him, I thought that this was how a rabbi must have spoken to my great-grandmother in the stetl.

'It also helps to stop brooding' he added. 'Do something entirely different for a while.'

'Good idea,' Sid said, after he'd gone. 'You could give us a hand in the shop. What do you think?'

'Vanessa could go more often to the nursery.' My voice drifted away.

But it was arranged. I dropped Vanessa off at Rodney House, and continued to Gorton. Working four days a week was a great distraction. Near the end of November, I woke with that familiar, unique sensation of something different, *alive* within me.

I raced downstairs to Sid who was reading the paper before work.

'We've done it!' I cried.

'What have we done?' He remarked, still glued to the newspaper.

'I think I'm pregnant!'

At the doctor's surgery I discreetly passed the urine sample in its scrupulously clean bottle to the gatekeeper – the receptionist. When she told me that the results would be back in a week, I sighed. And no, she couldn't tell me over the telephone, I would have to make an appointment to see the doctor. A week was an aeon of time but it came at last. The results were there, but no, there were no appointments for that day, I would have to wait until the following day, 4:30 in the afternoon, which meant taking Vanessa with me. I would have rather gone on my own, but there was no choice.

We went, another spell of uncertainty while Vanessa almost jumped off my knee every time the doctor's voice boomed over the loudspeaker system, calling the next patient. But at last it was us.

I knocked and went in. Normally, I would have waited for him to say, 'What can I do for you, Mrs Stern?'

But at once I demanded: 'Dr Griffiths, please tell me, am I pregnant?'

He raised his eyebrows, and with a measured look said, 'Mrs Stern, I'm happy to say that you are. It was positive.'

Vanessa was sitting straddled over my knee, her legs hanging down next to mine. My heart leaping, I gave her a great hug and she smiled in delight. I knew, of course, I knew already but I needed official confirmation. 'What about antenatal care? Where will I have the baby?'

'St Mary's.'

Horrible memories leapt into my mind: the gynaecological ward where they'd expected me to miscarry at twenty weeks; the children's ward where the paediatrician had said, 'It's not you. It's the baby who's not normal.' The humiliation of learning how to feed my baby on that very ward when she was three months old.

'Couldn't you look after me here?'

'I wouldn't dream of it. With your history, it will be St Mary's. The new hospital of course.'

I gave a sigh of relief.

Chapter 10

December 1970, my first antenatal visit.

Passing through the wide glass doors of the new antenatal building, I experienced a melange of excitement, wonder and apprehension. I was excited to be at the beginning of a second pregnancy and full of wonderment at this luxurious modern building, a five star hotel in comparison with the 'old' hospital, now dust and rubble. I guessed they would have the most up-to-date knowledge, the latest equipment. But I was in such a state of apprehension, my heart was racing. What would happen this time? Would something go wrong? Thoughts I hardly dared whisper even to myself.

Everything will be wonderful, I told myself fiercely.

In the waiting area, women sat in comfortable armchairs reading magazines. No one had stockings rolled round their ankles as we'd done in the old St Mary's Hospital. The cattle market, they called it.

I walked to the desk where I found a familiar face from the past: the midwife who used to preside over the women in the old hospital. My heart began to pound so loudly I felt that the women queuing behind me could hear it. Overwhelmed by the swirl of anxious memories from those terrible months five years ago, I stopped.

The midwife had no such qualms. 'Hello, Mrs Stern, it's lovely to see you. You're back with us again.' She drew my file of notes from the trolley. 'Here you are.'

Resolved to forget everything about the first pregnancy, I said, 'I guess this is a much better place to work.'

'It's wonderful. Makes such a difference to the staff. Everyone was miserable over there, always draughty and cold; I know it affected the patients as much as us.' She held up my notes. 'Lucky lady, you're with Doctor Warrell. He's a wonderful man!'

'I'm so relieved.' All the anxiety fell away when I heard that. 'I saw him several times when I thought I couldn't get pregnant.'

'And your first, how did it go?' Her face became sombre when I told her about Vanessa. 'It was the same for a friend of mine. The husband couldn't stand it, and ran off. Make sure such a dreadful thing doesn't happen to you.'

'How do you feel about this pregnancy?' Doctor Warrell asked after the routine examination.

'Very pleased.' I didn't allow myself to be over enthusiastic, fearing that certainty might invoke 'the evil eye,' though I didn't really believe in such a thing.

'We know your history.' He laid his hand on my notes. 'Even without what happened, women are apprehensive. It's entirely normal.'

When it was time to leave, he stood to shake my hand. 'I shall see you every appointment unless there's some emergency. There's nothing to worry about.'

Such a lovely man, tall, well-spoken, probably from a public school background, he often addressed me as *my dear* over the following weeks. Thank heavens, they passed uneventfully, my blood pressure, the growth of the baby, my weight. Everything was perfect.

A new energy entered our lives.

With Vanessa, I was inspired to work even more intensely than before, encouraging her to spend long hours in the chair.

'You can do it, Vanessa,' I would say as I knelt behind the chair. She slowly, slowly reached out for a brick or wooden toy. 'Good girl.'

We moved the chair to the dining room where I could kneel comfortably on the carpet, but how could I carry on like this until the baby was born? Recalling the woman who had found people to 'pattern' her child, I sent a message to the synagogue newsletter, asking for people interested to come and watch what we did.

So many people responded, I was touched. Every morning, I would tell them it would be tough going, against all their instinctive feeling about handling a child, any child.

'But it's the only way she will learn,' I smiled. 'If she cries, and she certainly will, we must take no notice. She has to learn to do what *you* want, not what *she* wants.'

Kneeling behind her, giving a running commentary, I explained the work. Many were shocked; few returned. But Vanessa was thrilled with all these people watching her and lifted her head constantly to smile, so despite her disability, she charmed them all. Of a dozen women who came, two remained: Mrs Hurst, a lively intelligent woman who had come to England before the war, a young refugee escaping the Nazis. She had experience of working with children in homes, and recognised at once what Vanessa needed. She came daily as my bump grew. Even showing me that Vanessa had a sense of humour, something I didn't know. Who would've thought that Mrs Hurst's account of being a refugee in England would be published and dramatised on Woman's Hour years later?

February 1971, Vanessa's fourth birthday, and I held a party for her, inviting all the little four and five-year-olds we knew. They piled their plates with sandwiches, argued over chocolate biscuits and demanded more ice cream. How articulate they were! When

Chapter 10

I took a birthday cake to Rodney House the following day, I saw how the staff still carried our little daughter like a baby, and I was upset. We needed to find a school or unit where she would be treated like the little girl she was.

Recalling that Miss Burgess, the chief physiotherapist, knew everything available in the area, I spoke to her following Vanessa's session. She asked if I'd heard about Pictor House, a school run by the Spastics Society, excellent, forward-looking, where Vanessa could stay until she was nine.

'It's just opened. For about fifteen years there's been a house with facilities for children like your daughter. Mainly run by volunteers. It has a wonderful reputation with huge support by people like Violet Carson, you know, from Coronation Street, and many of the theatrical people who raise money for charities. Last year I attended a conference about the early discovery and diagnosis of cerebral palsy.'

'Miss Burgess, I can't thank you enough. I'll make enquiries the moment I get home.'

'Let me know what you find out.'

A jewel of a discovery.

'Please come and visit us,' said the Matron when I called that evening.

A week later I left Vanessa for her trial visit; they promised she could attend three days a week if it suited her. It was wonderful. However much or little Vanessa understood about having a baby brother or sister, I felt she would be jealous. Better if she could be settled before the baby's arrival in August. After an interview with the matron and doctor, we went into a large bright room, where children like Vanessa were lying over wedges on the floor, or sitting hunched in wheelchairs, much as in her nursery although they were larger, older. But it was bright; the children clean and dressed like any child you could meet in the street while the volunteer staff was friendly and welcoming.

'Now Vanessa, I'll push you in the wheelchair to that space where you can see everyone. You're going to have a lovely time today.'

I had made this decision instinctively. I was growing up at last, leaving behind that crippling uncertainty and lack of self-belief I'd had in my first year of marriage.

It proved to be a brilliant choice. The previous year, the MP Jack Ashley, had pushed through an act of Parliament in which the education of children deemed 'ineducable or subnormal,' were to be included in the 1970 Education Act. Until now, they were cared for as 'sick' children, and allowed no specific education. This was a source of great anger to parents and many medical officers.

When the act was passed, the very month Vanessa started Pictor House School, qualified teachers like the new headmistress Mrs Vickers were appointed, and teachers trained to work with the 'mentally handicapped.'

Mrs Vickers was inspirational. She set up a one-year scheme of investigation into all aspects of the school. Vanessa's classroom was renamed the *Developmental Unit* and every kind of sense stimulation activity was introduced to the children. Light, music, odours, the touch and smell of sensory stimuli such as coarse cloth, velvet, and their reactions or lack of them all noted. To make physiotherapy part of the children's life, they were treated in the classroom, integrating physiotherapy with the child's individual programme. This very idea had inspired me to take the wooden chair to Rodney House, but with such dreary results.

Soon afterwards I was invited to meet one of the speech therapists.

'It's about the assessment of Vanessa's language development,' she said. 'We do this with all the children. If the child can speak, it makes our job easier. But for those like your daughter, we've devised ingenious ways to find out what they understand. Like these pictures, for example.'

On her desk lay a series of brightly coloured pictures: a door, a cup, a child, a grandmother, together with more complex things like a box of cereal in a cupboard, a person sitting on a chair. Stick figures with round simple faces, smiling, sad, surprised.

'We've shown these to her and were amazed. Vanessa used her eyes to show us she recognised every picture as we named it. You wouldn't believe this, but she got full marks.'

I wasn't surprised, always believing in my heart that Vanessa was an intelligent child, only hindered by her handicap.

'We think she has the comprehension of a two-year-old. You must have worked very hard with her.'

'Everyone has. Because I'd been a teacher, I knew this is what we'd have to do. It came naturally.' We laughed. 'My mother's a great back-up' I added. 'When Vanessa stays with her, she tells her stories about Tommy, a boy in a picture she's pinned to the kitchen wall. Whenever we visit, Mother asks where Tommy is, and Vanessa looks towards the kitchen.'

I told Sid when he came home and we grinned at each other.

'Phone the family,' he said. 'I know you're dying to do that.'

'I will. I'm very proud of her.'

Another transformation occurred with my decision to look for help in the house. Our friends the Gabbies, had a Dutch au pair girl who fitted in so well with the family, I was really taken with the idea. Especially after my experience of working as an au pair girl in a Breton hotel when I was a student. The little Breton girls who worked night and day became my friends. We didn't have much to eat, but I found a marvellous freedom in speaking another language, almost becoming another person. This added another layer to my love affair with France.

Anne Denis came in April 1971. Tall and good-looking, she had blonde hair, green eyes enhanced by eyeliner, long black lashes, and wore narrow jeans and boots; we talked together in the lounge while Vanessa sat on my knee, staring at her with interest. It was such a familiar story: a family she disliked, her main task to look after the children, and forced to take her meals with them, disgusting children's food, she said, like fish fingers or pizza made in a factory. The evenings she spent in her room like a servant, never with the parents.

Horrified that English people could treat a French person like that, I felt very sympathetic, but as we talked I wondered if living with us might not suit her. When she said she wanted to be an air hostess, and that's why she had come to England to improve her English, I told her she would work for five hours a day with us, doing light housework, helping to give Vanessa a bath when she got used to her, maybe feeding her if necessary. 'But you'd be part of the family. Eat with us, watch television if you wanted. Go to classes.'

'That will be very nice.'

She asked if she could smoke. I agreed without a second thought, it would be outrageous nowadays, but then even doctors smoked in their surgeries. She took a blue and white packet of *Gitanes* from her handbag, selected a cigarette, and lit it with one of those tubular lighters so familiar to me from my life in Paris.

'Maybe you'd prefer to look elsewhere?'

'*Elle est belle*, Mrs Stern, she's beautiful. I will come here.'

After a few pouty lips, Vanessa got used to Anne and she became devoted to Vanessa, often taking her to her room when she'd hold Vanessa on her knee while talking to her many friends. She would go through the intricate process of applying make-up, and to my daughter's utmost delight, varnishing her nails. Our house had become a kind of focal point, with Vanessa, the queen, surveying her subjects while French, German or Swiss girls crowded Anne's bedroom, smoking and laughing. It was wonderful having someone French in the house. Anne was more like a younger sister, so I accepted her excuses for being late. The bus didn't arrive or she'd taken the wrong train, when all the while she was sitting with friends in a Cheadle café, probably criticising their hostesses and longing to be back home.

They couldn't complain about the weather: from the beginning of May, there was a heat wave. We had to remember Vanessa's sunhat when we all sat in the garden.

With someone to babysit, Sid and I went out in the evenings, often with the Gabbies. While Vanessa had her admiring circle of young women, our social life grew wonderfully. One day I suggested to Anne it would be better for Vanessa to lie on the hall floor as usual, while I was cooking.

'Not to sit on your knee.'

'I can't do that. All my friends want to see her.'

So I gave in, allowing our daughter these social moments even if it felt that I was spoiling her, defying one of the objectives of the programme: to keep to a set routine.

But in view of what eventually happened, it was lucky that I did.

Sid walked in one evening, saying: 'We must do something about the house. Extend it somehow. We need a larger kitchen, an extra bedroom, especially when the new baby arrives.'

'And you already have some ideas?'

'Yes, but we need an architect who knows about disability, who can advise us.'

We found one who seemed ideal. He drew up plans for rooms with widened doorways for the wheelchair. He recommended a bathroom with a small moulded bath, which would replace the kitchen at the end of the hall. He drew plans for a square kitchen at one end of a modernised playroom. Domesticity had never appealed to me, I enjoyed housework even less, but we needed a particular kind of space to answer our needs.

Having already designed two dispensaries, Sid was delighted to work with the architect, discussing, measuring and planning, and was deeply involved in our new venture. I made a minimal contribution: I chose the kitchen cupboards. The architect recommended a specially formulated carpet which allowed wheelchairs to move freely along the floor. At work, Sid envisaged even more change: together with his brother Michael he was considering buying an old established pharmacy in Altrincham, a local market town because the Gorton pharmacy had been *leap-frogged* by another pharmacist, opening closer to Dr Burt's surgery than ours, and affected the business.

Anne came at Easter when I was almost five months pregnant. We had a little team of women working with Vanessa. The pregnancy was going so well, plenty of movement from the baby energetically exploring his or her space in my stomach, and my bump was shaping hugely. But I was driven to work even harder with Vanessa, desperate to see her make more progress before the baby arrived. I kept her long hours in the chair or crawled beside her as I moved her round the floor, activating her legs.

I was a woman possessed.

It had dreadful consequences.

One morning in May, I heard the front doorbell ring.

I was on my hands and knees in the dining room, holding Vanessa over my right hand and manipulating her arms and hands with the other, which meant I was supporting myself,

Vanessa and the weight of the baby, bending and lifting like some weird animal.

I heard Anne open the door to whoever it was: 'They're in the dining room.'

It was my mother- and father-in-law. But I barely noticed them.

'What are you doing?'

I raised my eyes at the sound of Rachel's horrified voice. They stood together at the doorway, their eyes wide, their faces locked in horror. Marching into the room, Rachel banged her handbag down on the dining room table. 'Susan! Are you mad? Look at you. You must *stop* all this.' She bent forwards as though to drag Vanessa from my hands. This was unheard of; they'd never interfered in any way. Besides, I doubt if Rachel could have lifted Vanessa from the floor, she was so heavy and awkward.

I straightened up, still kneeling on the carpet. 'I have to make the most of my time before the baby is born.' I spat the words out. How dare they tell me what to do with Vanessa!

Rachel threw a furious glance at her husband, and I saw his face was dark with anger.

'Rachel's right,' he said. 'You shouldn't be doing this now. You should be resting.'

'Give her away! You must give her away!' Rachel shouted.

Lifting Vanessa from the floor, I yelled, '*Give her away?* Don't you understand she means more to me than anything the world? I couldn't *ever* give her away.'

We had never quarrelled. I had never seen them angry. All that day I was deeply troubled by the confrontation we'd had in the morning, but I was determined that nothing, nobody would deflect me from this work.

How wrong I was. Someone else was angry with me, and it wasn't my husband.

It was the baby.

Although everything was fine at my next antenatal visit, three days after Rachel had implored me to *give Vanessa away*, I was shaken out of my sleep by something terrifying, something I had already experienced before Vanessa was born. Was it all happening again? I clutched my stomach with both hands. It was becoming hard, then harder, and pain surged around my back and down my legs. I tried to sit up but instinctively I knew that I shouldn't move. Very slowly, I lay back, my head on the pillow.

Contractions. I was twenty-six weeks pregnant and in labour. *Twenty-six weeks*. Could the baby survive?

In terror, I called out, 'Sid, wake up! Please wake up. Something's wrong.'

'What's the matter?' He'd been so busy at work, he could barely open his eyes.

I shook him.

'You must wake up! We have to call a doctor.' I was groaning now.

'You're in pain? Contractions?'

'Yes.'

We called out a duty doctor. Hours dragged by. I could barely breathe I was so afraid of what might happen. When he arrived, he said, 'You're having contractions, but I can't do anything about it. You girls generally want to get started, not stopped. I'll give you a sedative. Get some sleep.'

And left.

Next morning, Anne asked me quietly if anything was the matter.

'Just a few pains,' I said. 'We had to call the doctor. I'm all right now.'

'I'll get Vanessa dressed today. You take it easy.'

Sid was looking worried. 'What will you do? Michael won't be there until later, so I have to go to work.'

'I'm a bit better,' I said carefully. 'The contractions aren't so strong this morning.'

'You could get a taxi?'

'No, I'll be fine.'

But as I drove to St Mary's, the contractions swelling and hardening my stomach were far stronger than during the night. Like a mad woman, I careered through the lights on amber, parked as near as I could, and grasping my stomach with both hands, my breath coming unevenly, I pushed through the main entrance to the foyer and ran heavily to my friend at the central desk, jumping the queue in my anguish.

'I need to see Dr Warrell,' I cried, my words coming in short bursts. 'I'm having contractions.'

'This is an emergency.' The sister told the other women waiting in the queue. ' She must see a doctor at once!'

As they recognised what was happening, they immediately moved out of the way, and for a fleeting moment, I saw my fear and anguish mirrored in their eyes. Wasn't this every woman's deepest anxiety – to lose her baby? I waited for long moments until a nurse arrived to escort me to Dr Warrell's room where she tapped gently on his door. Peering round, she spoke quietly to him. 'It's all right,' she said, 'he'll see you now.'

'Come and lie on the bed, Mrs Stern. Nurse will help you up.'

Gently, the nurse uncovered my stomach. Dr Warrell bent his head close to my bump and listened. With a feather-like touch, he examined me. 'My dear, you haven't driven here on your own like this?'

I nodded, my heart pounding, feeling a pulse in my ears, in my throat.

'We'll send you for a scan. That will show us where we're up to.'

A porter wheeled me into the lift, pressing the button that would take us to the scanning department. I leaned back in the chair, my icy fingers gripping the sides, my eyes closed. What would happen? Would I lose this baby? Was this my fault?

I needed to change position in the chair, something wasn't right. Suddenly, I felt a gush of water down my legs and onto my feet. I cried out. The porter looked down, and then pressing the button, we flew to the top floor, to the delivery suite.

I was on a high delivery bed. People moved swiftly around me, conferring, calling out. I lay still with my eyes closed, my stomach hard as a ball with the contractions. A doctor came. There was an injection. I lost consciousness. Time passed.

When I woke again I was alone. I slept, knowing I should wake up, but it was as though my eyelids had immense weights on them. Then I heard a voice calling my name, a familiar voice. I made a huge effort, and saw Dr Warrell.

'Ah, you're awake at last,' he said gravely.

I forced myself to keep my eyes open but when I tried sit up, I could feel pain, like a shadow of a pain, its fingers pressing my stomach. I flopped back.

'Stay lying down, Mrs Stern.' He paused for a moment. 'We almost lost the baby, my dear. However, we were fortunate. Only half the waters escaped. We've stopped the contractions for the moment.'

'Is the baby all right?'

'For the meantime, yes. We'll keep you here until your body recovers its equilibrium. You must have complete rest.'

I knew what it was. In my heart, I knew. He or she was furious. Didn't like the place it was in. For five and a half months of this baby's life I had almost ignored his or her existence, obsessed as I was with my daughter. I was certain the baby had grasped what I had said to Rachel, a few days before: Vanessa is the most important thing in the world to me. And wanted to leave. Or maybe, the baby was saying, 'What about me?' I so hoped it was that.

Chapter 11

A small white room, a bedside cupboard, two chairs. Sun shearing through the window, beating down on Manchester streets. The intense heat of the room. Nurses, doctors, ward assistants, coming and going.

Terror. My mind aflight with anxiety, fear racing through every nerve in my body.

What would happen to the baby? Could he or she survive, if... I couldn't say the words ... the worst took place? Would he or she be properly formed? And would I suffer, as they always said, more than if the baby came at the right time? Hearing a trundling sound from the corridor outside my room, I was back in the gynaecological ward where I had expected to lose Vanessa, and I froze.

But it was Elaine, pushing along the tea trolley.

'Mrs Stern, you all right?' She was poking her head in.

'Yes,' I croaked. 'Sorry. I didn't hear you.'

Wedging the door open, she filled a cup from the spigot on the urn. 'There you are, a nice cup of tea to begin the day. You want two sugars?'

'One, please.'

'I'll help you up. Can't drink tea lying down, can you?'

Deftly, she slid back the metal bed rest, stacked up the pillows and helped me sit up. 'Don't you go worrying about anything, Mrs Stern. The Lord will look after you.'

I could hear her singing as she pushed the trolley, rattling its way back to the ward. After drinking the tea, my mind still frantic, whirling, I would slide down into bed, my head pressed awkwardly on the lowest pillow until the night sister, completing her round, would call in and reverse the process, telling me to lie flat which was more relaxing.

Full of self-pity, I said I wished I could.

She went to pull up the blind. The sky was muslin blue, like the skies in my beloved Provence, and for a moment, my heart lifted with memories of the South, of the Midi. At the door, she pointed her finger at me. 'Now you take it easy. Think beautiful thoughts.'

Beautiful thoughts? As my mind cleared from the night sedation, an even greater fear possessed me, taut, inescapable: Vanessa, my little Vanessa. What would happen to her? Who would look after her? What about our work?

And the memory of that morning when Rachel and Abe had stared at me in horror, and those words: Give her away, grew and grew in my mind until I wanted to scream. By ten o'clock, after five hours of this panic, I felt my stomach harden and harden, pain radiating down the sides of my belly into my back, and the contractions had started again. Every five minutes: a danger sign.

I would ring the bell, and a nurse would appear. 'What is it now, Mrs Stern?'

'Contractions again.'

'Let's have a look, shall we?'

She would sit beside me, place her hand on my stomach and time the contractions, holding her watch in her left hand.

After a minute, she would say, 'Not too bad. Keep resting.'

'What if they…?'

'What if nothing. Just keep calm. And don't worry.'

As though my anguish about Vanessa was affecting my body, it continued day after day. Weirdly, the contractions faded away in the late afternoon. I was almost happy. When I asked the nurses why this was they shrugged. Perhaps it was a subconscious hope that Sid would come in the evening, and I could tell him how frightened I was. At the beginning, only he was allowed to visit. He would come straight from work, staying for a while then going home, or sometimes to his mother's for a meal.

Our conversation was a record with its needle stuck.

'You've got to stop worrying about Vanessa. She's fine. Anne's managing very well.'

'Can she feed her?'

'Of course. She's watched you often enough.'

'Is Vanessa upset?'

'A little at first, but now she's always smiling.' A pause, I didn't answer, and he'd add, 'You must believe me.'

After he'd left, I would relax, reassured. Next morning the fear returned, rampaging through my brain, dominating my every thought. Like a spider whose web is violently broken and falls into a bowl of water, I floundered in every nerve of my being. For four years I had lived, breathed, dreamed about Vanessa. I had no other thoughts in my mind but how I could look after her, how I could help her progress. I wasn't a separate being.

Dr Warrell came regularly, together with his registrar and Sister Jones who was in charge of this ward.

He didn't examine me at first, only saying, 'I hear you've been having some contractions, my dear.'

'Yes, Doctor Warrell. Nearly every day.'

'I always send a nurse to monitor her, Doctor.' Sister Jones spoke quickly.

'That's excellent.' Turning to me, he continued, 'We'll keep you here until they subside.'

It was early June, and I had been in hospital nearly three weeks when the family began to visit. Sid had been coming every evening, telling me about the extension and the demolition and reconstruction work now in full flow. All was upheaval and chaos. I hardly heard his words, my mind driven by an awful memory.

'Your parents, what can I say when they come tomorrow?'

'About what?'

'You know. About giving her away. Do they still want to send Vanessa to a home?'

'Don't be silly. Of course they wouldn't dream of doing that.'

'You weren't there,' I shouted.

'Don't. You mustn't get upset. My mother was frightened for you, that's all. You know they'd never push anything on to us.'

'But she was almost right. Look what's happened.'

I was still uneasy although I needn't have been. The moment they arrived, Rachel walked directly to me, and taking my hands in hers, she said, 'I'm sorry. I was wrong the other day but I was so afraid for you and the baby.' She put her arms around me, hugging me as best she could.

'It's all right. I know you were very upset,' I said awkwardly.

She looked about. 'So this is your room. Very nice. Quiet. Are you comfortable here?'

'They're marvellous.' I was eager to reassure her.

Abe was still by the door. 'Shall I get the armchair for you, Rachel?'

She nodded. 'Anyway,' she continued, 'you shouldn't worry about Vanessa. Anne's marvellous with her. Treats her like a princess.' Settling herself in the armchair, she drew it close to the bed. 'She spends hours feeding her. Irons her clothes, dresses her hair with ribbons.'

My father-in-law brought the hard-backed chair from the other side of the bed, and sat down beside her. 'We pop round almost every day, and it's always the same, we find Anne talking and laughing, and so is Vanessa.'

'But the building work, you don't know what you're missing,' Rachel had a *you should only know* expression on her face. 'I don't understand how they can bear it, the noise, the banging, the shouting of the workers. All day long, yet Vanessa seems as right as rain.'

'Sid tells me you're taking little meals for them,' I said. Proof if I needed any, of their loving concern. 'Thank you very much.'

'That's nothing.' She shrugged. 'The least we could do.'

'Besides, we have to report back to you,' said Abe, a rare tone of mischief in his voice.

Once they'd gone, that relentless fear about Vanessa leaped into my heart, and the contractions continued. Even when my parents arrived the following day with the news that my sister Barbara had given birth to a baby girl, ten days after my precipitous arrival in St Mary's, I lay half-listening. They had kept it from me, worried that it might upset me.

'But why shouldn't Barbara have a perfect baby?' I asked them. 'What's she like?'

'Dark hair, for the moment, pale skin. So lovely.' Mother smiled.

'And everything's all right?' I knew Barbara had been worried in case something went wrong.

'She's fine.'

'I am so glad, and what are they calling her?'

'Elanor,' replied my father, seating himself in the armchair. 'Not the usual spelling. According to David, the name's from a book, *The Lord of the Rings*. I don't know it.'

'A kind of fantasy novel, I think.' Mother bent to open her capacious bag. 'Here are some copies of *Woman* and *Women's Weekly*. A little light reading.'

'And I brought you *The Humanist* to read.' Dad proceeded to stick it in the cubbyhole beneath the magazines.

'I wouldn't call that light reading.' She gave me a wry look.

We continued to talk. When Elaine appeared with the afternoon tea trolley, Dad stood up to collect his tea. 'It's a beautiful day, isn't it, Elaine? Can I add some more milk? This is a little strong.' He smiled engagingly at Elaine, who gave him a shy smile back.

'You help yourself, Mr Merrill. Glad you're enjoying the weather. Makes a lovely change.

'I brought her a home-made fruitcake. I wonder if you might have a knife.'

'There's one in the kitchen, at the end. I'll get it later.'

'I can get it,' Dad said, 'if you show me where it is.'

And off he went as usual, finding his way round when he needed something.

'I've got some plates as well. Cut a piece for Elaine,' he said on his return. 'I promised her one, when I passed her in the corridor.'

Dad stood up, probably weary of the conversation. 'Come on, Efra, Susan's looking tired.' Straightening himself, he manoeuvred his bad leg, and leant over the bed to kiss me.

'We'll be back soon,' Mother said, gathering her bags. 'If there's anything you want, you phone us.' Clasping me in her arms, she whispered, 'Don't worry. Everything will be all right.'

I felt so alone after they'd left. But relieved they didn't come every day because I couldn't keep pretending about the contractions. Luckily occupied with Barbara and her new baby, my mother worried less about me. But how I missed Vanessa – I wanted to hold her on my knee so much, to smile and receive her all-embracing smile in return. I missed her physicality, her awkward body which I knew as intimately as my own; I missed her presence, so vibrant that strangers were drawn to her, stopping to ask her name, telling her how pretty she was.

I continued to be on bed rest, my hands around my stomach, listening to the contractions, counting the seconds and minutes, counting on and on. The sun blazed through the window until it moved to the other side of the hospital but even so, it was stifling, and I would lie with the sheet rolled down to my ankles.'

In charge of this ward was Sister Jones. She was thin, had dark hair and moved quickly. Often her mouth was pinched with unexpressed frustration. Probably in her forties, she sometimes reminded me of myself. Whether or not she was married, I never found out. Flowers were permitted on maternity wards in those days, and visitors would arrive with posies of freesia, pansies, and lily of the valley. Later they would bring red and pink roses. She hated dead flowers, sweeping faded, curling petals from the windowsill and taking my vase to empty it in the sluice down the corridor. When someone brought a bunch of red and white flowers, she separated them. 'Red and white mean death. I can't have that on my ward.'

A few days after my parents' visit, she arrived with a new consultant.

'Dr Warrell is very busy at the moment but I'm sure you will like Dr Mais.'

'Pleased to meet you, Mrs Stern.' He shook my hand vigorously. Tall and sunburned, with blonde hair, he was Australian, bringing an element of warmth, of great expanses into the room. 'And how are you today?' He stood close to the bed.

'Just the same, I think, but I would love to take a shower. It gets so hot in here, and they won't turn down the radiator.'

Like my mother, I was always troubled by the heat and especially by this heat wave. As though our Russian ancestors, better accustomed to ice and cold than to sunny skies, continued to influence our senses. Finding it unbearable one day, I had crawled out of bed and switched off the radiator. Discovering my sin, Sister Jones was furious, telling me that it was essential to keep the radiators on, to make sure the babies were kept in an even heat. I was duly chastised, and never dared do it again.

'Let's see where you're up to.' Dr Mais turned to Sister Jones, who was standing by the end of the bed. 'How many weeks now?'

'Twenty-nine, Doctor.'

'And how are the contractions?'

'She's still having them most days. But they haven't led to anything,'

'Let's have a dekko. Could you pass me Mrs Stern's file, Sister Jones?' He pored over it, then strode round the bed, and sat down beside me. 'I think we can let you have a shower. You've been getting up to go to the toilet, haven't you?'

I nodded.

'Sister, starting next week, she can take a shower, but with someone to help her. Is that doable?'

'A student nurse, maybe, while she's making the bed. Is that all right, Dr Mais?'

'How about that, Mrs Stern? A shower every other day. The best we can do for the present.'

'That's wonderful. I'm sure it will help.'

He shook my hand. His was a warm, firm handshake. At the door he said, 'I'm here for some months so we'll meet again.'

I thought about Dr Mais when they'd gone. In other circumstances I might have noticed how good-looking he was, but not now. It didn't pass by the student nurses; it wasn't long before there were heated discussions, as they paused in their bed making to wonder if he'd go out with one of them and if so, who would he choose?

I had been there for nearly a month before I felt ready to see Vanessa.

Sid's parents were bringing her together with Anne one Saturday afternoon. While I longed to see her, I was terrified of how she would react, and how I'd feel when they came.

Nurse Davies was on duty most mornings; she had curly nut-brown hair, laughing hazel eyes, a droll sense of humour, and I had got to know her a little. She had come to nursing after working in a bank, and was older than the other nurses and very independent.

I was apprehensive and restless, that morning. I wanted to walk around to dispel this nervous energy. Not such a preposterous idea since I had been allowed to get up, at last. She watched from the door as I circled the room three times, my legs weak and wobbly, and told me to breathe calmly as I walked. Finally she said, 'Enough. Time to get back on the bed.'

They arrived. Rachel held the door so that Anne could carry Vanessa in. I caught my breath, my eyes filled with tears. Vanessa looked so cool, so pretty in her pink dress with its faint red check pattern in the weave, almost like muslin, and narrow tucks from neck to hem, all the buttons decorated in the same material. On her legs were white knee socks, obviously straightened by Anne before they came in, while Rachel carried her little white cardigan.

My heart raced; I wanted so much to hold her, but I knew I couldn't. I leaned over to grasp her hands. 'Hello, sweetheart. It's lovely to see you.'

For some moments, she stared at me, but then she made her famous lip and began to cry.

'You shouldn't cry, Vanessa,' Anne said, looking anxious. 'Mummy is so happy to see you. You must smile!'

Pulling out the chair for her, Rachel said, 'Anne, you sit there.'

'You want to sit on the bed with Mummy?' asked Anne.

'Better keep her on your knee,' advised Rachel, hovering behind. 'She might slip off.'

'I hope you're being a good girl for Anne,' I said, 'eating up all the meals.'

'She likes the little meat dishes Mrs Stern brings.' Anne and Rachel exchanged smiles.

'See, didn't I tell you that already?' said Rachel. As though chiding me for doubting her word. 'Look how chubby her legs are. She's eating fine.'

'I'm a bit forgetful now. In a bit of a dream.' I turned to Vanessa. 'Anne's making you look very pretty. I love those pink ribbons in your hair.'

A huge, delighted smile. I let out a long sigh of relief, and we chatted. Anne told me about the house, the builders, and their endless mugs of tea, the noise and dust as they pulled down walls and prepared to rebuild them differently, none of which I could imagine.

Nurse Davies popped in saying, 'Shall I bring some tissues if you want to give Vanessa a drink?'

'Thank you,' Anne said, 'but I have a large kitchen roll in my bag.'

'This is Nurse Davies.' I introduced her. 'She keeps me sane.'

They laughed with relief, and I knew this was just as troubling for them. Lost in my fraught feelings, it was as though I'd forgotten everyone's existence.

'Lovely to meet you, and what a pretty dress you're wearing, Vanessa.'

Nurse Davies' voice brought me back to the room, and my daughter beamed, always ready to engage with other people. When they left, she gave me her wide-mouthed smile, and I sank back on the pillows. But later, after supper, I lay on the hard bed and tears trickled down my cheeks. Why? Why did I have to go through this? Why was I here alone, away from my precious daughter, away from home?

I pulled the sheet over my head and I wept.

It was about one o'clock in the morning, and I was listening to the hospital sounds, the low voices, the buzzing of the generator, an occasional faraway laugh, when I heard someone walking heavily along the corridor, stopping at the lavatory across the way. She was gasping, beginning to moan. Then came a woman's hoarse voice, 'Help me, nurse. Nurse! Someone help me. It's coming. It's coming!'

Then terrible groans. Lighter footsteps followed, a nurse running to help and shouting, 'I'm here now, Lizzie.'

Another bang as the lavatory door slammed open. The groans were so loud they seemed to be in my room. Then a scream. 'Nurse, help me.'

More screams.

'It's all right, Lizzie. It's all right. Won't be long now. Soon be over.' I could hear the nurse's voice, calm, reassuring,

But I lay frozen.

The screaming died away. More footsteps, another nurse arrived. A heavy shuffling sound, reassuring murmurs, then silence.

Next morning, even before she had done my blood pressure, I pulled myself up to face Nurse Davies. 'What happened last night? It was horrible.'

'She lost the baby. She knew she would. We all knew it would happen.'

'How can you be so matter-of-fact?'

'We have to be tough sometimes. It's the only way. By the way, your blood pressure is up a bit this morning.'

'Is that any wonder? I can't stop thinking about her.'

She gave me a reproving look. 'Stop being like that. It won't do you any good.'

So I tried. I changed the subject. 'Thank you for offering to help with Vanessa, yesterday.'

'She's so pretty. I'm not surprised you're missing her. When you go down to the day room, that's whenever they let you, you'll find you're not the only one missing your family. Now, have you chosen your meals yet?'

Despite her cheery advice, I couldn't stop dwelling on the poor woman, how she had lost her baby in the lavatory. I could see it, hear it. And my stomach swelled, hardened, and pain licked around the edges into my back. The contractions became fiercer, gripping me, the pain sharper. I clutched my stomach, my sides, and began to groan, too.

Again and again, I rang the bell until finally, a nurse appeared. 'The pains are really strong.'

She timed them, said she'd speak to sister. But it wasn't Sister Jones who came to my room. It was Dr Mais. Briefly he examined me, then sitting down, he took my hand.

'Mrs Stern, it's entirely understandable that you should be worried about your little girl. And of course, you're extremely anxious about this pregnancy. Having a child like your daughter is a huge responsibility. Mothers like you become totally dedicated to their child's well-being, and caring for the most vulnerable is a mark of humanity.

But Mrs Stern, we are more than animals, we have souls, intelligence, if you like, and we respond differently.' He smiled. 'I like to believe I can help my patients, not simply as a doctor, mending their bodies, but mindful of them as a person, complex, profound.'

I listened, entranced. A doctor who cared about people's souls?

'I've never heard a medical person speaking like you.'

'I'm not your usual run-of-the-mill doctor. A bit of a maverick, they used to say in Melbourne. That's fine with me if what I'm going to say will help you.'

I was gazing at him, hardly aware of any contractions.

'What are you going to tell me, Dr Mais?' I had never spoken in such a familiar way to a doctor, but his manner, so easy, so friendly, encouraged this.

'Do you have religious beliefs?'

'I would love to have some. I know having a belief would help. Many of the nurses tell me they're Christian, and talk about their faith. I did start looking when I was about eighteen, and I've had unusual spiritual experiences, but I really need something now.'

I didn't exactly know what I meant by that, just that I felt it.

'There's a book I can recommend, which I've read a thousand times myself, and which millions of people have sworn has helped them. It's called *The Power of Positive Thinking*. I promise you, if you really absorb its message, you will be a different person.'

I looked at him in amazement. Could there be something that would make me stop worrying?

He told me about the book, that it was written by a man called Norman Vincent Peale who was searching for something to change himself from being a fearful, negative person, and when he couldn't find such a book, wrote it himself, based on his experience of altering his life. We talked about the mind, about fear and its opposite, confidence. Faith in oneself.

'I'm such a worrier, so uncertain. I come from parents who are anxious people. They had difficult childhoods. My grandfather lost his first wife and child in Russia, and after they came to London in 1905, tragically lost his second wife, Sophia, who had what they called childbed fever.'

'Puerperal fever,' he said softly.

I nodded. 'And he adored her. But my mother was fostered at a few weeks old and never knew her own mother. My mother is strong, very loving but she's frequently anxious and emotional. Though being emotional isn't bad,' I added quickly, 'but my father is very controlled and likes things to go his way.' We spoke about my father, his vegetarianism – our religion.

I continued: 'Dad's an atheist. He hates conventional religion and thinks religious people are fools.' I stopped and wondered if I was saying too much. I took a deep breath. I needed to tell him this. 'It's very hard for me because I am afraid of angering my father, but I am drawn to spiritual things, I'm searching for something deeper.'

'Like so many.'

'And then there's ancestral memory,' I said. 'Generations of people, my ancestors, fleeing, persecuted, killed – doesn't that add to the mix?'

'I agree, it goes back a long way but it doesn't have to stay with you.' His gaze was positive, enthusiastic. 'Can you get hold of the book?'

'I'm sure my husband can.' I smiled. 'I'm beginning to feel better already, simply from talking to you.'

'For the moment, take deep breaths. Let your limbs relax. This will help you and your baby.'

Chapter 12

Sid bought me *The Power of Positive Thinking* and I plunged into it, reading and underlining all the suggestions which spoke deeply to me. It did have a Christian message. I couldn't become a Christian but I began to read the Hebrew Bible and New Testament in the 1970 translation into modern English. Although I knew it lacked the beautiful poetry of the King James Version, it was enough.

'Be bold and mighty forces will come to your aid.' 'The thing I most feared came upon me.' So many expressions of hope from the Psalms and others, that I learned by heart. I didn't know whether nuns, priest or rabbis made this a practice but absorbing these ideas became a sort of spiritual training for me just when I needed it.

To my growing wonder, the contractions began to fade, and I marvelled that my body had become smooth, shaping as the baby grew, no pain, no swollen hardening as contractions took hold. My own body again.

I also knew that life was complex, with different influences having their effects.

It could have been the physical outcome of resting my body. Or an awakening when a doctor appealed to my desire for a spiritual way, or even that I had found someone who could give me reassurance, whatever it was, it worked.

Friends came: Jessica relating the discussions at the book club and bringing me a recording of our latest ironic choice, *A New Life*, by Bernard Malamud. One of the staff nurses who worked nights devoured books like me and when she'd finished her round in the early hours, we listened to the tape surreptitiously, like naughty girls, discussing the protagonist's alternatives. Did he make the wrong decision here? Was it because of his personality? Was he simply unlucky?

Slowly, slowly I realised I was beginning to enjoy my time in hospital, which was such a transformation when I considered how agitated I had been during the first six weeks. There was nothing I could do for my daughter Vanessa. She and her needs had been lifted from my hands, and I rested for the first time in four years. At long last I thought about the second baby, wondering who he or she was, what kind of personality this baby would have.

Meanwhile, there was great excitement: nurses and patients alike were agog with the news that young Queen Elizabeth was coming to officially open the hospital. Sister Jones told me that I wouldn't be able to see her since Dr Mais feared the emotion might bring on the contractions again. I said I didn't mind at all because we were republicans.

There were others who did. One Saturday evening, I had a visitor: a very old friend, Norma Hampson whose husband Harry played bass with Sid when I first knew him. Apparently, she was on the general ward which I'd never seen and when she peered round the door, I called her in, thrilled to see her. She walked slowly over to embrace me. Norma had lost her first baby the year before. Having read about still births in a magazine she'd had a premonition that this might happen to her. Imagine her horror when during her labour, the midwife casually mentioned that it already had. The baby was stillborn. Cold and clinical, without sympathy. At three in the morning, they had tried to contact her husband, but he was deep asleep and hadn't heard the telephone ringing downstairs. You were lucky if you had one telephone in those days.

After this tragedy, she'd been told to come into hospital the moment she was pregnant for the second time. By chance Harry had met Sid in the corridor and learned I was also in St Mary's.

'How are you?'

'All right, I suppose.'

'Norma, it's wonderful to see you. Have you been here long?'

'A couple of weeks.'

She sat down beside me.

I told her what had happened with me and thrust the book at her. 'You must read this. It's marvellous; it's helped me enormously.'

She held the book in limp hands, turned a few pages. 'You've underlined things already.' She placed it on the side cupboard.

'It's a kind of self-help, based on Christianity,' I gabbled on, 'especially on the Psalms.'

Enthusiasm had blinded me. I hadn't registered her worried gaze.

'I can't believe it,' she burst out. 'I've got to leave the day before the Queen comes. They've just told me.' She gave me an agonised look.

'What about bed rest?'

'They said I can do it at home but I must be extremely careful.'

Calm and confident, I told her she would be fine, that this book would help her as it was helping me.

'Perhaps I'll ask Harry to get it.' She smiled. 'It's great you're here. I'll come again.' She stood up with care. 'Better go back to the ward.'

We kissed, tears in our eyes, knowing what we had both been through.

But I was right; she would eventually have a healthy little girl later in the year.

My second visitor came on Sunday morning. It was my orthodox friend Hetty. She told me her baby was due to be induced the very day of the Queen's visit.

'Would you believe it, they've postponed it until the following day.'

We laughed, but I could see she was put out, and although the medical staff treated us like human beings, chatted with us and smiled (a far cry from attitudes in the old hospital), we still had little control over our bodies.

I asked Sid to buy *Natural Childbirth* by Sheila Kitzinger – but how I hated that woman! Perhaps it was due to my emotional state, perhaps not. Somewhere in the text there was a reference, not exactly in these words, to weak, middle-class girls in thrall to their fathers, fearful of their bodies. These women, she claimed, would have the most problems during the actual birth. She was talking about me. Never mind our socialist political views, I didn't have to work and reading her book, I felt scapegoated. Later I came to see that women in the 1960s and 70s who had the choice, worked when their children started school, often waiting until they were seven. Contemporary childcare wisdom emphasised the psychological benefits to young children when mothers stayed at home.

Sheila Kitzinger's words stung, nevertheless. I ignored that particular chapter and concentrated on the breathing exercises, repeating them several times a day.

Meanwhile, Sister Jones measured my stomach with a tape measure to check the baby's growth. Dr Warrell assured me that when I was thirty-two weeks pregnant, he would send me for a scan. 'You'll have the added assurance of seeing the baby in the uterus.'

A retinue of young doctors training to be obstetricians formed a respectful semi-circle around him that morning.

'Here's Mrs Stern, growing a baby,' he told them. 'Babies grow, when mothers rest.'

He asked one of them to examine me. The young doctor placed tentative fingers on my abdomen in imitation of the master, but keeping his eyes averted, either from embarrassment or because he didn't want me to see his ignorance.

'Thank you, Mrs Stern,' Dr Warrell said while they trooped out. 'You're doing very well.'

I had made it to thirty-two weeks, now it was the day of the scan. Good thing nobody took my blood pressure for it must have been dangerously high. Nurse Lawrence, who reminded me of a Dickensian midwife, older, experienced and tough, wheeled me to the radiology department and helped me onto the narrow bed while the radiographer did something with machines.

'I'm sorry,' he said when everything was ready. 'I have to put oil on your stomach. It's rather cold.'

When he applied it, I shivered from the shock but also from anticipation.

'Nothing like this with my first child,' I said.

If we'd seen how Vanessa was developing inside me, would it have made any difference? I blinked the thought away.

While he passed a kind of arm backwards and forwards over my stomach, the radiologist chatted. 'Brand new. We're lucky to have this in St Mary's. It'll open up all sorts of possibilities. Now,' he glanced over to the small television-like screen on a table behind him, 'there's the head and there's the umbilical cord. Can you see them?'

Staff Nurse Lawrence stared wide-eyed and nodded as eager as I, to watch the extraordinary images appearing on the screen, but to me it was more like a pulsating moonscape and when I told the radiographer, he laughed.

'Never mind. Dr Warrell will tell you the results tomorrow, but everything looks fine to me.'

Dr Warrell walked in with his entourage while Sister Jones followed respectfully.

'I'm glad to see you're feeling better, Mrs Stern. The scan is excellent. If you continue to thirty-four weeks in this way, I will seriously consider letting you go home.'

'Home?' I couldn't believe my ears. I had been cloistered in this room so long, I had forgotten how my house looked or what it smelt like. I had often seen it in dreams, changing, shifting, but always out of my reach.

'Now that you've been up for a couple of weeks,' he continued, 'I think you should find your legs. Don't you agree Sister Jones?'

She gave a rare smile.

'I would encourage you to walk up and down the corridor, perhaps sit in the day room for some minutes.'

'I'll arrange for a nurse to accompany her,' Sister Jones said.

'A good idea, and if this goes well, she can take a little stroll on her own.'

The following day sitting in the armchair by the window, I wrote to my friends in Paris and the Loire to tell them how much better I was feeling; that I had taken a shower on my own and could actually sit in a chair to have my meals. My eyes brimming, I put my letters on the locker, and thought about this stupendous news. Home in two weeks!

Popping her head round the door, Nurse Davies was asking if I was ready for my big adventure when we heard Sister Jones' agitated voice calling her to the office. At once. Nurse Davies gave me an exasperated look: 'I promise I won't be long, so don't go anywhere!'

'Where should I go?' I grinned.

I waited. There was more hubbub in the corridor and she didn't return.

Putting on my dressing gown, I decided to go alone, laughing at myself for thinking this was such a great thing. Reaching the day room, I felt a bit wobbly so decided to sit down. Timidly, I opened the door to find half a dozen women wearing an assortment of nighties and dressing gowns, leaning forward as they smoked – all of them were smoking – discussing something with great excitement. One of them looked up, 'Come in, love. We don't bite.'

I made my careful way round a low table where an array of cigarette packets, red and white Park Drive, blue Nelson Tipped, and the occasional golden Benson & Hedges encircled a large metal ashtray overflowing with stubs.

The woman who invited me in told me her name was Joyce. 'Did you see Vicky Robson go?'

I shook my head. 'Sorry, I don't know who she is.'

'She's run away!'

'Run away?'

They all nodded.

'Just wondered. Everyone's looking for her 'cos she's disappeared.' She peered at me. 'You the lady who's been here ages?'

'Yes, for my sins.'

'Don't be like that. It's no joke being in hospital.'

The questions came thick and fast: how long had I been there, what had happened to me, when did I think I would go home. Everyone smiling, nodding, and even offering me a cigarette, which I refused almost apologetically. I told them about the waters breaking at twenty-six weeks, being on bed rest for over a month.

'So how far gone are you now, love?'

'Thirty-two.' I smiled.

'You might be going home soon.' A woman in a lustrous red dressing gown that reminded me of Miss Havisham's wedding dress introduced herself as Mabel.

'Dr Warrell said I could walk around now,' I told them. 'That's why I'm here.'

Nods of approval when I mentioned him, many of them saying what a gentleman he was, how well he treated them. But I began to feel tired and thought I should leave. Drawn by their evident solidarity and camaraderie, I hesitated. Their conversation returned to Vicky Robson.

'Alice Wainwright, her over there, she knows where Vicky is, but she won't let on.'

Alice muttered, 'She made me promise, and you have to keep promises, don't you?'

'What if she's done herself an injury?'

Alice shook her head.

When someone suggested Vicky might have gone home, Alice drew in a sharp breath. Everyone fell silent, thinking about home, and Vanessa came into my mind, her pretty face, her lovely blue eyes, and I so wanted to hold her in my arms.

We sat with our thoughts until the grind of the lift interrupted them. It was followed by a clanking noise as the lift stopped and the door was flung open, then the sounds of a furious row, a woman's high voice, a man's deeper one, and Sister Jones' querulous tones made us all look up, the others exchanging glances. We heard a man yell, 'You make bloody sure this doesn't happen again or I'll report the lot of you! I'll sit by her bed, tie her in, if needs be.'

'That's quite unnecessary, Mr Robson. My staff will keep an eye on her. Would you please stop shouting? It's disturbing my ladies.'

'I'll bloody disturb them, I tell you, if this happens again.' We heard him make his way to the lift, banging the door shut.

Everyone exchanged amused but wary glances.

Vicky flew in, strong and wiry apart from her bulging stomach, her black hair tied in a ponytail, and wearing a flowery dressing gown. There came a collective cry of '*Vicky, what happened?*'

'Did you really go in your nightie?' asked one of them.

'I did.' She gave an impertinent smile. 'Just went. Took the lift to the ground floor, walked out. If I'd got dressed, they'd have seen me. Got a taxi.'

Everyone burst out laughing while I secretly envied her courage, even her defiance.

'Must have thought you were a lady of the night,' Joyce reached for a cigarette from her packet of Nelson Tipped, pausing as she lit one. 'What did he say when you got home?'

'Oh, him? He was asleep. On nights.' Vicky gave an upward tilt of the head, with a 'couldn't care less' expression on her face.

'So what did you do?'

'Made a cup of tea. Sat on the couch, breathing in all the smells of home. Really happy. But then me mum come in with our Peter in the trolley, and I got up to give him a hug.'

Everyone spoke at once.

'Will you all stop interrupting?' Vicky glared round at the eager faces, and we fell silent. 'Sorry folks,' she took a deep breath. 'I'm a bit mental today. My Peter was shouting, 'Mum, Mum!', but my mother pulled the trolley away from me. She'd gone deathly white, now she was bright red. "What you doing here?" But I went, "Keep it down. He's asleep upstairs." Then she kind of whispered, "Vicky, what the hell are you doing here, and in your nightie and all?"' Peter started crying, and I fell back on the couch, and I was crying too.'

There were murmurs of commiseration.

'I begged her to let me give Peter a cuddle, but she gave me such a look. I told her I couldn't bear it no more. I was desperate to come home but she said I was crazy, I had to go back and she was waking Ron up.'

Everyone sighed.

'He was like a madman. He ran down the stairs, dragged me off the settee and pushed me towards the door, yelling, "You're going right back or I won't be responsible for my actions."'

'Should have thought of that eight months ago,' someone said.

Much laughter.

'I told him I wasn't having no more kids, so be warned.'

'They don't know they're born, those men,' someone said.

Directing her gaze at me, Vicky asked, 'You got any kids?'

While I was there I was doubly careful to say nothing about Vanessa's disability. 'Yes,' I said, ' a little girl. She's four. I really miss her.'

'That's why,' proclaimed Vicky, 'that's why I went home. They don't get it here.' She turned to me again, 'You've been here a long time. Ever thought of running away?'

'No. I'm too much of a coward.'

They all spoke at once:

'No, it's them.'

'They don't understand.'

'You aren't a coward.'

Vicky sat back. 'Thank God, I've only two weeks left. If it had been months like you, I'd have probably thrown myself out of the window. Still the kids still need me, even if he doesn't.' She smoothed down her ponytail and I recognised the ringleader in her. Charismatic, defiant. How different I was, always doing what was expected of me. But then hadn't I almost sacrificed this baby for what I wanted for Vanessa? I said a quiet thank you that the baby had prevailed.

Now the talk turned to miscarriages, babies born in lifts, ambulances, on the kitchen floor. There was a pulse in my throat, my heart beating faster.

'Think I'd better go back to my room now,' I said.

There was a chorus of responses: 'Bye love. Come back soon. Nice to meet you.'

Making my slow way down the corridor, I passed Sister Jones looking even paler than usual, probably after the altercation with Mr Robson.

Stopping, she exclaimed, 'Have you been smoking, Mrs Stern?' A furrow of anxiety criss-crossed her forehead.

'No. I've just been to the day room.'

Taking a sharp breath, she pursed her lips. 'I might as well talk to the wall. I've told them a thousand times not to smoke. How bad it is for their baby, but nobody takes the slightest notice.'

Everyone wanted to go home, I thought, as I lay on my bed. Only this morning, Doctor Warrell had said that I could go home, officially, without fleeing in my dressing gown. Home after all these weeks. How would it be? Could I cope? But with Anne there I was sure I would manage. Smiling to myself, I gazed at the motes of dust dancing through the sun rays that poured through the window.

Chapter 13

And then – catastrophe.

A few days later, Sid arrived, his face sombre. He sat hunched in the armchair. At once, I was suspicious

'What's the matter? Tell me.'

'I'm glad you're much better, because we've got a problem.'

'You'd better say it.' I frowned. 'Is something wrong with Vanessa?'

'Absolutely not. Glowing.'

'Is it the house? Something with the building? Did the architect make a mistake?'

'Nothing like that. I wish it was. No, listen, Sue, it's about Anne. She's all right, but she had a phone call today, saying she must return to France.'

'Why? I thought she wanted to stay until after the baby was born. Maybe till the end of September.'

'Afraid she's got to go. Her father has died.'

'Heavens.' I sank back on the pillows. 'What on earth can we do?' I thought for a moment. 'There are night care facilities for Vanessa at Pictor House but nothing during the holidays.' The penny dropped. 'How is Anne? How is she taking it?'

'Upset, of course. But you know, I think Anne's almost more upset to leave Vanessa. She couldn't stop talking about how she'd let us down. She promised to find somebody to take over the moment she got home.'

'Tell her she mustn't worry. She must go and support her mother. We'll find a way.'

The next few days, I sat up in bed making complicated plans, asking my mother to enquire about social services, and even telling Sid that I could look after Vanessa myself. I discussed this with anyone and everyone who came into my room.

'We must be certain that all is well with this baby before we let you go,' was all Dr Warrell would say.

Unexpectedly, we found a solution. One of the men working on the house had a fifteen-year-old daughter, who wanted to become a nursery nurse. Coming with him one day, she had fallen in love with Vanessa, and begged to look after her.

'Do you think it's wise?' I asked Sid. 'She's terribly young. Only just left school.'

'Let's give it a try.'

Connie came, and Vanessa accepted her. Sid brought a beautiful photograph of them in the garden, their faces shaded by the willow tree. Connie had on one of my nylon overalls, she was turned away from the camera but I could see her smiling, she was holding Vanessa who wore her long-sleeved, blue dress decorated with white flowers with smocking above the waist. She was laughing, her blonde hair burnished in the sunshine. Both looked radiantly happy.

Doctor Mais was grinning when he walked into my room, followed by Sister Jones.

'Well done, Mrs Stern, you're thirty-four weeks. Ready to go?'

My stomach flipped over. I felt my cheeks flush, heat rose to my hairline and I shivered. Such a rush of emotions – pleasure, anticipation, fear – all in a second. I had been so desperate at the beginning at being torn away from Vanessa and overwhelmed by my anxiety for her, but now I felt confused.

I became aware of Sister Jones speaking softly to the doctor. 'Perhaps you should know that Mrs Stern is having an extension built. Could I suggest she has a trial weekend at home to begin with?

'Thank you, Sister. An excellent idea. How does that grab you, Mrs Stern?'

'Yes, I'd like to do that. Then if it's okay, I would stay until the baby's due.'

Sister Jones smiled. 'Can somebody take you home and keep an eye you whilst you're there?'

'My husband. And Connie, the young girl helping us look after my daughter will be there too. I won't be alone.'

I had bought the maternity dress before coming into hospital, months ago it seemed, and Rachel had shortened it. Its tiny turquoise and bronze flowers on a cream background had taken me back to Aix-en-Provence, to Claudie Chabas, one of the girls I taught in my year at the Lycee de Jeunes Filles. She was preparing for the examination for the elite Ecole Normale Superieure in Paris, to become a teacher of teachers, and was nineteen like me.

I went often to her home in Pertuis, a ravishing little village near the Durance River, surrounded by lush vegetable gardens in a rich, fertile valley. It was here that I first saw typical Provencale material, made up by her mother into curtains, bed spreads, even a skirt for herself. Tiny, tender flowers on a richly coloured background. Such sunlit memories. I had been looking forward to wearing this dress. I asked Sid to bring it when he came on Saturday morning.

While he waited for me, I pulled the frock over my head, and threw a quick glance at myself in the mirror. Smiling nervously, flushed with excitement, I giggled like a teenager, 'I hope Vanessa likes this,' I said to the person in the mirror.

We were approaching the main door on the ground floor when I had a sudden vision of myself at twenty-six weeks, running through this very place, wild with fear, gripping my stomach as though I could hold the baby inside, prevent it from emerging too soon. I inhaled deeply and closed my eyes to shut out the memory.

We reached the car and Sid helped me climb in. But driving home along the A34, one of the main roads south, I was overwhelmed by the noise, the frantic speed of the traffic, and I clung to the door handle. Passing gardens where the grass was richly green, the bushes and shrubs abundant with leaves, I had to close my eyes, for it was all in Technicolor. The sun glared through the windscreen and everything was too bright, too garish, too much.

Was this my home? I discovered a long low building where the garage had been. All unfinished, with stacks of bricks in front and builders' equipment littered around like giant's toys. I gazed at the transformation.

'This way. Be careful where you walk. Loads of bricks and rubbish about.' He guided me into the hall, where rubble littered bare floorboards. I paused at a strange, widened doorway into the new kitchen. 'Through here,' Sid guided me in.

At the far end of this long room, once the playroom and extended by a square kitchen, I saw Vanessa in the wheelchair, sitting with her back to me, her head flopping to one side. It was twelve-thirty, and Connie was perched on a low stool in front of her, giving her lunch.

When she saw me walk in, she gave me a shy little smile then lowered her gaze to the plate of food.

'Will you be all right now?' Sid asked. 'Connie makes great sandwiches. And perhaps you can take Mrs Stern's bag upstairs?'

'We'll be fine, Mr Stern. I'll take the bag up when we've finished. Hello, Mrs Stern,' she said, hesitant. 'Do you want to sit here?' She pointed to one of the kitchen chairs which looked abandoned in the middle of this vast floor.

'Thanks, Connie. I will, and don't worry, Sid. You get back to work. We'll be fine.'

'Bye, everyone. See you tonight.'

Vanessa stopped eating. Turning her head slightly as I reached her side, she stared and gazed at me with wide open eyes. I tried to imagine what she might say if she could speak. Anger? Accusations? But she made a lip and began to cry, great tears rolling down her cheeks.

'No, no, Vanessa, please don't cry.' I touched her arm, 'I've come to see you. Where's your beautiful smile?' She continued to weep, her hands flaying in the air, and I was so surprised, tears welled up in my own eyes and I had to blink them away. To hide my consternation, I said, 'Supposing we take her out of the chair, Connie? If she sat on my knee, she might feel better.'

I unlatched the wheelchair tray and tried to lift Vanessa out, but her legs caught in the pommel and I was too weak to hold her with one arm, and disentangle her with the other. I sank back on the kitchen chair, Connie lifted her up and I held out my arms. She placed her on my knee, but Vanessa arched herself backwards, rejecting all my attempts to hold her. She thrust herself away, and with tears rolling down her cheeks, she slid slowly to the floor.

Connie turned her gaze away, and I saw she was upset.

'Perhaps she'll let me feed her in the chair?'

It was useless – Vanessa kept her mouth tightly closed, refusing every spoonful I offered.

'You carry on, Connie,' I whispered, feeling my insides crumble. I made my faltering way across the floor and walked blindly through the unfamiliar doorway where I bumped my leg on a huge piece of masonry in the hall. A large purple bruise appeared on my shin, travelled down my leg and ended at my ankle in a kind of reddish blotch.

In the front room I fell onto the orange sofa, its colour seeming to blaze with further accusations, everything asking: *why did you abandon me?* I began to weep, my head in my hands, great hard sobs tearing from me, tormented by Vanessa's rejection. I didn't know what to do, what to think. I had been home for half an hour and I was lost. Tears streamed down my face and I couldn't stop. I had no handkerchief, no tissues, so I dragged the skirt of my maternity dress up to my face and was wiping my eyes when Connie came in with a plate of sandwiches. She stopped at the doorway and whispered, 'Are you all right, Mrs Stern?'

With a raggedy breath, I said, 'Of course, Connie. It's just so strange being here.' I couldn't share my feelings with someone I hardly knew.

She returned a few moments later saying that Vanessa was having a rest, and asked if it was all right to bring her own sandwich into the lounge. I told her it was lovely to have company but we sat in silence, hearing ourselves chewing, embarrassed and uncomfortable.

Then, giving a little cough, her brown eyes focused on mine, Connie said softly, 'I try to do everything you tell me, Mrs Stern, everything you've written on the piece of paper.'

'I know you do.' I smiled. 'It's all new and very hard, a lot to learn quickly.' I was moved by her depth of feeling, her desire to please me.

She lifted her head, shyly returning my smile. 'It is, and I've never seen anyone with a little girl like Vanessa. Anyway, that lady's been coming while you've been in hospital. You know, Mrs Hurst, and she's showed me what to do.'

'She visited me a couple of weeks ago, and she told me Vanessa had a sense of humour. Would you believe it?'

Connie's face lit up. 'She loves me to do silly things, like pretending to fall over. It makes her laugh.'

I was so delighted she enjoyed being with Vanessa, my despair faded away. Connie was only fifteen, what did she know about looking after a profoundly disabled child?

She leaned forward. 'Is everything all right with the baby now?'

I guessed she had wanted to ask me that earlier but was too scared. 'Everything's fine. If the baby arrives next week, it would be okay.'

When Sid came back at half past six, Connie went home for the night. Together, we bathed Vanessa but she cried and arched her back in the water, and sobbed when we put her to bed. This upset me so much I told Sid I wasn't sure about coming home for good. Thank heavens, Sunday was a better day, Vanessa was happier, eating her meals, smiling at me and I relaxed.

Connie returned next morning and I went back to St Mary's.

I sank down on the bed. Nervous, my hands fluttering, I knew my blood pressure was up. Doctor Warrell arrived soon afterwards, saying, 'I hear you've been home this weekend, Mrs Stern.' Approaching the bedside, he peered at my leg. 'What's all this? Looks as if you've been having a battle with a piece of masonry.' He glanced at Sister Jones, a smile playing around his lips. 'Sister has just told me. I wanted to see the extent of the...' he smiled again, 'the damage.' His expression changed. 'But we won't have all our good work undone by builders, doubtless doing excellent work on your house. I think we'll keep you here, after all.'

'Stay here? Until term?'

'Yes, until the due date. When is that, Sister?'

She searched through my bulky file. 'Eighteenth of August, Doctor Warrell.'

'Thank you. We can keep her a little longer?'

'Of course.'

He turned to appraise me with his calm blue eyes. 'I think that's the best plan, don't you? Only a few weeks to go.'

I felt so relieved. 'I thought you'd need the bed.'

'If Sister says she has room, that's all that matters.'

Sid found me curled on my side, facing the window when he came that evening.

'What's the matter?'

'I can't go home because of my leg.' I showed him. 'Doctor Warrell said they didn't want their good work destroyed by a piece of masonry. I feel terrible. I'm leaving all the work for both of you. I'm a coward.'

'Don't be ridiculous.' Miserably, I turned to look at him and saw he was smiling as though a great weight had been lifted from his mind, 'Don't you realise? It's the best thing. I was afraid you might go into labour while you were with Vanessa and Connie. I'm so relieved.'

'You don't feel bad that I'm not sharing the care of Vanessa?'

'Absolutely not. She goes to school most days. Connie can manage to feed her, change her, and even bathe her now. They're happy together.' He grinned, his hazel eyes twinkling. 'I'm glad you'll be here, even though I have to rush home for my dinner after visiting you.'

I began to spend time chatting with the nurses, listening as they shared their secrets, told me about their love affairs, their hopes for the future. The family came as always and I could see how relieved they were. And whenever they could, our friends dropped in when they had an appointment at the Infirmary or were visiting someone, always bringing me interesting gossip or unexpected news about themselves. At quiet times I read,

136

practised the exercises religiously, and did everything I could to help this baby to make a perfect entrance into the world.

One afternoon I heard, 'Hello, anybody at home?'

Someone was peering round the door, her hugely rounded stomach barely covered by her dressing gown. She had a curiously concave face with straight, fine features and her eyes were bright and searching.

'I am Mary Gonshaw.' I guessed that under normal circumstances she would have walked quickly into the room but now she held onto the door, moved slowly to the chair and sat down heavily. 'Even older than Methusaleh, I'm afraid. Thirty-five and medically known as an 'elderly primigravida'. For some reason, they've called me in because, as you might have guessed, I'm expecting twins.' She gave me a wicked smile. With her fair hair, almost white and cut short, she looked like a mischievous fairy in a pantomime.

'Congratulations. Although I get about now, I haven't met anyone having twins. I'm Susan Stern by the way, though friends call me Sue.'

'Very pleased to meet you, Susan or Sue. You looked very comfortable before I so rudely interrupted you.'

'Exercises in preparation for labour, whenever that will be. I've done them so often, I can do them in my sleep, so I'm glad you called in.' With my left hand, I indicated the childbirth book.

'So how come you're here?'

'Half the waters escaped ten weeks ago but everything's going well, thank goodness.'

'You've been here since then?' A look of anxiety crossed her face but disappeared at once. 'I wouldn't care for that.' She shifted herself on the chair, obviously uncomfortable with the weight of the two babies. Giving me a sharp enquiring look, she continued, 'What do you really think of them, the medical staff, particularly the consultants?'

I stared at her in surprise, but I sensed that this was an informed question from someone who might have connections with the medical profession, and I tried to respond appropriately.

'I've had complicated pregnancies. This time the consultants have been wonderful: they've explained what was happening, what they could do. Concerned, and what I've valued most, they've been approachable. The nursing staff is just the same. I'm convinced I've had better treatment than the women in the private wing.'

'Really?'

She was bright, and I guessed she had definite views. I wondered what work she did.

'Good,' she said. She turned her gaze to the bedside cupboard where I had a pile of books. On top of them, I had balanced a framed photograph of Vanessa. She was 'standing up,' supported by Sid, while he leaned against her bedroom radiator, the turquoise and gold curtains closed behind them.

'You have another child?'

'Yes, my daughter. She is with my husband, the only photo I have of them together, as he's always the photographer.'

'May I?' There was an odd questioning look in her eyes.

'Of course.'

Carefully, she picked up the photo.

'Is he French?'

'No. I'm always surprised when people say that. Born in the East End of London, but very dark-haired like his parents.'

Still focused on the photograph, she said, 'And how old is the little girl?'

'Taken last summer, when she was about three and a half.'

She peered at the photograph for some moments, and I became uneasy. What was she looking for? Did she know something?

At last, she returned it to its place, careful not to dislodge the books. There was a pause. Then lifting herself from the chair using both hands as leverage, she said, 'I'm delighted to have met you. Do you walk about? Are you allowed to do so?'

'Oh yes, thank goodness. It's some time since I was on complete bed rest. In the last few weeks they've encouraged me to walk up and down the corridor, be sociable. It's a waiting game. Only three weeks to go, and the baby could arrive any time.'

As she walked slowly to the door, she said, 'Please come and see me in my room. I'm only next door and it would be good to break up the monotony. Actually, it would be very good to get to know you.'

I heard her walking heavily to her room. I picked up Vanessa's photo, my hands shaking and my heart pounding. What did she see?

From then on, I visited her often, we drank tea, talked about the authors we liked – she was a great Jane Austen fan – and occasionally, discussed politics. One afternoon she made her laborious way to my room. She was holding a complete packet of ginger biscuits which she proceeded to open, dropping a few beside me on my bed and telling me she was waiting for the afternoon cup of tea to arrive, and we would have a feast.

It was then, for the very first time, that I heard the words: *hospital for the severely subnormal.* They struck terror in my heart.

Mary was sitting as best she could in the armchair while I stretched out on the bed, my head propped up with the pillows. Very quietly, but looking at me directly, she said, 'I hope you don't mind my asking but I've been thinking about your daughter. She's exceptionally pretty but I feel, well, I have some experience of these things in my work and I was wondering exactly what her problem is.'

I had noticed her looking at Vanessa's photo on several occasions, and wondered what she was thinking, but something told me not to ask.

'What are you talking about?' I said after some moments of silence.

'It is the way your daughter is standing in the photo, supported by your husband. Not like any three year old I know.'

I couldn't breathe; I searched for an answer and finally came up with: 'She has mobility problems.'

'I see.' Her voice was soft. 'That's a shame, she looks so happy.'

'She is.' I glared at her.

There was a long pause. I shifted on the bed, telling myself this was simply a question and not something I had to fear. I swallowed. 'What made you ask that?'

Mary held out the ginger biscuits. 'Do take one or I'll eat the whole packet myself. A peace offering.'

'All right.' I exhaled.

'I'm not known for my diplomacy. Too outspoken they tell me. But it has its advantages when I want something done. The thing is, I'm a psychiatric social worker, for my pains. I work in a large subnormality hospital where I've seen children and adults very much like your daughter.'

My heart thrummed. Something dark seeped into my mind.

To protect myself, I changed the subject. 'You're not from the North are you?'

'From Cambridgeshire originally. All my family are down there, so I don't expect many visitors.' She laughed. 'That's why I'm glad you live next door. Someone I can talk to, someone congenial.'

Another morning, after the doctors had been, she was having coffee with me when suddenly she said, 'What do you envisage for the future?'

'How do you mean?'

She was dipping a digestive biscuit into her cup, 'I mean, for you, your family?'

'Teaching, preferably adults. And I want to write, seriously, I mean.'

'You're avoiding the issue.'

'Am I?'

'Your daughter. What will become of her when you're too old to look after her?'

I gasped. Only Rachel and Abe, so anxious about me and the unborn baby that they'd suggested 'giving her away', had said anything like this. And only while I was pregnant. Nobody had ever said such a thing.

'She'll go to the Spastics Society School. Maybe until she is sixteen. I can't think further than that.'

'All the families I've supported have been exactly like you. I understand how difficult it must be. From what you've told me about her, for a child so disabled, there's only one thing in the future, it's a subnormality hospital.'

'Never!' I cried.

She persisted in bringing this up until I demanded she let it alone.

A few days before the baby was due, Nurse Davies peeked round the door.

'They're clearing the ward before the new doctors arrive.' She gave me a meaningful look. 'It's always in August. They're organising the timetable for inductions.'

I drew a sharp breath. 'What happens then?'

Mary was with me, drifting in and out of sleep, but when she heard the word *inductions,* she cried, 'Don't allow them to do it! Let the baby come when it's ready.'

'They always do it around the due date, so best not to get too concerned about it, Mrs Gonshaw.'

She left us and I heard her quick steps as she probably went to give the good news to someone else. Mary rose like a ship on the horizon, her twins growing enormously, 'Don't let them force you into it. Keep your own counsel, Susan. They're not gods or kings, these doctors, even though they might think so.'

'You should have been a lawyer. You'd have been an excellent advocate for the defence.'

'I did think of it,' she agreed, 'but I've always been too fascinated by how the mind works to have battles over personal wealth.'

'You could defend the poor,' I grinned.

'Very true.' She gave a great yawn and clung to the door. 'This blasted sedation. I'd better go before I fall to the floor and you couldn't possibly lift me up. Not in your state of health.'

When Sid arrived that evening, I asked him what he thought about me having an induction.

'Do what the doctors tell you,' he replied, dropping into the chair.

Why did I ask? How could he help me decide such a thing, when he had a load on his shoulders: the new shop, Vanessa, the almost completed work in the house?

After he had gone, I lay musing. It was the tenth of August. I had been in this room since the nineteenth of May. How much longer? I took an enormous breath, straightened myself as well as I could considering my bump and said, 'I've had enough. Baby, I want to see you now. I want to go home.'

It would be an induction.

On Friday, when Dr Warrell came in, he said, 'I hear you're happy to have the baby induced, my dear.'

'I've been here such a long time, I just want to get home.'

Dr Mais was with him and they conferred, pointing to the notes, speaking quietly together.

'I'm leaving you in the good hands of Dr Mais,' said Dr Warrell. 'We shall do it next Thursday. Several ladies are going upstairs around that time and we have to order it with care. Dr Mais will explain it to you. I hope that's all right?'

Dr Mais outlined the procedure to me, emphasising that it would be monitored moment by moment. 'Do you have any questions?'

'I don't think so. By the way, my husband won't be there. It's not his kind of thing.'

'Why should he? Since the beginning of time, it has been the focus of women's knowledge – for midwives, for wise women. It's not a man's domain. But will you be upset?'

'Not at all!'

'That's okay then.' He picked up the book he'd recommended to me. 'Do you think this helped?'

'Definitely, even though I couldn't become a Christian, it focused my thoughts on something good.'

'Brilliant work. You've done extremely well, Mrs Stern. You've reached term, the best thing for this little fella.'

'Fella? A boy?'

'You know what I mean.'

'I heard you're leaving St Mary's, Dr Mais,' I said sadly as he stood up.

'Yes, I have a post in the south of England but I'll miss everyone here. It's been a great learning curve. Not till the end of August, so I'll surely get to see your baby before I go.'

Chapter 14

Today's the day, I thought, the second I opened my eyes, and my heart beat wildly with apprehension and excitement. I'm actually looking forward to this, was my next thought, which was madness I knew. Whoever looked forward to delivering a baby? I had told Sid he needed a night off since he would have plenty of nights 'on' in the next few months. When my friend Jessica, the one I called my kindred spirit, had come for a few minutes to see me, full of encouraging thoughts, I was delighted. She even described her own experience of giving birth.

'Everyone is amazed when I tell them I love the birthing process. You become part of the universe; it's the most extraordinary feeling.'

I glanced at her, remembering how awful it had been with Vanessa. 'I hope that happens to me,' I replied softly.

She had reached the door of the room when she said, 'One thing you should remember tomorrow. Pain is part of creation. It is fear that is destructive. Have courage!'

I was thinking this when I heard Elaine rattling the tea trolley down the corridor and singing hymns as she usually did. She carried in a cup of tea. 'I'll be thinking of you today, Mrs Stern.' She glanced upwards. He'll be with you. And it's such a beautiful day, sunny and warm.'

After she'd left, I thought how ironic this was. Going into labour day after day for six weeks, terror-stricken that the baby would come too soon, and now he or she was about to be induced. I frowned, and a niggling doubt pushed its way into my mind:

suppose something happened, suppose the contractions stopped, supposing the baby was starved of oxygen? Brain damaged?

Stop it! You know last night Doctor Mais said I would be monitored the whole time. Relax. I shall take a look at Elaine's 'beautiful day.'

Going to the window, I pulled up the blind and hot sun poured in. I could just make out the trees around Whitworth Art Gallery, several early cars en route for Manchester, night workers and nurses waiting at the bus stop. Empty streets. The students, who'd later amble along Wilmslow Road to the university, still fast asleep. I thought about my time at Manchester University as a postgraduate student, loving the courses on child psychology and child development, my teenage experiences of a complicated family life supplying me with abundant material for essays. I recalled going to a ball with a boyfriend I had met in Mokarlo's, one of the new coffee bars that had sprung up in the 1960s; he wanted to marry me but I had refused. I wondered what had happened to him.

'Good morning.' A nurse wearing a dark blue uniform was at the door. 'I'm your midwife for today.' Pale skin, almost sallow, but she had beautiful bone structure, an actor's face, mobile and expressive. Her dark hair pushed back beneath her cap, a careful expression in her hazel eyes. I felt that she took her work seriously. 'Are you ready?'

'Just get my dressing gown.'

'Morning. You've got a nice day for it, I'd say.' It was the porter who'd entered behind her. The midwife threw him a warning look but, smiling broadly and unperturbed, he positioned the chair close to the bed, and I settled myself in it.

In the lift, I recalled that dreadful morning three months ago, when I sat in an identical chair. That day when it all began. Waters pooling round my feet, splashing onto the lift floor, the porter's shocked white face ... his hand slamming the lift button for the top floor … the delivery suite … contractions … blackness.

My heartbeat racing, I looked down. Nothing.

Everything's all right now. They'll induce the baby. They'll keep watch over me. It will be fine.

Slowing, the lift rattled as we reached the fourth floor. There was a pause, and the door slid open, light from the corridor beaming in. The porter guided the chair out, and turning left, we raced along, passing several closed doors until the midwife striding beside me called, 'Here.'

I found myself in another white room with a trolley for instruments and a stand beside the bed for drips or transfusions. I knew what they were now. I noticed something like a television screen on the wall, opposite the bed. The midwife helped me from the chair. The porter manoeuvred it until he reached the door, where he gave me an enormous wink and disappeared into the corridor.

Monitors, a drip attached to my hand, straps around my waist, the induction was set up. The midwife said, 'The beauty of monitoring is that I shall be in and out all the time, checking everything, making sure all goes to plan.'

For a couple of hours, it all went smoothly but around one o'clock everything changed.

'I can really feel them,' I told the midwife when she popped in. 'I don't know what to do.'

'Excellent.' Throwing a glance at the screen, she said. 'That's what we've been waiting for. It's time to discuss some pain control.'

They linked me up to another screen as a fierce contraction took me by surprise. From far away, I heard the midwife speaking. 'How about something to take the edge off the pain?'

'Do you mean gas and air?' I muttered.

'An injection of pethidine.'

A picture of the mother and baby on the cover of *The Experience of Childbirth* appeared starkly before me. A hidden voice pronounced: *No, no pain killers. Avoid them. Think of the effect on your baby.*

I let out a shuddery breath. 'How long will this go on?'

'It depends on your body, the baby, the stage you're at.'

'Hours?'

'Could be.'

'Tell me about this pethidine. Are there any dangers for me or the baby?'

'We don't give it if baby's nearly there, which isn't your case. Like aspirin or paracetamol it reduces the pain, makes the contractions bearable. Some women even find it enjoyable.'

'How do you mean?'

'A narcotic effect. Makes you feel good.' She laughed.

My body was working hard, *travailing* I recalled suddenly. Breathing over the pain was useless. I didn't want a desperate out of control process, as it had been with Vanessa. If pethidine could give me some feeling of control, I would have it.

'Yes.'

'I'll get it ready. In twenty minutes, you'll feel such a difference.'

She was right. Within half an hour, I could feel the struggle going on within me, the regular tightening and hardening, but it was just bearable, especially the back pain, and where, I demanded to myself grimly, was that mentioned in the book?

Hours passed. No screaming, no hanging onto sheets or bed heads. The midwife came and went. The contractions were immense, continuous. She looked at the screen. 'Not long now.' Then, 'Time to go to the delivery suite.'

'Mrs Stern.' The midwife is talking. 'Just follow my instructions.'

'Yes?'

She's standing very close.

A memory: the pushing ceased… they used forceps…Vanessa…

'Right,' shouts the midwife. 'Push now!'

And here comes that immense body surge which tells me to push, to bear down as they used to say, the words spilling through my mind. Bear down… bear down… bear down…

I am expelling a football.

'Have a little rest,' she says. 'Ready? *Now.* The head's there.'

I am splitting apart.

'That's it. The head's out. I'll turn the body. Push again!'

Huge, huge effort. Someone is making horrible groaning sounds.

A strange slithering, stretching, rushing feeling.

'It's a boy,' I hear the doctor call.

A boy! That wonderful first cry!

I opened my eyes and saw him. Little arms and legs moving as he yelled a good strong baby sound. I began to cry and laugh at the same time. I called, 'Is he all right?'

'Perfect. Your baby is perfect. I'll cut the cord and clamp it. Now you can have him. Just for a moment.'

She placed him beside me on the pillow.

I saw his black hair, glistening as it stuck to his head. His small body. *My baby is all right.*

The doctor put the baby on the scales. 'Six pounds three ounces, a respectable weight.'

He stopped crying. He opened his eyes and his mouth. Taking everything in.

This one is ready to grasp the world, I thought.

'We'll clean him up,' the doctor said, 'and bring him to you very soon.'

'She can go back to the ward, can't she?' asked the midwife.

'Absolutely.' Even the doctor seemed delighted. 'Excellent, Mrs Stern. You've done much better than last time.'

They exchanged smiles, everyone was so happy.

Sid arrived as they moved me out of the delivery room. My heart was bursting with joy, with success, with pethidine. I was beaming, I felt wonderful.

He stood back in astonishment. 'You look fantastic. I can't believe it. You look as though you've been on holiday. Sunburned.'

'It's the pethidine,' said the porter, the one who'd brought me upstairs ten hours before. 'Are you ready to go back, madam?'

'Of course I am.'

Wheeling me along to the lift, he said to Sid, 'You take care, sir, some of them get to like it too much'

They laughed, and I tried to see their faces from upside down as I lay on the trolley. What secret were they sharing that I didn't know?

'Pethidine, it's the same class of drug as morphine, heroin, that sort of thing. Makes you feel good, at first,' Sid said.

'I'm very glad I tried it. Who knows, I might like some again!'

'Here he is.' Nurse Lawrence trundled a cot into my room. She wrapped him papoose-like in the sheet, and placed him in my outstretched arms. I held him, my eyes on his tiny 'old man's' face, and watched him breathe, noting his beautifully shaped mouth, his minute ears, the black hair not quite dry. Already, there was something sure and solid in his tiny body. I couldn't take my eyes off the baby, couldn't get enough of looking at him, feeling him so close, so warm. Lifting my gaze at last, I saw Sid was leaning forward, waiting. 'Come on, it's your turn now.'

He took the baby from me, a great smile on his face. 'Another Sterny,' he murmured. 'That's what they called us in school.'

'You're in a hurry. By the way, when they asked me about names, I said we hadn't decided yet.'

Not true. We had decided on Anthony, for a boy, after my maternal grandfather, but tradition stipulated we had to keep his name to ourselves until after the circumcision. To hide the baby from the Evil Eye. Again the power of names, I wondered, as I watched Sid smiling at his son.

I had suggested the name Jonathan but Sid thought there'd be loads of little Jonathans and he preferred something original. A loner, he eschewed crowds and conventional groups, taking his own decisions after careful thought. A nonconformist.

'Time for photos.' He produced a camera.

In the album are photos of baby Anthony, two hours' old: I'm sitting in my shorty nightie, bare legs dangling at the side of the bed and he's cradled in my arms, my gaze on his face, my mouth shaped almost in a kiss.

Nurse Lawrence was back. 'Breast or bottle?'

'Bottle,' I muttered.

'All right, I'll be back shortly.'

'So you've decided?' Sid said with relief.

'Finally,' I bit my lip, still conflicted by this most difficult of decisions.

A midwife had come a few days before to examine my breasts. 'You're well-endowed for it,' she said. 'Best for baby. I'm sure you know all that.'

'Of course I do,' I told her sadly. 'I've worried about this for days. Weeks. I would really like to feed the baby myself but I have a profoundly handicapped daughter at home. Feeding her can take hours. With the bottle, anyone can give the baby his or her feeds.'

'It's a shame though.'

I had gone over and over this until I was silly and tormented by guilt. Already this baby's life was being juxtaposed against Vanessa's, shaped by her and her needs.

She handed me the tiny bottle, the baby turned towards it, and sucked with such persistence he'd soon finished, without giving me time to wind him. Sid and I stared at each other in amazement. 'Marvellous,' I said. 'A feeder'

Slipping off the bed, my feet bare, I began to walk up and down with baby Anthony over my shoulder, patting his back. There came a small burp. 'Did you hear that? A proper burp?' I turned him towards me. 'You're a wonderful, wonderful boy!'

It was after eight o'clock, and Nurse Davies was on duty.

'Has his nappy been changed yet?'

'Do you think I should?'

'Why not?'

I pulled back the bed covers and turned the baby over. He cried, angry at being disturbed, his arms and legs weaving and curling. I undid the disposable nappy and a spray of pee flew over his legs, onto his tummy and the clamped cord.

Sid began to laugh, 'You'll have to get used to that.'

Nurse Davies handed me some cotton balls. 'No need to wash him tonight.'

'Good thing I don't need safety pins. He's a wriggler and I'm shaky.'

Once he was tucked in, he slept again.

My husband was leaning back in the chair, his eyes closed.

'Go home. You look exhausted.'

'This day has been far worse for me than for you, let me tell you. I was so worried, I couldn't concentrate.'

I knew that despite his unflappable attitude, he felt deeply. I realised that after Vanessa, it must have been a hugely traumatic time of waiting. But I countered, 'Cheek, I would like to see you go through childbirth.'

Whether it was this wonderful, amazing day, or the pethidine, or even the thought of going home, I couldn't fall asleep that night, my mind recapturing the baby's birth, Sid's face and the extraordinary thought that I would actually be leaving the hospital after all these weeks. But I couldn't imagine our new life. I was institutionalised. I realised with a start that I knew little about how things had been for Sid: his preoccupations with the new pharmacy, the constant concern about Vanessa but which he kept to himself. How had he done this? I would have spilled out all my anxieties, all the little events of the day if the tables had been turned. But no, he would sit back in the chair when he came and calmly listen, saying the occasional word. How many men would have been so resilient, so accepting?

Trying to breathe over my anxieties, I imagined how we would be together in this new life, this almost new house, wondering if I had become a stranger, and how would Sid feel then? I pictured Connie. Would she feel comfortable with me being there? And what about my precious daughter, whom I had hardly seen? Would *I* feel strange with her? No wonder I couldn't relax. But holding the image of my marvellous new baby in my mind, I finally let myself drift into the welcoming arms of sleep.

Next morning the baby was sleeping soundly. I gave him the ten o'clock feed and was watching him sleep when I noticed something odd: he looked suntanned. Was it the pethidine? My heart in my mouth, I threw on my dressing gown and went to find a nurse. 'He looks brown. Is he all right?'

He was jaundiced.

Such a blow, but that afternoon the family arrived and I forgot about it. Rachel and my mother took it in turns to hold Anthony, remarking on his calm but wrinkled old man's face and his black hair, those miniature fingers, and above all his *perfection*. They didn't use the word, but I knew they really meant 'normal'.

Hundreds of cards arrived, from friends, from relations, from the girls in the pharmacy, even from people we barely knew, all so delighted, so thrilled for us. The Gabbies who had visited so many times told Sid they would come round when we were home. There was also a congratulatory letter from the synagogue reminding me about the circumcision, and my heart began to thrum.

The jaundice took five days to clear in addition to the week I had expected. Five days felt like an age. Every moment, I would move the little blanket away from the baby's face, checking to see if his skin had become paler. At long last, the doctor said, 'He's fine. You can take him home.'

Chapter 15

'Goodbye,' said Sister Jones, a little awkwardly.

'Goodbye,' chorused the nurses who had followed her in, large smiles on their faces.

'You would think I was the Queen herself!' I replied. 'But it's lovely to see you all before I go.'

They had become my friends; I wanted to give each one of them a hug. But in 1971 it wasn't what we did. Instead, I said, 'I can never thank you enough, you in particular, Sister Jones, but all of you!'

'Just doing our job.'

The others murmured their agreement.

'You must look after yourself. You'll have your hands full,' said Nurse Davies.

'She's got me as backup,' Sid said, a twinkle in his eye. Anthony yawned, gave a little snuffle and started to cry. 'We'd better get a move on. Time to put him in the carrycot.'

'See you soon,' I called, as they went back to work. I had already said goodbye to Mary the previous evening; we had exchanged addresses, promising to meet as soon as she was settled with the twins.

'Let them come,' she entreated to whatever deity she followed. 'This very moment!'

'I'll send you positive thoughts to help.'

One final look around room twelve, my bubble home for more than three months, and I followed Sid to the lift and out into the sunshine.

Connie was by the front door holding Vanessa in her arms. I got out of the car and made my wobbly way towards them.

'Hello, Vanessa, it's Mummy. I'm home, at last.' I showed her the baby. 'This is your new little brother.'

I wondered how much she understood. But she smiled, Connie gave a shy smile and I touched Vanessa's hand. In the new barn of a kitchen, Sid placed Anthony asleep in his carrycot, on the floor, returning with all the paraphernalia I had acquired in St Mary's. Relieved that the car journey had rocked Anthony to sleep, giving me some moments to look round.

'It's wonderful.' I said to Sid. 'Designing it, then making sure the builders followed the plans. It's great.'

Connie spoke softly. 'Would you like a cup of tea? And shall I take Vanessa upstairs for a rest?'

'I'd love a cup of tea.'

Then she asked if she could look at the baby. We peered into the carry cot together.

'He's just like Vanessa,' she murmured.

It was wonderful to be home. To see the sky, the clouds passing, to hear the peace. At first, I noticed the planes landing and taking off from Manchester Airport, but they soon faded into the gentle background murmur of the suburbs. No more constant traffic noise. No more persistent hospital rumble, no more women's cries, no generator or footsteps on polished lino. I lay luxuriating in the essence of homeness, wondering if there was such a word. If not, I smiled to myself, I would invent it.

Then that hungry baby cry. 'Won't be long,' I told him as he began to stretch and fling his little hands around.

Later I went down to see Vanessa.

Despite my euphoria at being home, already she was there, occupying her usual place in my mind. But there were no more smiles. She glared at me, her mouth fixed, her eyes wide, anger unspoken.

'Come on, Vanessa, do you want to sit on my knee?'

She didn't.

'Shall we play with the toys?'

'Nnnnn.' Her noise for *no*.

For an hour I tried to cajole her into a good mood.

'She wasn't like this before I went into hospital,' I told Connie who was watching in silence.

I tried giving Vanessa some tea but she clenched her teeth, refusing everything. What had happened to her? Breathing fast, I rose from the chair. 'Connie, you'd better feed her. She won't have anything from me.'

The following evening, I tried to bathe her but she lay rigid in the water, and then pushed backwards.

'Sid,' I called to him, 'where are you? Vanessa's just slipped out of my hands.'

He told me she had been like this for some weeks, he couldn't work out why but he had kept it from me, not wanting to make me anxious before the baby came.

As if this wasn't enough, there was the circumcision. My heart pounded so loudly I thought everyone could hear it. We had notified the synagogue as soon as Anthony was born and I had to hold myself together when I telephoned Rabbi Rabinowitz to ask him what we should do.

'Mazeltov, Mrs Stern. We're delighted for you. You didn't need my wife's advice after all.'

'I'm sure that going to work with my husband was the answer.' I paused. 'I also went to the mikveh with an orthodox friend.'

'Excellent. I know my wife would have recommended this.'

'Well, can you tell me what happens now?'

'The synagogue office will contact a *mohel*.'

'A *mohel*?'

'The one who performs the circumcision. He'll phone you shortly since your baby is two weeks old.'

'Is he … a doctor?'

'No, a learned, pious man especially trained. He will have done hundreds, maybe thousands of these over the years. You've nothing to worry about.'

I wasn't convinced.

'If you can get ten men, *a minyan*, so much the better. Tell your friends. The *mohel* will want to do it in the early morning, if possible, but you'll be up already with a young baby, won't you?'

'I'm sure I will. Will you be coming, Rabbi?'

'I'll do my best but you never know what might turn up. You'll also need the baby's Hebrew names. Now, a little enlightenment: your son will use these names in his Jewish life: for the circumcision, when he studies *Torah,* I hope, and when he marries. All the significant moments in his life. Tell me the names you've chosen.'

'Anthony Jonathan.'

'You can have Aharon for Anthony and Yonatan for Jonathan. I'll write them down and a friend can collect them from the office. One last but most important thing, have you chosen the *sandek*, the godfather as it were, who will hold the baby during the ceremony?'

'We've asked Cyril Raines, Sid's cousin who lives in Cheadle. I believe he's delighted.'

'Let me know as soon as the arrangements are finalised.'

An hour later, the telephone rang. 'I am Mr Fogelman, the mohel. I can come this afternoon, at two o'clock, to examine the baby.'

Promptly at two, an Orthodox man from North Manchester, wearing the broad black hat, black suit and with a greying beard was at the door. At once, he asked to see the baby, following me up to the bedroom, where I had spread a towel on the bed.

'Just remove the nappy, please.'

Anthony began to wail, disturbed from sleep as I lifted him. Laying him on the bed, I took off the nappy. With absolute concentration, Mr Fogelman examined him. 'He's all right. We can do it. But you mentioned he was jaundiced, Mrs Stern?'

'After two weeks the hospital doctor told us he was clear.'

With the lightest of touches, he pressed the baby's cheek. 'That is correct. Otherwise we could not carry out this *mitzvah*. All right, you can dress him.' He waited in the hall until I was ready. 'I will need the boy's Hebrew names. Do you have them?'

'My friend is collecting them from Rabbi Rabinowitz.'

'Good. Then tell your husband I'll be here at half past eight tomorrow morning. I hope you can get a *minyan*. It will be better.'

'We're contacting all our friends, and the synagogue office is letting people know.'

'Until tomorrow, Mrs Stern. Goodbye.'

I was sitting in the kitchen, taking comfort in a mug of tea when the phone rang once more. This time it was Cousin Sylvie, Cyril's wife. Bright, knowledgeable in Jewish custom and practice, she wanted to find out about arrangements.

'Did anyone tell you about the *lechaim* for afterwards?'

'Oh dear, is that something else we must do?'

'Lechaim is the toast we make when we drink to life. You only need some Kiddush wine and kichels, those sweet crumbly biscuits you buy in the Jewish shop.'

'I am sure that Paula, my friend, will get them for me.'

'We will get them. Now don't worry, Susan, the baby will be all right. They always are. I'm so looking forward to seeing him.'

Next morning, my back shivery, my hands trembling, I fed and dressed baby Anthony while Connie prepared Vanessa for school. Soon I could make out the Cockney tones of Rachel, Abe and Sylvie, the heavier northern timbre of Cyril's voice.

Rachel came to the bedroom. 'How is he?' She bent to smile at the baby.

'All right for the moment,' I muttered.

'I'll come for you when they're ready. Don't go down yet.'

'I couldn't resist having a peep.' Sylvie was at the door, her brown eyes shining through her glasses. 'Lovely! Though I don't know who he looks like.'

'Go back downstairs,' Rachel ordered. 'You'll see him soon.'

She closed the door behind Sylvie. My heartbeat began to race as I to heard cars arriving outside, men's voices in the hall. Greetings. Rachel went to the top of the stairs, returning quickly. 'The mohel's here. He's just talking to Sidney. Asking for the baby's Jewish names.' Her gaze reassuring, she glanced at the baby in my arms. 'He'll be all right, I promise you. Let's go down.'

I already knew it was the custom for women to wait in another room, often in the bedroom. I had once seen a young mother in her nightwear, sitting crouched on the landing, her arms around her chest as though to protect herself. My heart pounding, barely able to breathe, I followed Rachel to the lounge where the men had gathered. As though sensing something, the baby started to make small tentative cries. Rachel stood close to me with Sylvie on my other side. The room was crowded. There were no women. I knew my friends were busy with small children, and for a second I recalled what Hetty had told me about women's obligations. Cyril was sitting on a chair, his back to the window, facing the crowd. I could just see the green silky cushion on his knee with the gold embroidery and the flowers. Mr Fogelman was talking to Sid. Rabbi Rabinowitz smiled as he saw me come in.

'She's here.'

The men turned when they heard this. Rachel carried in the baby as Sid, white-faced, watched. She placed him in Cyril's arms, and together they laid him on the cushion. The *mohel* approached, and dipping his finger into a small glass of Kiddush wine already prepared, rubbed some on the baby's lips as a kind of anaesthetic. Anthony stopped crying. His back to us, Mr Fogelman bent over the baby, I closed my eyes. Cold shudders ran up and down my back. I heard words in Hebrew, the men responding with *amen*.

There was a sudden sharp cry.

Oh my God. I had to get to him. I started to push through the crowd of men, but Rachel caught my arm, 'You mustn't go.'

There were cries of Mazeltov! Mazeltov!

Mr Fogelman said, 'The father can take him.'

His face grey, his hands shaking, Sid carried our baby wrapped in the shawl and placed him in my arms. I clung to him, pressing him against my heart but the baby continued to cry, his eyes closed.

'Feed him,' whispered Rachel. 'Now you can feed him.'

With my head bent over as though to protect him from any other dreadful attack, I climbed the stairs to my room.

Why, oh why, had I decided against feeding him myself? That would have been the greatest comfort of all. As though she guessed my thoughts, Rachel appeared at the bedroom door.

'It doesn't matter what you do. He'll get over it.' She closed the door behind her, and folded her arms, watching as I gave him the bottle.

Another knock at the door and Mr Fogelman appeared. 'Is it all right if I come to check the baby?'

Laying the baby on a towel, I stepped back.

After some moments of intense examination, Mr Fogelman smiled.

'This is very good. Everything is as it should be. I'll come on Sunday to check him once more. But don't give the baby a bath until then.'

'She can top and tail him, can't she?' demanded Rachel.

'Just be careful. I'll leave you some dressings.' He lifted his hat and revealed a large black skullcap covering his head. 'Goodbye.'

The day passed, but that night I lay awake for hours, holding Anthony as he slept and wakened, feeding him when he cried, slept, cried again. Yet the following evening, to our surprise and utmost relief, he was calm, himself once more.

A week after the circumcision, I stood in the kitchen, my gaze passing uneasily from the stove to the cupboard, wondering what on earth I would cook for the evening meal. Meat for Sid and Connie? But then I had to make something separate for me. Fish? That would need an expedition to the village, and I wasn't ready to take the baby out in the car. I decided on cheese cutlets, they would suit everybody.

But I continued to stare at the gas burners. What should have been a wonderful new beginning had turned into a nightmare for all of us, except the baby (I hoped). I thought I knew my daughter, attuned as I was to her every feeling, every need, but now her reactions proved me wrong.

Sid had brought Vanessa to see her new little brother while I was still in hospital but you couldn't tell by her reactions if she had understood. Although we'd recovered from the trauma of the circumcision, this had no bearing on Vanessa's life. She continued to display the intransigence she had shown when I first came home.

'Vanessa, my lovely girl, it's Mummy. I'm here at last. I'll look after you and the new baby,' I told her, but she only stared, her blue eyes hard and unhappy, her body rigid.

I tried giving Vanessa one of her meals each day, but she kept her teeth clenched, so that Connie had to take over.

Every morning I brushed her hair. 'So you'll look pretty at school.' I played her beloved game as we sat in the chair in her bedroom, flattening out her hot little hand to trace the bear's steps around her palm as I chanted, 'Round and round the garden, like a teddy bear. One step, two steps, tickle you under there.' I tickled her beneath her chin which usually resulted in an enormous grin, a delighted shout.

Nothing. Not a smile, not a glance, she would throw herself backwards, pressing her heavy head on my arm but I was so out of practice, my arm would give way and she almost slipped to the floor; I needed all my strength to manoeuvre her into a sitting position. Then I tried taking Anthony to her as she sat in the wheelchair, getting her to touch his face; she would make a lip, her way of showing she didn't like where she was or what was happening. I repeated what they said at school, 'Vanessa Stern, we can sit on that lip. It's a doorstep!' Yet her eyes remained hostile.

Nothing I said or did could reach her.

I felt broken. Astonished that she had the capacity for such anger, such jealousy. A new Vanessa revealed. My hormones still erratic three weeks after the birth, I was tearful, irritable, even brusque with her and Connie. Like a needle stuck in a record, I repeated over and over again: 'She wasn't like this before I went into hospital.'

How could I have said this to a girl of fifteen when she'd worked so hard to look after our disabled child? But puzzled and rejected, I even suspected Connie was criticising me for my bumbling hesitation, and I had no way of knowing what she

162

thought because we hardly spoke. I didn't realise how hurtful this was for her; she went about her work, silent and watchful, keeping her distance.

The previous evening, almost in despair, I had shouted at Vanessa as she flopped and fell in the wheelchair, 'Stop that, Vanessa. Now you *really* look handicapped.'

Catching a horrified look in Connie's eyes, I tried to regain some composure, but she slid through the door saying she would take Vanessa's clean clothes to her bedroom.

'We only know about handicap,' Sid said that evening. 'We've no experience of how an ordinary child would behave in these circumstances.'

There came a flash of realisation. If Vanessa could talk like any four-year-old, she would have shouted, 'I hate you, Mummy. You went away. You left me here. I hate you.' She had only her body to convey her emotions but this was hugely successful. It helped me to recognise this, but how to get through to her again?

What a new beginning. Only Anthony, our wonderful baby, was happy and content, eating and sleeping. Thank goodness for him. So it was hardly a surprise as I stood by the gas stove that morning, to hear Connie murmur, 'Mrs Stern, can I speak to you for a moment?' Her voice was low and hesitant.

'What is it, Connie? Is something the matter?'

'I have to ask you something.' She looked down. 'I want to go home, Mrs Stern.'

'Is it anything I said? I've been bad-tempered lately. Can we talk about it?'

'No. Not that. I want to enrol on a course for nursery nurses and Mum says they begin soon.'

What a relief. I couldn't have coped with arguments or accusations at this moment although I felt such guilt at how I had treated her. 'Your mum's right. Further education courses usually begin at the end of September.'

'You don't mind?'

'Of course you must do that. Isn't it why you came in the first place, to get some experience? Connie, it's a great idea.'

'You're not angry, Mrs Stern?'

'Oh, Connie, how could I be? You've been wonderful while I've been in hospital. Such a difficult thing to look after someone like Vanessa and you've done it so well.'

She smiled and her face cleared of anxiety. 'I loved being here. I really love Vanessa.'

Chapter 16

Connie left, and I felt lighter, relieved to be on my own however chaotic it was. Slowly Vanessa regained her confidence, although there were frequent occasions when you'd see her lying on the floor, yelling for her meal while I was encouraging Anthony to finish his bottle just a little more quickly. If mealtimes coincided, my strategy was to give the baby half his bottle, then feed Vanessa the first part of her supper, (holding her head with one hand while I spooned food into her mouth with the other), then I would give Anthony the rest of his feed, and put him back in the cot. Finally, Vanessa would have stewed fruit or pudding and finish with a drink. I had wanted to feed Anthony myself and felt huge guilt that I didn't, but I had been right: it would have been impossible.

Mealtimes lasted two hours. At times, Vanessa would yell while I was feeding Anthony and I would shout, 'Why can't you wait a moment?' pretending to myself that she understood, and wasn't she the older one after all? There were hours when they screamed together, Anthony's little hands clutching the blanket, Vanessa on the floor or banging her head against the wheelchair.

Which one should I go to first? They both needed me. I was torn in two.

When Vanessa was at Pictor House School, I could breathe a little, delighting in her little brother. Never was a child more adored. Even at the age of three weeks, I felt a great strength emanating from him. In the evening, when he reached out for the bottle, his fingers gripping mine so tightly, I'd call to Sid,

'Look how he's grasping my hand already.' I couldn't help but marvel at him. He gazed at his hands, he could form a circle with his fingers and stared intently at the mobile or pictures I placed round his pram. Because of my experiences with Vanessa, I was determined he would be both loved and stimulated from the moment he could focus his eyes.

One day Sid was feeding him. 'He smiled at me. Is that possible?'

'I'm sure they start long before the books claim they do. Let's see.'

He smiled at me, too.

At last Vanessa settled down, her good humour returned. Sid told me that even before Anthony was born she had been unhappy at school, jealous if the staff gave attention to another child. As though knowing intuitively what was happening, she had been querulous, crying all the time. This term, back in the Developmental Unit, she was content and playful.

Some of us have the great good fortune to find the place – city or mountain or land – where they become their true selves. For me, it was *la belle France.* Speaking another language liberated me from the role of 'good, obedient little girl' that had always restricted me. Liberation didn't mean throwing myself into a life of sex, drugs and rock and roll when I lived in France, even though it was the era of existentialism, the sombre French version of the sixties counter culture. I should have been bolder!

But the spring term of my second year I spent in glorious Paris, followed by a year teaching English in beautiful Aix-en-Provence, where I had friends of every nationality. At seventeen, I had worked in a hotel at Dinard where I met a group of Catholic students, members of Pax Christi, who invited me to join them in community work around the ancient cathedral of Vézelay, with its tiny fantastic sculptures of biblical characters, where the second crusade began. Significantly, I found myself drawn to people who had the certainty of a religious belief, not in defiance of my father, but from a real spiritual hunger. And living in France helped me understand Béatrice, the girl Anne found to take her place after her sad and sudden return to Paris.

She arrived one sunny autumn day and seemed to sail into the house, her long hair flying. Wearing glasses, tall and thin, she was a junior Olympic athletics champion in Paris, an achievement totally ignored by her autocratic colonel father.

'Tell me what I can do to help you,' she asked next morning, while I was feeding Anthony at the table.

'Filling the washing machine, hanging out the clothes, a bit of cleaning, ironing maybe, though I don't do much, tidying up the toys'

'Can I help you with Vanessa? Anne told me about the work you do with her. Can I do it too?'

Vanessa was at school, Anthony had finished the bottle. I sat back, a rare moment of relaxation which I treasured. With him in my arms, I went to the wooden chair, collecting some toys from the table, and sat again. 'Watch what happens when I give him this rattle. Here you are, Anthony, isn't this lovely?'

I shook it; he grabbed it with his fist, his gaze intent. My hand over his, I shook it gently, and he tried to bite it.

'You see how he reached out, held it, and tried to explore it with his mouth?'

Béatrice nodded, and leaned in even closer; I guessed she wanted to hold the baby.

'Lots of movements involving his eyes, his hand and arm come from his huge desire to explore the world.' I loosened the rattle gently from his fist, shook it again and Anthony bent forward to recapture his prize.

'He is trying to get it back,' Béatrice said.

'We've had to teach Vanessa all this. Important fine movements. When she comes home tonight, I'll show you how we work in that special wooden chair and table over there. You see how the chair has a straight back but no padding? Vanessa has learned not to fall onto it because it hurts.'

Béatrice gasped. 'You can do that to her?'

'It teaches her to sit like other children. It looks a bit like a torture chair but I promise you it isn't. Last year I got her to stay sitting forward like a baby of about five months. That way, wherever her hands are, they touch something. Just like an ordinary baby when he discovers his own body or objects, by chance, and learns about the world. We have to provide this special environment for Vanessa so she can do the same. Hopefully she'll discover her own hands and learn to use them.'

Béatrice was still focussed on the chair. 'Does she like to pick things up?'

Taking my coffee mug from the table, I banged it gently. Anthony turned at once, his eyes alert. 'You see how it's attracted his attention? Vanessa does enjoy banging things but all the rest of the activities we're trying to teach her, she does only to please us. It's very hard for her. These tiny things I'm telling you about are the great milestones. With most babies it's just instinct. I've learned that our brains develop while we do this. It's wonderful really.'

'I always thought the milestones were sitting up, crawling and walking and talking of course. It's extraordinary.'

'Right, Béatrice, end of lesson for today. Now for the boring morning stuff. Putting the washing in the machine and hanging the nappies out in the garden. I'll show you where everything is.'

Our lives took on a satisfactory routine. In the evening Béatrice would retire to the hardly-used dining room and would study for a couple of hours, her books laid out in orderly piles, just as I had seen in other French homes. After she had been with us for a few weeks, we took her to the Catholic Chaplaincy at the university to meet people of her own age. Getting to know boys other than the sons of the close-knit military families in Paris presented her with challenging questions. After several of these Sunday night outings, there'd be intense conversations around the washing machine on Monday mornings.

'I've been talking to some people about,' she paused, hesitant, 'about sex!' Her pale skin flushed pink.

'Anything in particular?' I knew what was coming.

'I have to ask you, Mrs Stern. I hope it's all right? *Maman* won't talk about this.'

Even with seven children, I thought, but I said, 'I'll do my best to answer you.'

Despite her strict Catholic upbringing, she wanted to be modern like Anne. One morning, she said, 'Do you think it's all right to sleep with someone before you're married?'

I imagined her life in Paris: a crucifix above every bed, a picture of Mary with the infant Jesus on the dining room wall. I had stayed in just such a house, when I visited a student friend in Toulon. Nineteen like Béatrice – it was a turbulent, searching time for me, when I had to make similar decisions. I recalled the late nineteen fifties when most of my friends were married by the age of twenty-one while I was at university. People certainly got pregnant before marriage, but it was a disaster. The fifties had been a time of: 'We did everything but…'

I shoved a load of nappies into the machine.

'Béatrice, you don't have to have sex with him to prove anything. Is he putting pressure on you?' She shook her head, her eyes troubled. 'Good, because if he is, I think you should find a new boyfriend.'

Another conversation about the pill took place the following day.

'Wouldn't that be the answer?' she asked, her dark eyebrows drawn together above her glasses.

'You could forget to take it,' I said, 'and what would happen if you got pregnant?'

'My father would throw me out.'

'Then wait till you find the right one.'

In the Developmental Unit at Pictor House School, the new work was going apace. Vanessa had her individually planned programme, which was often demanding. In the afternoon, on her return, we took in it turns to kneel behind her as she sat in the chair, putting the sticks and rattles into her hands, and over time, we saw some slow progress. Vanessa learned, with huge effort, to pick up and hold toys as she'd done before my hospital excursion. Many evenings she stayed with her head bent, too tired to do anything. I told Béatrice that even sitting in a chair or a wheelchair was progress. 'She sees the world like anyone else. It must be good.'

Fast-moving, practical, a better nurse than teacher, Béatrice found all this hard and as Vanessa responded better to me, I changed the routine: after breakfast, before the taxi came, I would work with her for half an hour in her room. It was a relief that she accepted this, considering how hostile she had been when I first came home. We renewed our contact with Doctor Wilson, and I was ever hopeful that Vanessa's brain would acquire the new essential patterns for using her hands like any normal child.

In addition to the innovative work initiated by Mrs Vickers, attitudes towards disabled children were beginning to change. My mother was a picker up of potentially useful newspaper articles, and in a piece from the *Manchester Evening News*, I learned of workshops for parents of handicapped children, taking place at the newly formed *Hesther Adrian Research Centre* at Manchester University. Its purpose was to enable parents to assess the developmental levels of their children.

In January, I joined the course.

Knowing already where Vanessa was in her developmental stage, I preferred the group gatherings in each other's homes. Because of our useful kitchen, the first was held at our house. We renewed our acquaintance with Barbara and Nigel Smith, whose progress with Peter I had so envied and admired, and shared our stories with the other parents. Vanessa was more disabled than most, many of whom could talk and walk but all had problem behaviours, usually stemming from the child's disability and our response to it as parents.

With Vanessa, it was her habit of waking at four every morning. For years, I had given her warm milk, thickened with cereal and Bournvita, and we'd both gone back to sleep. Now with Anthony's night feeds continuing until he was three and a half months, I was up and down for hours. There was also Vanessa's demand for immediate attention: a behaviour I had created because I couldn't bear to hear her crying.

'You must leave her,' stated Barbara Smith, her tawny eyes glowing. 'After three nights of crying, the pattern will be broken. No reinforcements.'

I couldn't do it. Vanessa screamed so terribly I feared she would have a fit if we left her so long. Her fitting in the early months was always with me, the horror never disappeared.

Other parents had similar problems; there was the little boy who slept half the night with his mother, pushing her out so he could sleep the rest of the night with the father; the child so sedated to prevent him crashing his head on the wall, he was completely unaware of anyone. We all had something to deal with, and it helped to know that we struggled with similar issues.

Yet despite Béatrice's help, I was often exhausted. The crying, the nappies, the demands from one child or the other ever inescapable. No different from other mothers of little children I knew, but I longed to be more practical, a better manager. Béatrice left us at the end of March, '*Maman* wants me to be home in time for Easter. I wish I could stay with you forever.' She kissed everyone three times on each cheek, as though we were family. Getting into the car en route for the airport, she called, 'I'll come back as soon as I can.'

1. Vanessa's famous lip. Age fifteen months

2. Ready for bed! 1970

3. Holiday in Bournemouth 1970

4. The Stern Family 1973

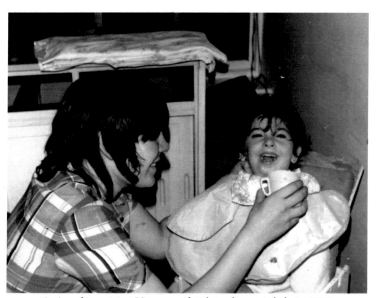

5. Anneliese giving Vanessa a drink in the special chair. 1973

6. With the boys 1977

7. In the motor caravan 1978

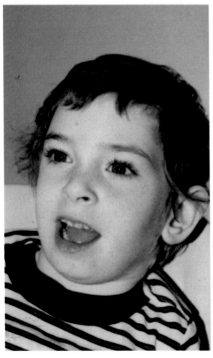

*8. School photo 1980.
Vanessa aged thirteen*

Chapter 17

I was always convinced that Vanessa was intelligent but that her handicaps stopped her from expressing all she understood. Anthony seemed miraculous to us and that was entirely understandable. Even his daddy came to realise what a genius he had fathered. By February, when he was five months old, I could sit Anthony in Vanessa's small wheelchair for his meals. He would lean forward, his arms wide, his eyes following whoever was in the kitchen.

Obsessive compiler of photograph albums, I loved creating books of pictures. The latest, red with 'gold' on the cover, where I happily slipped photos of Anthony into the plastic leaves. By the time he was seven months, we had a wonderful record of his growth and development. We had taken photos of Vanessa on our orange sofa in the sitting room; now there were several of Anthony in various Babygros, or the matinee jackets knitted by my mother, tumbling sideways or reaching out for the camera, ever eager to explore. There were many with Grandma Stern: all smiles, she held him in her arms, his well-rounded shape signifying to her sturdiness, resilience, survival.

'Look at those *pulkas*, (thighs),' she would sigh. 'I could eat him.'

One of my favourites showed him in a 'big boy's jumper,' sitting crouched over, as Vanessa did (a natural, age-appropriate position) as I trimmed his nails, careful not to let him grab the scissors. Every movement he followed with fascination. Another, at nine months, showed him standing in front of the TV, balancing with his left hand on the screen while twiddling the knobs with the other.

Later he'd use the length of the kitchen as a racing track, crawling at enormous speed, and tiring of this, he would disappear into the hall, climb the stairs and come down on his tummy. Coupled with what I had learned with Vanessa and the fascinating child development course I'd taken for my postgraduate education certificate, and naturally inclined to allow children and adults do what was right for them, I gave him every freedom to explore and play wherever he wanted. Once, when the doctor visited me, he said, 'He's like a spider all over the house.'

But how wonderful this was. How my heart rejoiced when I watched him feeding himself, never mind the mess on the tray or the floor. From the age of four months, I would place him on his tummy beside Vanessa, careful to leave enough space so that she wouldn't roll over or hit him with her arms. I could see her watching him out of the corner of her eye but to Anthony, Vanessa was as much a part of his surroundings as we were. He was never jealous of her, although often furious when I answered her wails rather than his lusty yells for attention.

He was ten months old in June 1972, when we decided to take a holiday in Cornwall, in a children's hotel friends had recommended to us. Everything was geared to families with little children: the children's dining room, a loudspeaker system and all the bedrooms had baby listening devices connected with the reception. And there was the uttermost beauty of Cornwall, its little coves, its beautiful air, cliffs, sand and sea.

'This has been a gruelling year what with opening the new pharmacy, the house extension and Anthony's arrival,' I told Sid before we booked. 'This time we need to go away without Vanessa. I'll look for some respite care for her.'

Chapter 17

The Princess Christian Home in Fallowfield, South Manchester, a training centre for nursery nurses, offered short-term care. Unfortunately, Pictor House School hadn't yet created its holiday accommodation, otherwise that would have been our choice. The Saturday afternoon before our Sunday departure, I wheeled Vanessa into the hall of the Princess Christian home, lifted her from the wheelchair and, with a nursery nurse, went to the bedroom where there was a cot for her, one of four in the room.

'Look, Vanessa, this will be your bed for the few days while I'm away with Daddy.' I showed her the cot. 'That's yours. The others are for the children staying here.'

She made a lip. Then she made an *nnn* sound.

'Vanessa, it's lovely here. And your daddy is very tired. He really needs a holiday.' Turning my insistent gaze to the young girl, I implored, 'When she goes to bed, please lay her on her tummy. Not on her back or she'll cry all night. Please make sure about that.'

'Of course. I'll note it in the admission book. Don't worry, Mrs Stern, I'm sure she'll be all right.'

Downstairs, I kissed Vanessa. 'Have a lovely time. I'll come for you next Sunday evening.'

I ran out of the door with her miserable wails in my ears, but I was uneasy as I drove home – something the nursery nurse had mentioned as we walked into the dormitory rose in my mind, beginning to haunt me.

'A little girl died here yesterday and we were all so upset.'

How terrible for the parents. If only she had told me when we arrived; I don't know if I would have left Vanessa with them.

A long journey to Cornwall but by Monday evening, we felt we were truly away. We had taken Anthony to play in the sand pit. We'd walked into the village, the salt smell of the sea in our nostrils, the sun at the back of our heads, and we'd even walked along a cliff path, so we could show Anthony the sea below.

I was about to put him to bed when a voice on the loudspeaker system erupted into our room.

'Mr Stern, Mr Stern, please go to reception immediately.'

I couldn't breathe. Blood rushed to my face, to my head. Sid went white. Exchanging shocked glances, I grabbed Anthony, and together, we shot into the corridor, pushing our way through the crowds of families until we reached the reception desk.

'What is it?' Sid demanded. 'Why did you page me?'

'A Mr Stern has called. I believe it's your father. There's a long-distance call waiting for you in booth A.'

'Did he say what it was?'

'No, but if you go to the phone box along that corridor, you can speak to him yourself.'

Sid was already lifting the receiver as I squashed myself into the booth, Anthony clutched in my arms.

'Hello. It's Sid. What is it?'

If he'd been white before, his skin became the colour of stone. He listened, barely speaking. I could hear nothing. I kept whispering, 'What is it?'

But he continued to shake his head, mouthing, 'Later.'

He replaced the receiver.

'Tell me. What is it? Who is it?' I was holding Anthony so tightly, he probably couldn't breathe.

'It's about Vanessa, she was ill when she got to school but now she's in hospital. They're dealing with it.'

'How is she? What did he say happened?'

'Let's get back to the room. I can tell you everything there.'

Trying not to panic, we forced our way through a wall of parents and children until we reached our room, slamming the door behind us. I stared at him, wide-eyed, terrified.

'What happened?'

A flash of anger in his hazel eyes. 'When she got to school this morning, they found she had a temperature of 105 degrees, and was dehydrated. Luckily the matron recognised this immediately, called an ambulance and now she's in the Duchess of York, on the ward she was in before.'

'Oh God. How terrible. We must go home.' I turned as though to start packing at once, letting Anthony slip to the floor.

'No. Wait a minute. They're feeding her every hour. There's some improvement, already. The hospital told Dad we shouldn't cut short our holiday. We can phone them whenever we want.'

I sank onto the bed. 'How could this happen?'

He sat beside me. 'The matron at Pictor thought she'd probably cried all night because they couldn't feed her properly. She was hungry and afraid.'

'Did they put her on her tummy?'

'They didn't. Or so the matron thought.'

'But I *told* them she mustn't lie on her back. I told them she cries and gets more and more agitated and hot.'

We stared at each other in consternation.

'We could have lost her,' I shuddered.

He nodded. His eyes were dark. 'Luckily they know her at Pictor House. Anyway, Dad phoned the hospital just now, and they told him she was asleep. So that's an improvement. '

Later, I phoned the ward while Sid stayed with Anthony. The sister suggested we call them twice a day. If there was any deterioration, they would contact us at once.

'I'm sure you need a holiday, Mrs Stern. Stay there. Try and enjoy it. Vanessa gave me a little smile this evening so things are looking up.'

I couldn't eat that night but the following days, lulled by the gentle atmosphere of Cornwall, and able to telephone the hospital twice a day, we almost relaxed and enjoyed ourselves. By

Thursday morning, Vanessa was no longer dehydrated, we heard, eating and drinking normally, sitting smiling on a nurse's knee as she watched the others playing in the ward.

Walking along the cliff path, pushing Anthony in his buggy, and feeling the warm breeze on our faces, hearing the sharp cries of the gulls and cormorants, I said, 'How lucky we are to have such a wonderful National Health Service. Such excellent communications, we can phone them, they can phone us, and we'll know immediately what is happening.'

'Let's enjoy the rest of this holiday,' Sid said. 'We've three days left, even if one is driving home.'

We enjoyed our first holiday with Anthony unimpeded by Vanessa's constant demands. But we didn't forget her: in every conversation I found myself saying, 'Yes, but we have a little girl at home who is handicapped.' And they would tell us about someone they knew, a friend or a relation, who had a child like her. We didn't realise how many disabled children there were in the world.

Back in Manchester, I went to collect Vanessa; she was lying on her back in a metal cot, head pressed against the corner, legs caught in the bars. Other children in pyjamas were playing on the floor and I so wished someone could have propped her up in a chair so she could be part of the group, not left alone. But the world saw her as a baby. They didn't know what we knew. I always believed that she had the potential to do far more than she could. So strong was this belief, I couldn't see her as others did.

How can one describe the magic of a child's first word?

It happened when we returned from the holiday. I was holding Anthony in my arms and pointing to a frieze of animal pictures on the kitchen wall. Like all responsible and somewhat precious seventies parents, we bought our toys from Galt's, where everything was made from natural materials. A red duffel bag of Galt's wooden bricks, with spindles, wheels and cubes, would soon become Anthony's favourite plaything.

That day I was chanting the names and numbers of pictures of animals on the frieze when Anthony piped up, 'Tortoise.'

I stared at him, 'Did you say tortoise?'

'Tortoise.' He grinned, pointing and repeating with gusto, '*Tortoise.*'

'You wonderful boy. Tortoise. Your very first word.'

'Tortoise. *Mummy.*'

'Mummy?'

I was ecstatic. I squeezed him so hard he looked at me in astonishment. Then came *Daddy* and *Nessa.* Within a couple of weeks, he had a repertoire of short sentences: want that; drink please; more drink; get down. They were surely enough to negotiate his world. I continued to marvel at how swiftly and easily Anthony learned until one day guilt hit my heart. What about Vanessa? I had barely worked with her since Béatrice's departure three months ago. I must begin again and at once.

As I knelt behind her chair, urging her to pick up the little wooden train or a coloured brick or to bang on various tins, Anthony would crawl at great speed and grab whatever he wanted at that particular moment. Useless to cry: 'No. Vanessa needs that.'

It was clear I needed to look for more help if I wanted to continue this essential work.

This is how we met beautiful Elisabeth, a friend of Béatrice. She was twenty-one, spoke excellent English, and brought the aura of Paris to our suburban home. She told me that her family came from the Midi, her ancestors were Italian. She reminded me of the dark-haired women I had met in Provence, moving slowly, gracefully, and I felt an instant connection with her. She said she'd found her English degree too arid, too dry and was starting a course at the *Ecole de Tourisme* to be an air hostess.

I told her that although I loved the literature, talking and travelling in France, I'd felt exactly the same about my degree at Leeds University.

'I prefer to be with people,' she said smiling.

Vanessa adored her, and their rapport was swift thanks to Elisabeth's ease with English, her serene, gentle quality which endeared her to everyone.

There was another reason for her coming to England.

'I have a friend in Paris,' she said. 'André, a craftsman jeweller. We've been going out for some time and I think I want to marry him.' She hesitated. 'But he's of gypsy blood and my grandmother's family tree goes back to the 11th century and the kings of Provence. My father says he'll disown me if I marry him. I have come here to discover my true feelings.'

She met an art student and was out every evening. I guessed she was having an affair, which was fine with me because she knew what she was doing, and when she came home in the early hours, I said nothing. She wasn't an innocent young girl like Béatrice but sophisticated, worldly-wise in the best possible way.

For Anthony's first birthday tea, we invited the family and the Gabbies with their little girl Nadia and baby boy Neil who was a few months older than Anthony. It thrilled my heart to see his grandparents' delight when we lit the candle and he reached out to grasp it, smiling and shouting, 'Candle. Candle!'

The day before Elisabeth returned to Paris, Anthony took his first steps to her outstretched arms, and her dark eyes gleamed as she held him. I ventured to ask that evening if staying with us had helped her decide about her French boyfriend.

'Yes, I shall marry him whatever my parents think. Thank you for helping me see clearly.'

Sure enough, sometime later, we received a photo from Elisabeth, radiant as she left the church with André. She had made her own wedding dress, (in true French fashion) all the invitations, and had even arranged the reception.

Anthony began to walk. He ran, jumped, climbed and whirled, often dragging his blue Mothercare blanket with him. After Vanessa left for school, I would fill the washing machine while he emptied the kitchen cupboard on the kitchen floor and built intricate towers with cans of baked beans and spaghetti in tomato sauce, an occupation which absorbed him for half an hour.

He was a natural little boy with superabundant energy, needing constant occupation, often demanding. He needed boundaries but because I was ever drawn to doing something with Vanessa, her total physical helplessness calling to me to help her move and play, then Anthony couldn't come second. There was an equally powerful force in him, and I felt like a yo-yo between them.

At the weekend with Vanessa at home, we spent mornings daubed with paint. Anthony was really too young to do this but he was so enthusiastic, standing in his vest and nappy, covered with red, yellow and blue powder paint, a rainbow stretching over the floor across the demarcation lines of newspapers, where he'd been 'painting' in large slabs of paint. It made him so happy. He learned the joys of water very early. Pushing a chair towards the sink, he'd shout, 'Taps, water, jugs. I need jugs, Mummy.'

A friend gave me a photograph of Vanessa and Anthony at her daughter's first birthday party. Five mothers with seven or eight little children, all the one-year-olds like Anthony sitting on their mother's knee – except for him. Vanessa was on my knee while he stood close to me, and I enfolded him with my right arm. Tears filled my eyes when I added this photo to the album. It should have been Anthony on my knee, not Vanessa. That's why,

I thought, I gave him so few restrictions. No wonder he used all his energy, even naughtiness to get my attention.

Although Paula, our friend round the corner, had gone back to work as a solicitor, often leaving one of the children with me, teaching even part-time, wasn't yet an option. But I needed adult company, somewhere I could go occasionally where Anthony would be with other children. While Béatrice was with us, I had begun to help out at a multiracial playgroup in Longsight, run by Kath Robinson, a warm, friendly woman, involved in local politics. It was held in the basement of a church, and when Anthony was a year old, he came with me. He joined the others, running and jumping, clapping his hands to the music. Sitting on hard chairs around the room were many of the mothers, both Indian and Pakistani. In hospital, I'd promised Asian women who'd come to chat, that I'd teach them English when I was home, but it never happened.

At the playgroup I would spend time with these mothers, troubled by their isolation, their inability to communicate whereas their tiny offspring spoke English with the rest of the children. They reminded me of Sid's grandmother who spoke Yiddish to everyone, including the milkman. She'd come to England from Warsaw in 1912, now it was 1972. Surely there were ways of teaching English to these women in their own homes, if they were reluctant to go to a class? I promised myself that I would do this as soon as I could.

This playgroup was one of many sprouting up all round England. The PPA, Preschool Playgroup Association was barely nine years old. One woman, Bella Tutaev, had written to the *Manchester Guardian* about the need for places where children could play together while women could work part-time. Within a year, one hundred and fifty women came together in London to set up this now-thriving organisation.

When she saw how I loved playing with the children, meeting the other adults, Kath asked, 'Why don't you go on a course for playgroup helpers at Fielden Park College? I'll introduce you to people there.' Who would have thought that Kath would serve on the city council for many years and would one day become Lord Mayor of Manchester?

Most interesting were the practical activities: we fashioned cardboard boxes, toilet rolls and powder paint into mini castles, trains, or even dinosaurs. Like the television programme *Blue Peter*, it was very much the vogue to encourage children to make things themselves. I believed it to be an offshoot of the sixties counterculture, or perhaps a continuation of the self-help ideas of the war since it focused on easily obtained materials we had at home: plastic bottles, cardboard boxes, poster paint, bottle tops, plasticine.

Chapter 18

When Vanessa was five and Anthony fifteen months, I was spending all my waking hours with young children, frequently drained by that insidious weariness that possesses mothers and especially those with disabled children. I needed an exciting event, a bright prospect to look forward to.

Sid was watching *News at Ten*, his gaze riveted to the screen, when I said, 'Let's have a party.'

'A party?'

'For your birthday, in three weeks time.'

'Do we have to?'

'I want to talk to some civilised beings.'

'Our friends? Call them civilised?'

'Don't be like that.'

'All right, I suppose so. How will you do it?'

'We've finally got a freezer. I'll cook everything at night.'

Sid wasn't particularly keen on large gatherings but I was fired up with the idea of having some light and laughter. It was November, the dark month of the year, long nights, and no sun. By now I had learned to make several vegetarian dishes, like Pizzaladiere and asparagus flan, from Robert Carrier cookery cards, very much the trend at the time; women had boxes of cookery cards on their windowsill to consult when necessary. I could make cheese and onion rolls with puff pastry, and salads were easy. I was proud of a certain sliced tomato, orange and onion salad I had eaten when staying with our family in Algiers.

For dessert there would be fruit cakes and fruit salad. It was a lot of work but I so longed for adult company, I felt it was worth it.

Sid's birthday was on Monday, the party would be Saturday evening.

An evening we would never forget.

Our friends came, we played music, people laughed and talked, we were grown-ups together. That night, doing the washing up after everyone had left at around two in the morning, I stopped mid-wash. My face flushed, a strange thought gripped me with its talons, and even seemed to pierce my hands deep in the suds and hot water.

'Don't stop,' Sid said. 'I'm dropping. Keep up the momentum or I'll fall asleep on my feet.'

'Sid.'

'What's the matter?' He was leaning against the draining board, a tea cloth in his hand, eyes half closed.

'I think I'm pregnant.'

'Don't be ridiculous.'

'I am. I'm sure of it.'

I could hear my heart, beat, beat, beat and the pulse in my throat, knock, knock, knock in the silence.

'What did you say? You must be mistaken.'

'I'm not.'

He turned back to the washing up, his gaze narrowed angrily.

Days passed, and feeling ever more apprehensive, I went to the doctor, clutching my little bottle of urine and watching it being stowed away to be transported to the pathology lab at Stepping Hill Hospital. But I couldn't bear to wait. Bundling Anthony into the car seat, I drove to the hospital and found the laboratory.

'Please,' I begged the austere woman behind the desk, 'I need to know.'

Perhaps because she saw Anthony in my arms, she softened.

'I'll do what I can. You'd better wait there.'

An hour elapsed. I was about to leave with a very impatient, cross little boy, when a nurse returned handing me a sheet of yellow paper.

Positive. I stared at the markings on the paper in consternation.

A tangle of thoughts careered round my mind. Another baby… I'm pregnant again… how old will Anthony be? *Pregnant.*

'Mummy, hungry.'

Turning my gaze to my son's tear-stained face, I scrunched the yellow paper into my bag and went to find the car. Where was it? I was so agitated I had forgotten where I had left it. But I eventually found the car, and panicked even more. How will I manage? He won't be two years old, and Vanessa, although she will be six, she's as helpless as a newborn baby.

Instead of going straight home, I stopped in the village, dashed into the sweet shop and bought a small packet of chocolate biscuits, tearing it open and thrusting one into Anthony's hand. Unheard of – giving him chocolate before lunch. Then I ran to the doctor's to ask for an appointment.

'Please, as soon as you can.'

'That'll be Friday, at half past four.' The receptionist stared at me over her glasses.

'Have you anything sooner? *Please.*'

'Sorry.'

I had already told Sid that I was going for a pregnancy test that morning. Now I was desperate to tell him the result but how could we talk while he was surrounded by other people? Dispensing medicine was a serious business, but still, I had to telephone him. It seemed like hours before I could whisper down the phone, 'I've got the result.' I heard the sound of tablets being counted into a bottle, his brother's voice speaking to one of the assistants, traffic noise from the streets. 'I can hear you're busy,'

I continued. 'But I've got to tell you. It was positive!' There was such an interminable silence, I shouted, 'Did you hear me?'

'Yes, I heard you.' Now it was my turn to go silent. 'I'll phone you later, when it's quiet.' His tone was abrupt. A pause. 'Are you all right?'

I closed my eyes. 'I'm okay. A bit shocked. Look, I had better go. You're busy and Vanessa will be back any moment.'

I waited a week to see Doctor Griffiths.

Anthony scrabbled around on the floor of the surgery, examining the waste paper basket, banging on my legs as I sat facing the doctor. To my amazement, Doctor Griffiths laughed when I told him how worried I was. Shocked by such a response, I glared at him.

'This is the best thing that could happen,' he said. 'Anthony will have a normal brother or sister.' I continued to glare, confused and hurt that he hadn't listened to me. 'How old is he now?' He winked at Anthony, who gazed back, solemn-eyed.

'About fifteen months.'

'This next one is due early July?' I nodded. 'Mrs Stern,' His gaze from beneath his thick black eyebrows was intense, 'there's absolutely no question that you should have this baby.'

'I do want the baby. It's just…. I don't know what to do. I don't know how I'll manage.' Tears welled up in my eyes, and I focused on Anthony's busy hands.

'I'm certain you will,' he said.' He gave a rare smile. 'I'll refer you back to David Warrell and you'll be absolutely fine.' He paused. 'We'll see you through this one, and then, no more.'

When I told Sid what Doctor Griffith's said, that Anthony would have a normal brother or sister, he agreed and I was astonished.

Two weeks later, my sister Barbara phoned, her voice buzzing with excitement. 'I've got something to tell you.'

'Go on.' Guessing she was pregnant again.

'I'm pregnant.' Her voice rose in a kind of acclamation.

'Mazeltov!' I cried, as delighted for her as she was herself. 'When?'

'At the end of July. Around the twenty-eighth.'

I closed my eyes. This baby I was carrying would arrive three weeks before hers but I couldn't tell her. Steadying my racing thoughts, I said, 'That's fantastic. I'm thrilled to bits for you.' Good thing she couldn't see my face. We had told no one yet, and I rushed on, 'How are you? You had a lot of morning sickness last time.'

She groaned. 'I've got it again. Hope it'll stop soon.'

An insidious anxiety about the pregnancy crept silently into my heart, my soul and even into my everyday thinking. New Year, January 1973, was cold and dank with metallic lowering skies and icy rain or snow, all of which accentuated my growing sense of unease. I woke with dull dread in my heart and went through the hours of the day like a zombie. Looking out of the window, I saw bare dismal gardens, which echoed my increasing sense of desolation. The house mocked me with its disorder – piles of clothes on beds, toys all over the floor, clothes shoved into bedroom cupboards. I had become a slattern.

The bookshelves, especially the bookshelves, were higgledy-pig-gledy with books piled high or leaning sideways; often Anthony pulled some out, spread them around the floor to build a house but left them there. The tin of Bournvita, Vanessa's favourite chocolate drink, would stick to the kitchen shelf. Accusing fingers were saying, 'It's chaos here. Do something about it. Do something.'

Bone weary, worn out, I could do nothing. What was happening to me? Had the fear of pregnancy been absorbed into my subconscious, despite my decision? Talk yourself in, I thought, as Rachel would have said. Be positive. I searched the bookshelf for *The Power of Positive Thinking*. But the words resembled spiders moving across the page. The mantras were voices from a distant time, meaningless.

I made lists of jobs to be done, food to buy, meals, fixing the lists with drawing pins to the kitchen door, and almost spitefully – they fell off.

Sid would come home, asking, 'What's for dinner?'

'Food.'

He stopped asking.

Now I hated cooking. Never a 'cook,' enjoying creativity in the kitchen like Paula, I wanted to give Sid baked beans every night but felt guilty at serving only 'thing' on toast. Still, I stalked grimly around the kitchen.

When Paula popped in one afternoon, she stared at the growing chaos. 'Surely you need some help again?'

'I'm fine.' The thought of having another person in the house was unbearable.

A week later, however, she told me she had found a girl from Brittany. 'Do you want the address?' She shoved it in my hand. 'Go on. You might as well.'

There was a common belief in France that Bretons were stubborn and hard-headed, although the girls in the Dinard hotel where I'd worked in 1956 were lovely. I wrote the usual letter telling this girl from Rennes about Vanessa, asking if she wanted to come given these circumstances. She replied saying that she did, and brought Breton toys for the children and a bottle of liqueur for us. It seemed like a good beginning.

I plodded through the days. Despite having help, I was in a dark place. Our new au pair girl hardly spoke, doing her share, running off to Cheadle in the afternoons, out every evening. There was no rapport between us. Even when she accompanied us on a day trip to St Anne's, with my in-laws, she stayed silent while helping Vanessa drink from her beaker, or bringing me bibs and nappies to change the children in the car. She must have picked up on my dreary state of mind; perhaps she'd encountered it at home. It must have been devastating to rediscover it in the north of England, if this was the case. And I, usually so sensitive to others and their feelings, was too deep in my own misery to reach out to her, a shadow at the periphery of my vision.

One Friday night, I could stand it no longer.

'Sid, I'm going out for a while. I'll go and see a friend.'

'Are you all right?'

'The usual tiredness. Maybe a chat will brighten me up. You don't mind?'

'No, I'll doze in front of the television.'

I took the car. I wouldn't go to my mother or my sister Barbara, they lived the other side of Manchester; nor did I want to burden my mother with my troubles once again. Where could I go? Who could I talk to?

On impulse, I drove to the house of my close friend Jessica, who had supported me before and during my pregnancy with Anthony. Uncertain, I sat outside her house in the dark, and then with a great intake of breath, I walked to the front door, where I pressed the bell once, ready to run if she hadn't heard me. Thank goodness it was Jessica who answered.

With the slightest lift of the eyebrows, she said, 'Sue, are you OK? Come in. Don't stand on the doorstep. It's bleak outside.'

'I know it is Friday night,' I muttered, still wavering. 'I hope I'm not disturbing you.'

'Of course not. Come in. Come into the lounge.'

I followed her. The room was peaceful with its green decor, its walls illuminated by various lush Modigliani prints, Jessica's favourite painter. Everything was calm, orderly, in its place. I sat on the edge of the sofa while she sat in an armchair close by.

'What is it?' Her voice was soft.

Frowning, my head down, I hesitated once more. Finally, I managed to say, 'I just need to talk to someone.' Then, beginning to cry, I told her, 'I'm... I'm sixteen weeks pregnant, and I don't know what to do. I just can't stand anything any more.' While I sobbed, she stayed silent, her gaze focussed. I dragged a handkerchief from my pocket and wiped my eyes, but I couldn't stop weeping. Finally, between sobs, I managed to get out, 'Nobody knows about the pregnancy except for Sid.'

She bent her head. 'I'm not surprised that you're pregnant again. But what's really the matter? Being pregnant?'

'Even though I've made up my mind this pregnancy should be normal, normal in every way,' I shook my head, 'I feel just horrible. I don't know what the matter is with me.'

'What does the hospital say?'

'Everything is fine so I can't... *won't* spend time lying around like I did with Anthony.'

'How's Sid?'

'He's all right, I think. Don't know how he puts up with everything.'

'Anthony?'

'Full of life. Tantrums when he can't get his own way. I lose my temper with him. It's part of the problem. Me. *I'm the problem.*'

'Tantrums are normal at that age. How about Vanessa?'

'She's okay. Going to school. Coming back. Not really making any progress.' Jessica gave me a sharp look but said nothing. 'It's me. Listen, the house is in a mess, I hate cooking, and everything, everyone is getting on my nerves.'

I began to cry again, my head choked with tears. At last, wiping my eyes, I managed to look up.

'Let's talk it over.'

Over those weeks, I went to her house and with common sense and understanding, she helped me unravel the anxieties and fears that were ready to destroy me. As we talked, I saw that my fear of childbirth had come from my grandmother Sophia, after whom I was named. Following three difficult pregnancies, she'd died of puerperal fever, that dreaded illness of the nineteenth and early twentieth century, when she was only twenty-eight.

My relationship with Vanessa and Anthony seemed to reflect how I felt about my parents when I was very young. As though I was pulled backwards and forwards between them. Both needed something from me that I was too small to give. My father needed my acquiescence as a reassurance to his well-being; my mother often saying that she'd never had a mother, and I chose to look after her.

I couldn't have known how this would be replayed in my relationship with my children. Like my parents, they also needed so much from me. I was scared to say *no* to Anthony, just as I couldn't refuse my father, whom I rarely defied. And at the age of four, I had learned to be my mother's carer when she'd sit crying after arguments with my father. Looking after Vanessa was similar in some ways to caring for her.

At last, my fear of childbirth disappeared. When the little kicks and movements became stronger, I grinned. *Don't need to remind me you're there*, I would say to the baby, *I know*. It was time to pick up my life again. We tried to help Anthony understand that he'd soon have a brother or sister. But he was so little himself, he would be twenty-two months when the next one was due in July. Could he understand?

One doubt wouldn't go away and kept popping up when I had a rare, spare moment. How would Vanessa react to another person who would probably displace her in my heart? I forced myself to stow this worry away in some invisible box in the depths of my mind.

Chapter 19

I've talked about destiny, sometimes called karma, or beshert, as they used to say in Yiddish, while on the other hand, I have described how I wanted to become more decisive, able to make choices for myself. A little of each must have led me into new, exciting directions very shortly after I began to enjoy life again.

It happened one beautiful spring day, when the sky was palest blue and an early sun brought colour to the houses across the way. I could hear the rich warbling calls of blackbirds seeking a mate, ready to establish their territory and I decided that as soon as Vanessa had gone to school, she was now picked up every morning by a volunteer driver whom she knew and liked, I would take Anthony out in the new twin buggy we had just bought, and make our leisurely way to the local village. The excuse was to buy some potatoes, the real reason was to enjoy this lovely morning, the walk, the daffodils making glorious patches of gold in the borders, and our son's fascination with all he saw.

This is how I met Scouse Cindy.

I was thinking about Anthony who was nineteen months old and already speaking well. He needed constant occupation for he darted from one thing to another, exhausting every activity in double quick time. What would he do when the next baby arrived? I was sure he would benefit from being with other little children, but how would I find them?

I stopped pushing the buggy. Supposing I set up a mother and toddler playgroup? Have it in our house, or in the homes of the other mothers whoever they'd be. I was so excited by this brainwave that I set off at top speed and rounding the corner, I bumped into somebody pushing a very old, upright trolley overflowing with shopping. I saw a pretty little girl, blonde as her mother, trailing along some yards behind her.

'What a smart pushchair.' The young woman smiled at Anthony. 'Don't you look comfortable sitting there?' Anthony stared at her solemn-eyed. 'Where's your other twin? At home with his Nana?'

'No,' I smiled, 'we have a little girl who is handicapped and she's at school.'

Then her eyes widened, her gaze riveted on my stomach. 'And you're expecting another one? Heavens, I can't even manage her.'

At this point the little girl began to scream hysterically for no obvious reason and Cindy, as she was called, said, 'Do you fancy a coffee? I'm dying for some adult company. *Dying.*' Her eyes and mouth crinkled up in mock desperation. 'Or do you have to get somewhere?'

I liked her. Interesting, lively and I guessed from her accent she came from Liverpool. I had met Scouse humour before and from this short conversation I imagined she would have it in abundance. 'Love to,' I said. 'The potatoes can wait.'

We drank cup after cup of coffee and I soon learned her story: they were both teachers but her husband had higher aspirations. He was currently reading Turkish at Manchester University. He thought it an unusual language to teach and would surely bring them great riches.

Stepping over the children, she lifted a photograph from a small teak sideboard and passed it to me. 'That's Ben, complete with guitar, pretending to be a virtuoso'

I saw a debonair-looking man, hair curling to the collar, long sideburns, and a look of intense concentration on his face. She returned the picture to its place. 'Lucky devil. I'd give my right arm to be back at work full time.'

'What do you do?'

She explained that she taught shorthand and typing evening classes at the local adult centre, but there were no nursery facilities and she had no money to pay for a childminder during the day. They subsisted in the free flat, payment for acting as caretakers to the nearby block of flats.

Our conversation was interrupted by an argument over some bricks which Anthony had snatched from Rebecca, the little girl, and was using for a complicated castle he was building.

'Why don't I make them some sandwiches?' The children munched them as we talked. 'What were we saying?' Cindy sat back. 'Oh yes, I teach four nights.'

'I wouldn't mind teaching at night,' I heard myself saying with surprise.

Cindy threw me a quick glance. 'What do you teach?'

I found myself telling her about my varied teaching experience: English in France, and at the College of Adult Education in Manchester, and French to juniors before I got married.

'I could ask if they've got any vacancies,' she said thoughtfully. 'Shall I do that?'

With a sudden rush of emotion, I said, 'That would be brilliant.'

I suddenly remembered the burst of inspiration that had led to all this. 'Cindy, I must tell you why I nearly collided with you before.'

'Go on,' she said.

'I was dreaming about setting up a mother and toddlers group, so Anthony would have other little children to play with when the next one arrives.'

'What an ace idea.'

'Would you come?'

'Me? I'd be your first customer. But how would you do it?

'Advertise in the post office near me.'

'I wouldn't dare do anything like that but I'd back you all the way.'

We smiled at each other. Another new venture. I was delighted I had met Cindy, that she had confirmed my brainwave. Exchanging telephone numbers, we promised go to the sub post office up the road.

Within a week we had eighteen replies.

They came: doctors, teachers, secretaries, women who never divulged their occupations before motherhood, so many young women yearning for adult company. It helped to see that other little children had tantrums or waddled around in squishy nappies. Cindy made mug after mug of coffee. The babies crawled or toddled, bibs around their necks, biscuits chewed or flung to the floor. We talked about everything, our homes, our husbands, but an underlying theme was how we longed to return to work. We discussed every stage of development, sometimes in secret acrimony if our child was last in the line to accomplish it.

The Mother and Toddler Group was born, and Cindy and I were, as she said, very chuffed with ourselves!

Six weeks before the baby was due, I stood by the telephone biting my lip and tense with uncertainty. With tears in my eyes, I lifted the receiver, and dialled Doctor Wilson's phone number. As soon as he answered I began to speak in such a rush, I knew he was wondering who was at the other end of the line.

'Hello Doctor Wilson. It's Vanessa's mother here. I want to… ' I stopped and frowned and began again, because I hated what I was going to say. 'I'm very sorry to tell you this, but we'll have to stop Vanessa's visits to you.'

'Hello, Mrs Stern. Is there something the matter?'

I sighed. 'Not really. We're simply making no progress, and it's been like this for months.' When he didn't say anything, I rattled on. 'But we're so grateful for your suggestions and your help. Since we started with you six years ago, Vanessa has certainly learned to sit in a chair, thanks to your work.' He still didn't speak and I began to feel worse, wondering if this was some terrible blow to him. 'And she can definitely pick things up.' Less and less, I thought, but I didn't tell him that.

'I'm very sorry that you're leaving,' he said slowly. 'If you ever wish to come back, I would be glad to see you.'

I knew we couldn't go back but I said something else just to make things a bit better. 'Actually Doctor Wilson, I'm expecting our third child in about six weeks' time. I will be rather busy over the next few months.'

I looked down to see that I was holding my stomach with one hand.

'Congratulations, Mrs Stern.' Thank goodness he sounded more cheerful. 'I do hope everything will be fine.'

'Thank you, Dr Wilson. Thank you so much. Goodbye.'

Why, I asked myself, why was I so upset at leaving Dr Wilson? The programme had offered such a brilliant possibility and now I was letting it go. Miserably, I acknowledged that I had lost the drive I'd had in the early years. Then there was so little time to be with her, most of it taken up with feeding and dressing. I knew, with a heavy heart, that despite all my passion, all our work together, Vanessa hadn't changed.

Another parting occurred.

One afternoon, carrying her suitcase, Madeleine strode into the kitchen.

'Madeleine, are you going somewhere?'

'Yes. Leaving this house. Never coming back.' There followed a torrent of French, and I felt my mouth fall open in amazement. 'You've treated me like a servant. A slave. I work longer than any other au pair girl. You pay me nothing. I can't stand this any more.'

'But why didn't you come and talk to me? We could have sorted it out. I always believe in talking through a problem. I'd no idea you felt like this, Madeleine.'

It was certainly the first time she had revealed herself in any way. She continued to glare, her pale skin flushed with anger. I asked her where she was going.

'To a pub in Cheadle, where I've been working every evening. From today, it'll be full time.'

With this, she swung round and walked out. I heard the front door bang, the windows rattle. Working in a pub? She could have punched me in the stomach. Peering through the kitchen window, I watched as she marched along the road, and filled with her sense of injustice, her short, square figure was a little more upright as she disappeared around the corner.

Dropping onto the bench by the table, I thought back to when she arrived. It must have been just as the depression hit me. Perhaps I hadn't been aware of her; perhaps she'd been drawn into my depression. I wondered if she'd encountered such a thing at home. My mind flitted around all these possibilities but I had been so wrapped up in my own little world I hadn't noticed Madeleine. We had photos of her helping at Vanessa's birthday party, building a castle for Anthony in the sand at St Anne's, without a single word of complaint. The real reason was that I hadn't made a relationship with her. Heaviness settled in my heart and I heard the words of my conversations with Mary, my pregnant neighbour in St Mary's hospital: what will happen to Vanessa when you can't look after her in the future?

With barely three weeks to go, I heard the telephone and recognised Cindy's lively voice immediately.

'Hiya Sue.'

'Hello Cindy.'

'Good news. I bumped into the principal of Cheadle Adult Centre last night and he wants you to come and see him.'

'Thank you. That's brilliant. Do they actually need a French teacher or was it all your charm?'

'The latter, of course...' She broke off to chuckle. 'But I guess they might need someone. Anyway, it's always good to show your face. Look, here's the office phone number.'

That's how at eight months' pregnant I found myself sitting on the edge of a chair in the principal's office. A friendly, older man, he was most solicitous, 'Would you like something for your back? My wife always needed a cushion in these circumstances. I'm sure I've got one hidden away in that cupboard.' He threw a glance at a wall cupboard, so crammed with books they were falling out onto the floor.

'No, thank you. I shall be really fine like this.'

'You sure? Well, Mrs Stern, I've heard great reports of your teaching. Would you like to tell me something about yourself? When did you qualify?'

As I talked, I realised that most of my experience had been concentrated on teaching English as a Foreign Language, rather than French which is why I was there for an interview, after all. Wondering if he would ask me to leave, only here on false pretences, I told him of my time in the south of France.

'Aix-en-Provence, did you say?' His eyes were suddenly alert.

'Part of my French degree. I taught English in the Girls High School in Aix while studying at the university. After I'd qualified, I worked at the College of Adult Education in Mosley Street, Manchester, teaching English to foreign students. The Lower and Proficiency Certificates,' I added.

'How about French?'

My heart began to thrum, 'Teaching practices were in Bury Grammar and Bury Convent. Then a pilot project in Manchester with primary children near Moss Side. They curtailed it after a year.'

'The cuts,' he drew in a sharp breath. 'Always the cuts. Let's go back to your time in Aix.'

'Do you know the Midi?'

'We go every year, trailing our caravan, and we love Provence.'

Vistas of translucent blue skies, of cypress trees – those dark sentinels on the horizon – and of shuttered white villas rose in my mind. We talked so long about Aix, St Remy de Provence, climbing the hills to Digne, the home of my friends, that we both looked at our watches, and he jumped up from the chair saying, *Mon Dieu*, it's seven o'clock, and I have a class. Well, Mrs Stern, so pleased to meet you. Would three evenings suit?'

I was amazed he would appoint me so soon after the baby, but I suspected our mutual admiration for all things French had convinced him.

'Thank you. That would be wonderful.' A doubt sailed into my mind: was I mad to accept three evenings? No, I would definitely manage. Somehow.

Something was about to happen which would transform our lives. Vanessa's gift to her daddy. Or rather, the idea of one, and a solution to a problem we'd had for more than a year. When we travelled by car, she was perfectly happy so long as we kept moving but the moment we stopped, she would scream hysterically. We never knew why she became so agitated. Sitting beside Anthony happily strapped in his car seat made not the slightest difference.

'She might feel safer if she could travel in the wheelchair,' Sid suggested. 'If we had an estate car, I could fix it in the rear.'

He decided to visit his local garage, where something made him pause. A beautiful motor caravan waiting to be serviced. Back home, with some excitement, he said, 'Supposing Vanessa could sit in her wheelchair fixed securely to the floor, able to see us, and we could see her. More like being in a room. Wouldn't she feel better?'

'But how?'

'This motor caravan, (or camper van people call it) might solve our problem. She could sit in the chair with plenty of space around her, as we drove. We'd be at the front but you could reach her. Anthony would be strapped in a seat close to her. What do you think?'

'Sounds brilliant.'

'Then I'm going to find out.'

He subscribed to one of the increasingly popular motor caravan magazines, and some time later spread out the latest edition on the kitchen table. 'Look at this. You can buy plans for building the interior yourself.' With unusual excitement in his voice, he pointed to the page.

Gazing at these grainy black and white photos, I frowned, 'You mean you'd make the furniture? Can't you buy motor homes all ready? Everything within?'

'You can, but there'd be no space for a wheelchair. Besides, I really fancy the idea of doing the fittings myself.'

I grinned at him. 'You must have been a cabinetmaker in a previous existence. You told me how you were fascinated by tools, that if you'd had your way, you would have been Mr B&Q by now. It's just up your street. But have you got the time?'

'I would make the time. One more thing, would you really fancy a holiday in something like this? If it worked, we could take Vanessa with us.'

'I would love it. Our own little home on wheels, cooking what we want, eating when we want. Fantastic.'

Sid exchanged his car for the blue Commer van which now stood in the drive. Using it daily for work while spending evenings and most Sundays building the furniture, he altered the blueprint to accommodate a wheelchair. The evening that I got the job, it was in the final stages of completion. Bubbling over, I had to share my news with him the moment I got back. The garage doors were open and knowing he was working there, I manoeuvred myself out of the car to speak to him. With a measure in his hand, he was bending over his workbench with absolute concentration. Holding my bump, I made my slow way towards the darkened interior where the evening light spilled through a far window, coming to rest like a tiny searchlight on a piece of rosewood furniture, and I stopped. The rosy grain of this small wardrobe looked like velvet.

I leaned against some planks of wood close to where he was working, one hand supporting my aching back, the other my bump, and gazed around: there was a low cupboard with two doors destined for cooking equipment, camping plates and cups. Beside me stood the wardrobe; on the other side was a small wall cupboard with shelves for tee shirts, and underwear.

'This is the base for a two-ring burner where we'll do simple cooking.' He pointed at squares of beautiful rosewood on the bench. 'The doors,' he added, stretching out his measure and focusing again on his work.

'It's absolutely great!' I cried. 'Miniature furniture, not like in a doll's house, but to fit inside the van. Absolutely perfect.' I stroked a piece of wood, admiring its velvety sheen, its soft touch. 'You've done wonders.'

'I'm quite pleased with it.'

I shook my head; the movement reminded me of the weight of my body, my gathering weariness. I inhaled deeply.

'You'd better sit down.' He glanced over his shoulder. 'What happened this evening? You haven't told me.'

'Tell you when you come in.'

By the time he'd put the tools away, I was asleep. The news of my new role as a working woman had to wait until the following day, when Sid said, 'Don't you think three nights is a bit much? We don't know how we'll be in the autumn.'

'True.' I had been pondering this as I drove home. 'Two evenings is enough to begin with. I shall telephone the college and tell them.'

Chapter 20

The baby was due to arrive on the fifth of July, my thirty-fourth birthday. Because Mother's sister was visiting England for the first time since 1934, when she'd eloped with an American medical student, Rachel had invited the family for Friday night dinner. Quite a crowd: my parents and aunt, my unmarried brother-in-law, Michael, whom Anthony adored, but he was safely at home with Ria, a young Dutch au pair girl we had acquired unexpectedly. Then there was my father-in-law Abe who always helped Rachel with the food and the immaculately laid table, while Sid and I completed the party.

Tonight, to follow the soup, Rachel had prepared fried fish and two kinds of fish balls, *gefilte* fish (boiled fish), and chopped and fried, together with a special spaghetti omelette for me and my parents. The cutlery gleamed in the evening light; there were tiny glass dishes of pale green pickled cucumber and *chrain*, horseradish with beetroot, made in typical Eastern European fashion, a spicy, rich, pink garnish for the fish. Decorated with graceful tiny flowers, the china tureens of vegetables added to the elegant table while Rachel's famous fish glowed golden on beautiful platters.

Standing by the table in her usual way, about to serve Michael, Rachel stopped and stared at me, fish slice held aloft. 'What are you doing? You've been doing it all evening.'

For the past two weeks I had been having practice contractions. This evening they'd been coming regularly. With each one, I froze, counting and breathing as I had recently learned at the National Childbirth Trust classes.

'She's doing her breathing,' Sid answered. 'She's been doing it for the past fortnight.'

Rachel raised her eyebrows but said no more. We carried on chatting and eating. Every time there was a contraction, I stopped.

'How often are they coming?' It was my mother, leaning in, her blue eyes wide.

'About every five minutes.' I threw a quick glance at her face.

'Susan, are you going to have that baby under the table?' My mother always had good colour in her cheeks, now it intensified. Straightening up and using her fork as a pointer, she said, 'Go to the hospital. *Now.*'

It was so uncharacteristic of her to give orders, I took a sharp breath. 'But the contractions will cease if I go.' This was what had happened with Vanessa and I'd forgotten it until this moment at the table.

'Every five minutes?' She shook her head. 'You must go at once.'

Everyone put down their cutlery and stared at me in alarm. Only my father continued to eat, masticating each mouthful thirty-six times as usual.

'Come on.' Sid pushed back his chair and helped me stand. 'Your mother's probably right.'

I gave her a wry smile, heaved myself off the chair and made my slow exit to the car.

We had left Ria in the kitchen, happily drinking coffee with a Dutch friend. Her eyes widened when we walked in; she looked even more astonished when I reappeared with my case, and waved to her from the door.

'Hopefully, this will have disappeared,' I said, patting my stomach.

'And you'll have the baby?'

'I hope so.'

Back in St Mary's Maternity Hospital, we approached the reception desk.

'How often are the contractions coming?' asked the duty nurse.

'Every five minutes though I think they've stopped.' I backed towards the entrance but Sid gave me an exasperated look.

'Well, whatever's happening, you'd better go to the delivery suite, on the fourth floor.'

'All right.' I bit my lip. 'I know where it is. Isn't there a lift along there?'

'That's right.' She sounded relieved. 'Well, good luck.'

Upstairs, a nurse led me to a small room at the end of a corridor, its broad sash window overlooking Wilmslow Road. 'Doctor will be around shortly.'

I glanced at my watch. 'It's nine-thirty. I've had one contraction since we got into the lift. Maybe they'll send me home?'

Sid frowned, and I saw he was even more worried, rubbing his chin with his hand, glancing around as though a solution could be found in this room, with its high bed and small side cupboard. But then the doctor appeared.

'How are things?'

I explained what was happening. Knowing what the next move would be, Sid stationed himself in front of the window, pretending that something urgent out there needed his attention.

'Let's have a look,' said the doctor.

I clambered with difficulty onto the bed and lay down. Turning briefly, the doctor called over his shoulder. 'This won't take a moment.' It was quick, and straightening up, the doctor nodded approvingly. 'You're doing fine.'

207

'But nothing's happening.' I heaved myself up against the pillows. 'Don't you need the bed for someone else?'

'Not at all. We'll keep you in, see how you get on.' He walked over to Sid. 'I've decided to keep your wife here for observation. We'll let you know if there are any developments.'

With a heartfelt sigh of relief, Sid said, 'Thank you.'

I wasn't surprised; in his place I would probably have felt the same. But once the doctor had left, I groaned, 'I knew they wouldn't let me out of their clutches. But the doctor's right. Go and get a good night's sleep.' I laughed. 'It could be the last for a very long time.'

After he'd gone, I stretched out my legs, trying to get comfortable. Why were hospital beds so lumpy and hard? I was wide awake, listening to the hospital sounds, the noise from the street. After a while, sliding myself off the bed with care, and holding my bump with both hands, I managed to balance on the polished floor. In the past few weeks I had begun to walk straddle-legged as the ligaments loosened ready for the birth.

Dragging the upright chair to the window, I sat gazing out.

Friday night. Even though it was twilight I could make out the striated sky over Oxford Street where the cinemas' neon lights illuminated it with vivid blues, yellows and reds. Buses filed their way along Wilmslow Road, taking people into the city. Later I heard singing as they left the pubs, laughter, the occasional quarrel, girls shouting, but finally, it grew quiet, and I shivered. Realising I was cold I steered the chair back beside the bed and climbed in. Then I pulled the sheet up to my chin.

Still trying to get comfortable, I turned on my side away from the lights of the cars travelling towards Rusholme. I was calm, without fear, actually looking forward to this birth. How different from those frantic days in November last year when I discovered I was pregnant and was terrified. Stroking my stomach, I whispered, 'Baby, I am so happy you're here, almost ready to meet this great big world. Are you a boy or a girl? I don't mind so long as you're healthy.' I gave myself a pat on the back: you've grown up a little. Found some inner strength.

Practising the breathing, I drifted into sleep.

'Nice cup of tea, Mrs Stern?'

Surfacing, I saw it was the night nurse on her six o'clock round. She was standing by the bed, a cup in her hand. 'Anything doing?'

'Nothing. All calm on the baby front.'

We laughed.

'Well, here's your tea.' She placed it on the side cupboard.

I reached awkwardly to take it. 'Thank you. I'm hopeless without my morning cuppa. Nurse, do you think I could go home? The contractions have stopped. False labour, I guess.'

She threw me a sharp, appraising look. 'Let's see what Doctor says when he comes. Well, I'm off to catch some sleep. Maybe see you tomorrow?'

I gave her a rueful look. 'Sleep well.'

The doctor arrived at precisely eight o'clock. After pressing his ear to my stomach, he said, 'I'm going to start you off. You don't want to be lying around here for days, do you?'

I was so taken aback that I could only gape at him. I watched as he attached a line to my hand, finally demanding, 'Are you inducing me? Supposing I don't *want* to be induced?'

'You're almost there,' he said lightly. 'This is but a modicum of encouragement.'

I wished my friend Mary, the psychiatric social worker I had met two years ago in this very hospital, had been there to stay his hand, but I recalled that even she had little power when they'd sedated her near the end despite all her arguments.

'Nurse will pop in and out to see how you're getting on.'

By twenty past eight, the contractions were coming in enormous waves. I concentrated on long slow breaths in and out, but now pains were running down the back of my legs. Backache labour, I knew responded less to the breathing. But it helped me control my emotions, so I persevered, my head turning towards the light as it came through the window.

After a while something changed. Oblivious of the light and the pain, my mind and body had merged into a heaving world in which the *Me* had disappeared. I felt as though I was flying through a universe. The pain was intense and I was inside it. Curling on my side, I drew up my knees.

'It helps to lie like that,' someone said. 'Do you need anything to ease the pain?'

'Think so,' I whispered.

'Let's see how you're doing. Good heavens, the head's there.'

I felt myself being pushed to the delivery room at great speed, my legs lifted and strapped up, a midwife talking to me. 'You're ready, Mrs Stern. Push when I tell you, then breathe quickly. Now, push.'

I was pushing despite myself. I was sure it wasn't enough but the midwife called, 'Good, the head's out. Now breathe, and push again.'

Then came the splitting sensation which I no longer feared – and the shoulders were there.

'One more push!' she cried.

I felt the whole body slip out, then the afterbirth.

Finished!

'Good girl,' the midwife said. 'It's a boy, a lovely little boy. He's perfect.'

I heard that wonderful new-born baby cry and opened my eyes. He was exactly like Anthony and Vanessa when they were born.

'Can I hold him?' I raised myself onto my elbows.

'Just one minute.' The midwife placed him, wrapped in a nappy, on the scales. He lay quite still, his eyes closed, almost comfortable, I thought.

The telephone rang and the midwife nurse went to answer it, chuckling as she got back to me. 'It was your husband. Wanted to know how you were doing. Couldn't believe you'd had the baby and everything was over.'

I lay back elated and overjoyed. But what did she mean about having the baby already? Opening my eyes, I peered around for the wall clock. 'Is that the right time?'

The nurse lifted her watch pinned to her uniform. 'Yes, five past ten.'

'I started at half past eight. Has it taken only an hour and a half?'

'Gets easier the more you have. It'll be forty-five minutes next time.'

I was about to reply when the midwife approached with the baby in her arms. 'There you are. One beautiful baby boy.'

I folded him close to my heart. Full of wonder at this new tiny Stern. *Richard,* I thought, gazing at his face, glimpsing his dark blue eyes which opened for a second then closed. We'll call him Richard, a strong definite name. I held him until we were back on the ward. No need for special attention this time, I was on a general ward with the other women.

As it was Saturday, Sid managed to have the afternoon off and arrived with his parents.

'Hello little Sternie.' He lifted the baby from the cot with professional ease. His parents watched, full of smiles.

In the evening Cindy brought chocolates from the Mother and Toddler group, and related how good Anthony had been when he'd come with Ria while I'd had an ante-natal appointment. 'He's clever,' she said. 'You know Julie, the doctor, Oliver's mum? She did some little tests on the children. Games, really. And your

Anthony cottoned on right away. She thinks he'll be a bright child.' Looking down at the baby, her gaze became unusually tender, 'Can I hold him for a minute?'

'Of course, you can.'

She lifted the baby gently. 'Aren't you the handsome boy with that dark hair and long lashes?' With careful hands, she put the baby into the crib. 'There's something I've been meaning to tell you. We might go abroad when Ben qualifies.'

'Abroad?'

'Australia.'

'Blimey,' I said.

'I know. That would be the end of our unique association.' She made a wry face.

'We could still remain *The Professional Sluts*, even when you're in Australia.' This was her name for us since we didn't tidy up the toys or wash out the mugs the moment they were used.

'I could write to you, *Chairwoman of the Professional Sluts Association*, and you'd know it was me,' I added.

She jumped up, put her hands at the back of her hips, thrust out her chest and stood in beauty contest mode. 'Notice anything?'

I stared. 'No bra?'

'Correct. I've burnt it. Well, I stuck it at the back of the drawer.'

'So you're a women's libber now?'

We had talked about the Women's Liberation Movement for weeks and she longed to go to a conference but hadn't the money. With a solemn expression on her face, she announced, 'Your turn next.'

'Cindy,' I said, 'I don't wear a wedding ring anymore.' I held my left hand aloft and she nodded in approval. 'But how can I possibly get rid of my bra when I'm feeding the baby myself?'

'OK, I'll let you off. But the moment he's weaned.'

She hugged me when she left, and I wondered how it would be, travelling to the other side of the world, far from your family and friends. Something I had never entertained but if it meant making a living, that's what you'd do. Cindy had become such a cheerful, funny friend with her quirky Scouse humour, I would really miss her.

Chapter 21

We went home when the baby was three days old. With Sid's help, Ria was managing to get Vanessa off to Pictor School where she would stay alternate nights until the end of summer term. The sister on duty played little games with her, and she was very happy there.

When I walked into the kitchen, I found Ria reading at the table while Anthony balanced precariously on a chair by the sink. Water gushed away merrily.

'Hello, Ria. Hello, Anthony, we're back. Ria, Anthony's soaked. Please can you take him off the chair and turn off the tap?'

'Oh you have the new baby.' Lifting her head, she realised what was happening and went to remove Anthony from his perilous position. 'Come and see, Anthony. Your Mummy is here with your new baby brother.'

He struggled to extricate himself from her arms and ran to where I was lifting the baby from the carrycot. I sat down with relief at the table. 'Come and see Little Richard,' I said. 'That's his name. Isn't he tiny?'

Ria looked fascinated, smiling and watching with more animation than she'd shown any time in the few weeks she'd been with us. Perhaps she was like our friend Paula who loved babies.

'See his tiny hands, his little, little fingers,' she said.

Anthony reached out and grabbed the baby's hand and he woke up and began to cry.

'What's the matter with him, Mummy?'

'He's hungry. It's time for a feed.' Carefully I lifted Anthony's fingers. 'Why don't you stay down here with Ria and build a big castle with the bricks?'

'Yes,' Ria said, 'come and help me empty the box onto the floor. You like that.'

I gave Anthony a hug, 'Remember how I told you about having a new brother or sister? You're going to help me look after him, aren't you?'

'Yes.' He nodded solemnly.

In the bedroom, I settled in a nursing chair we'd bought from one of the mums at the toddler group. Richard had fed well in the hospital and I loved the almost sensual feeling of his drawing at the breast. Reflecting on this as I sat quietly in the corner of the room, I was startled when the door opened sharply and Anthony bounded towards me. 'What are you doing?' he demanded, eyes wide.

'Giving the baby a drink. Do you want to see?'

I drew the cot sheet away from the baby's face, and Anthony, unusually still, watched, a little frown creasing his forehead. Then he shouted, 'Take it back to the hospital. I don't like it.' He clambered onto my knee, one hand ready to push the baby away.

'No, Anthony. When he's finished his drink I want you to help me put him in the carrycot, then *you* can sit on my knee. Why don't you ask Ria for some juice?'

Thank goodness, this worked and he marched off to demand a drink.

Of course, we had tried to prepare both Anthony and Vanessa for the new arrival, telling them they would have a new little brother or sister, someone they could talk to, be with, and for Anthony to play with when he was older. But what could they understand, especially Anthony, a baby himself?

The next day at three o'clock, Vanessa came home from school. 'Hello, my sweetheart,' I said, 'I have a surprise for you.' I lifted her out of the wheelchair, supporting her head with my shoulder. 'Here's your new little brother. He's called Richard.' He was asleep in the carrycot near the radiator. Taking her hand, I moved it to brush his face with her fingertips. The baby stirred, made a tiny mewing sound, a sucking moment with his lips, but slept on. 'Isn't he lovely?' She wriggled, licked her own lips, and tried turning towards the shelf where her feeder beaker lived. 'Are you thirsty?'

Ria was hovering behind me. 'You want to give her a drink? Shall I get it?'

'That would be lovely. Could you warm some milk and add a spoonful of Bournvita, please?'

With Vanessa on my knee, I told her about Richard. 'And he looked just like you when you were born.'

Anthony trundled up on his wooden red kiddie bike. 'Me, Mummy. She looked like me.'

'You all looked the same. Three peas in a pod.'

Ria laughed but Anthony looked puzzled. 'We're not peas, Mummy.'

'I know you're not. It's what people say when children look like each other.'

He thought about this for a second, then trundled to the carrycot and peered at the baby.

'Come on, I'm sure Vanessa would like to stretch out a little.' Lifting her from the wheelchair after tea I laid her on her tummy across one of the triangular foam wedges where her limbs could relax, and with her hands on the ground, she could lift her head and look around. Tonight I lay the baby in his Babygro on a soft blanket beside her. 'Now Richard's lying next to you on his blanket.'

Her eyes widened, she made a lip and she *growled.*

'Vanessa. What's that horrible noise? Richard won't hurt you, he's too small.' Anthony flung himself down on Vanessa's other side. 'Look, Anthony's here too.'

Nothing I said could change her reaction, she continued to growl like a little dog. This was what I had feared but hoped would never happen. She was jealous, just as she had been with Anthony two years before, but she'd got used to him. I closed my eyes, hoping against hope that she'd eventually get used to the baby.

Upstairs in our room, I collapsed on the nursing chair and began to rock Richard in my arms, as much to comfort myself as to help him sleep.

A day later, I discovered Anthony standing by the carrycot, a set of real, tiny screwdrivers with different coloured plastic handles in his hands. What had possessed us to give them to him? Under pressure from little children, I knew we all make mistakes. Fascinated by Sid's work in the garage, Anthony had made several attempts to join him. As a diversion, Sid had presented him with the screwdrivers in a little case; they were his most precious possession, lying on the table at meal times, pushed under his pillow at night. But how idiotic we'd been, what a dangerous weapon they were.

'Anthony, come away from the carrycot.' I grabbed him. 'Please give me those screwdrivers.'

He shoved them behind his back.

'You don't want to hurt the baby, do you?'

The conversation ended in a tantrum of screaming and kicking, as I wrestled them from him. Reasoning was useless at this age.

But often I would say, 'You're the big boy now.' And I believed it. He spoke fluently, was very active; in comparison with Vanessa and even with other two-year-olds he was advanced and capable. Between Vanessa and Richard I expected him to be more grown-up than was possible.

Richard's circumcision was the following Saturday, eight days after his birth. While Hetty was in Saint Mary's, she had told me her husband had recently trained as a mohel, an expert in carrying out circumcisions. Because she was my friend, I felt I should ask him to do this. But orthodox Jewish people didn't travel on the Sabbath and we couldn't ask him to walk fifteen miles from his house in Broughton Park to ours in South Manchester. We hatched a cunning plan: with my father's agreement, and for once he didn't protest, we went to my parents' house in Prestwich early on Saturday morning which allowed Mr Gruber to walk the mile or so from his home. He must have guessed we had driven but he made no comment.

Though large, my parents' living room was filled with hefty box furniture; it was something of a squeeze to make room for all the family and friends who could make it that morning. Of course, my mother and Rachel were there. Meanwhile, sitting on the stairs, I waited for my mother to tell me it was all over. It was an old solid house and thank goodness, I didn't hear the baby cry out. This time my father-in-law had the honour of holding the baby on the beautifully embroidered cushion, while the deed was done.

Once we were home, little Richard woke so many times in the night, crying with pain, that I fumed to myself, 'How barbaric this is. What possesses us to do such a thing?'

But breastfeeding at least, gave him some comfort.

Next morning Mr Gruber returned to see him. Richard was lying on a towel on our bed; Mr Gruber undid the nappy to reveal a large red patch on the baby's skin.

I gasped. 'What is it?'

'It will pass,' Mr Gruber said.

But it didn't pass. The red patch became eczema, and over the following weeks it appeared on the baby's arms and face, raw and weeping. It even affected his feeding.

He would feed for a few minutes but then fall asleep, waking half an hour later, crying, and I would feed him again. With broken nights, a lively toddler and Vanessa coming home from Pictor House School for the holidays in a week's time, I was overwhelmed. We struggled on.

Meanwhile, we had a visitor, only for a week, but another person to feed. A few days after Richard's arrival, Ria's sister came for a brief holiday. Ria had asked earlier if she could stay and thinking she might do a bit more when her sister was there, I had agreed. Looking much like Ria, tall and blonde, she brought beautiful wooden toys for the children but it was her sole contribution the entire week. Rachel and Abe took pity on me. They offered to take everyone to the seaside for the day. On their return, they were furious.

'They talked Dutch all the time. I had to *tell* them to feed Vanessa.' Rachel folded her arms, her face grim.

'They didn't even play with Anthony,' added my father-in-law angrily.

I said nothing, but the night before her sister was leaving, Ria asked if she could go back with her to Eindhoven.

'I thought you were staying the summer,' I said, giving her a set look. 'But it's probably best if you went home.'

It was the first Saturday of the holidays, half past ten, and I was still in my night clothes. Sitting on the little black sofa beneath the kitchen window, I was trying to feed Richard while Vanessa lay screaming on the floor, her arms flailing and Anthony was climbing on top of me in his soggy nappy and pyjamas, demanding yet another drink.

'It's all right, Vanessa. I'll be with you in a moment.' Turning to Anthony, I said, 'Sit down beside me. I'll give you a drink in a minute.'

He continued to bang my shoulder, grabbing my chin to make me look at him, 'I want it *now*, Mummy. I want it now!'

There was a tapping at the window. Turning with difficulty, I saw the anxious faces of Rachel and Abe, desperate to catch my attention. There was such a racket in the kitchen, and I was so distracted I hadn't heard the bell. Carrying the baby, with Anthony dragging at my dressing gown, I opened the door. 'I don't know where to begin but I'm so glad you're here. I've been up since about three.'

'Come on, Anthony,' said his grandpa. 'Look what I've got for you in my pocket.'

'You haven't got anything,' Rachel muttered under her breath.

'A few coppers, there's some change in my pocket. That'll distract him.'

'All right, I'll go and talk to Vanessa.'

We got through the day somehow but they couldn't come every day. When Sid returned from the pharmacy, we talked over what we could do.

'Surely,' he said, ever the optimist, 'there must be somewhere Vanessa can go for a couple of weeks. Until things settle down.'

'If they ever do,' I said, full of self-pity. 'I'll ask around.'

We'd had no support from any kind of social services, apart from the Spastics Society social worker, who came once a year. So I contacted the synagogue and was amazed to discover there was something called the Jewish Social Services. When I telephoned, they told me of a short stay facility, Laski House, just off Cheetham Hill Road in North Manchester. 'It's for disabled and abandoned children, or for parents who need a break,' the woman said.

Since my mother lived locally, I asked her to visit Laski House, tell me what she thought of it. Later she phoned back. 'It's quite satisfactory, rather bare, but the children seem happy enough.'

We arranged for Vanessa to stay for the rest of the holidays.

A few days after this, leaving Anthony and the baby with the Sterns, I drove to North Manchester with Vanessa, her wheelchair, foam cushions, cups and all her necessary paraphernalia in the boot, to meet the my mother at the gates. My heart plunged when I saw it: a tall, soot-blackened Victorian house, it stood in dusty grounds, its dilapidated flight of steps leading to a front door overgrown with weeds.

'We go in by the 'servants' entrance round the back,' my mother said, carrying as much as she could. I pushed Vanessa round in the wheelchair and we went in. Children were playing in a lobby crammed with chairs, its interior sombre on this summer's day. A young girl looking hardly older than fourteen came to meet us and I wondered if she was one of the children, but no, she was a supervisor.

'Hello, Vanessa,' she said, catching Vanessa's hand. 'Are you coming to stay with us?'

I lifted her, and she immediately stiffened in my arms as she made a lip. She was suspicious and began to cry.

'Don't cry, Vanessa,' said the young girl. 'It's lovely here.'

Mother and I exchanged doubtful looks but we followed her through a long bleak hall, up uncarpeted wooden stairs, to a bedroom. Three of four beds stood on bare floorboards.

'Those two are free.' She pointed to one by the window, one against a far wall.

'Could Vanessa have that one, by the wall?' my mother said. 'It would be better. When she stayed with me a couple of years ago, she wriggled to the top and got stuck between the headboard and the wall.'

'That's fine, make yourself at home. It's tea time now. I had better go.'

We ranged the foam cushions between the wall and the bed, and chairs along the open side so Vanessa, hopefully, couldn't fall out.

'This will be your bed now, Vanessa.' Although she still had little feeling in her hands, I took each one, moving them over the cover so she'd have some sense of ownership. This was hers. 'We'll leave your bag of clothes on top of that cupboard.' I showed her. 'With all your dresses and pairs of tights, so you won't scrape your knees on the wheelchair pommel.'

'Let's go downstairs,' said Mother, 'and find the dining room.'

A high-ceilinged room facing the road, its long windows smeared with grubby fingerprints and where many small tables, like mini card tables, were set with plastic plates, mugs and spoons. The girl was distributing sandwiches to each plate. Children were filing in, most of whom could walk, though there were others in wheelchairs, but all looked as though they could feed themselves. There were some children with Down's syndrome; others perhaps, with learning disabilities but the rest seemed free of obvious problems. I remembered being told about abandoned children, and sighed. But they appeared lively, chatting, jostling, and happy enough.

'I'm afraid Vanessa can't eat sandwiches,' I said. 'Would it be okay if I made some scrambled eggs for her in the kitchen?'

'Of course. We often make baby food for the little ones. Help yourself to whatever you need.'

My heart throbbing, I tore myself away after I had given Vanessa her tea. Sadness slowed my step as we walked to the gate but my mother took my arm, knowing how wretched I was feeling at leaving Vanessa in such a place.

'I'll come every day on the bus to feed her,' Mother said. 'I'll cook her little meals. I'm sure the food isn't very nourishing. Those sandwiches were made of white bread; they obviously don't know about a good diet.'

'Are you sure you can? It won't be easy on the bus.'

'Or Dad can bring me. You know how much he loves Vanessa. He'd do anything for her.'

Not only did my mother go most days, but at the weekend, she took Vanessa back to their house where she was always happy. I longed to find some clean, appropriate place like Pictor House, where she could stay at times like this, but it didn't seem to exist.

Anthony's second birthday was on the nineteenth of August, and I was so happy we could hold a party for him, even though I knew Vanessa would have loved it. But it was his special day, his day in the sun. I invited the toddlers from the group, together with family and friends; quite a gathering for such a little person.

It was a hot bright Sunday morning when Sid set up our present for Anthony in the garden – a red and blue Mothercare Wendy house. Furnished with his little chair and table, in his pyjamas, he sat there eating breakfast and playing with toys until we had to drag him inside.

For the party I had baked a chocolate cake decorated with Smarties, the sum total of my artistic abilities, plus dozens of fairy cakes. Sid had contrived a long low table from a door or piece of wood he had in the garage, and which we'd covered with paper tablecloths. The children were too small to play games so it was the party tea that was paramount. Sitting on cushions on the floor, they could reach the sandwiches, while a dozen mothers and grandmothers officiated, giving drinks, wiping noses and calming fractious toddlers when they couldn't get what they wanted. While the others smeared their lips with chocolate biscuits or drank from paper cups, I caught Anthony about to push back the chair and make his escape.

'Where are you going?'

'To my Wendy house.'

'Let's light the birthday candles, shall we?'

He sat down, and forgetting himself for a moment, blew out the candles while everyone sang *Happy Birthday*.

The day before the start of the new school term, Sid brought Vanessa home from Laski House.

'Can you take her while I get her stuff from the car?' he said.

I had been tense all morning. Making sure the baby was asleep in the carrycot and Anthony occupied with Lego, I lifted her from his arms. 'Hello my sweetheart,' I said. 'Did you have a lovely time visiting Grandma when she took you home at the weekends?'

She beamed at me, wriggling to show her pleasure.

Without looking up, Anthony shouted, 'Hello, Nessa.'

Another smile.

Then I made a terrible mistake: without giving her the opportunity to feel she was back, I carried her over to see Richard who was fast asleep in the carrycot.

'Look, do you remember your baby brother? He's bigger now.' She frowned, made a lip, swivelled her eyes to gaze at the sleeping baby. 'Do you want to touch his hand?' Recalling how she had reacted, growling when I came back from hospital, I was careful to let her initiate the contact.

She threw herself backwards. Wide-eyed, glaring, she began to cry. She had remembered him all right, and looking down at her distressed little face, anguish suffused my heart. I imagined what she might have said if she could speak: *I hate you, Mummy. You put me in that horrible place for ages. Now there's this baby.*

I hate him too. She might have raged, run up to her room, and slammed the door making the house shake.

Not an uncommon response by a furious, intelligent six-year-old.

Abandoning his Lego, Anthony raced over and began to jump on the spot.

'*I'm* big now. Look how well I can jump.'

'Of course, you're big.' Leaning forward, I put my other arm around his shoulders, 'And you're a wonderful jumper. Why don't you show Vanessa what you've been building?'

'I don't want to.'

Richard was making tiny, distressed sounds and wearily, I took him upstairs, out of harm's way, and went to help Sid. I hoped against hope that the young German woman we had found through the German Labour Exchange, my last reluctant attempt at finding someone to live with us, might be some kind of support over the next few months, or how would we possibly manage?

Chapter 22

Anneliese arrived, and she was a godsend. Tall, sturdy as a pony, she had smiling brown eyes, rosy cheeks and always wore something red – a short-sleeved checked shirt, dark red t-shirt, a reefer jacket. The oldest in a Bavarian farming family of eight, she slipped into our life like fingers in a silk glove. Nothing daunted her.

'I missed the required mark to be a doctor by two points,' she told us the day she came, 'so I'll become a nurse, then I'll study medicine.'

She settled with us at once and soon learned to feed Vanessa, who still hadn't outgrown that primitive reflex of pushing out any food with her tongue. Whoever fed her had to spoon small portions into her mouth, repeating the action until she'd swallowed them. Often it required scraping food from her chin, a slow business. Few of the previous au pair girls had the courage or skill, and I had always done this. Now I was free to concentrate on the boys. Anneliese loved them all: taking on Vanessa's work in the wooden chair, playing with Anthony, showing him flowers and plants, such as they were, in the garden: collecting shells, telling him about the sand and the sea when we took a day trip to the seaside. She adored Richard, delighting in her role as mother substitute when I was teaching in the evenings. She could carry two of them up to bed in her arms.

'I don't need evenings off,' she said immediately. 'I have the English classes at the local centre. And you have so many books I can spend my evenings reading.'

Because her English was fluent, there was never a problem with communication. Just before her arrival, full of guilt, I had made what felt like that dreadful decision to give Richard the bottle. His erratic feeding had made me despair. We'd also had those traumatic early experiences with Vanessa which led to her diagnosis of cerebral palsy. I knew this wasn't the case for him because he'd been carefully examined by the doctors at his birth. But the eczema was getting worse, especially when Vanessa came home. I never knew if it was a reaction to the heightened atmosphere, my increased anxiety, or simply the progress of the condition.

At the end of Anneliese's first week with us, I undressed him only to find the creases beneath his tiny arms were bleeding. In response to my call, Sid brought cotton gloves which the baby wore, tied around his wrists. When he started to suck his thumb, even through the glove, this normal behaviour at least reassured me there was no disability, since Vanessa had never put her hands in her mouth. But I was deeply concerned about the eczema and his feeding.

'It's time we consulted Doctor Griffiths,' I told Sid.

There followed several weeks of toing and froing to the surgery, prescriptions for various creams, none of which worked.

'I'm writing a referral for the Skin Hospital,' Doctor Griffiths finally said. 'The Hospital for Infectious Skin Diseases,' he added, giving me a sharp look over his glasses.

I wanted to cry, 'No. Not there.' Skin disease had a terrible resonance in my father's family. My grandmother had died in 1929 when she was only fifty-one of the skin disease erysipelas, which could so easily have been cured by a course of antibiotics. Her death had broken my father's heart and was one of the reasons for his obsession with health, with survival.

At least Anneliese could look after Anthony while I drove into the centre of Manchester. The Skin Hospital had been opened in 1905. Tall dark windows, pseudo-Greek pillars at the main entrance, a grim but imposing aspect designed I felt sure to overawe patients, to make them feel grateful to their betters. I reminded myself that it was probably built, as the Victorians said, by public subscription, just as my paternal grandfather, keen to be of communal service, had been one of those fundraising for the Jewish Hospital.

I found myself in a large square waiting room with dark wood-panelled walls and where corridors stretched away to invisible consulting rooms. People were sitting in silence, the occasional whisper escaping from someone seeking the 'conveniences.' Richard continued to sleep in my arms until a nurse approached, asked his name and beckoned me to follow her down a dark passageway. 'You can go in now,' she said.

I knocked at the door.

'Come in!' A woman's voice.

The doctor rose from behind her mahogany desk to shake my hand. 'Please sit down, Mrs Stern. Tell me why you're here.' At the end of my account, she said, 'May I examine the baby?'

I followed her to the brown leather examinations bed where she spread out a towel, and I undressed Richard. With utmost gentleness, she examined him. 'Now would you remove the nappy?' After some moments, she said, 'Thank you. You can dress him.'

Richard had hardly cried, now he looked at her, his blue eyes wide.

'You are a relaxed little fellow.' She smiled, but her gaze was serious when she told me, 'It is eczema and quite severe, I'm afraid. Let's see what this cream will do for him.'

So began yet another series of visits to a hospital.

Meanwhile, Anthony had entered the 'terrible twos' with a bang. Exploding all over the house, he was barely in one place for more than five minutes. He had become the middle child with all that implied. Before, while Vanessa was at Pictor School, he had been the focus of my attention. Now he had to compete with Richard as well as with Vanessa, doing whatever he could to make me see him, to remind me that he was there.

One evening in November, when Anneliese was feeding Vanessa in the wheelchair and I was sitting at the table, giving Richard a bottle of formula, something terrible happened. Perhaps to provide an invisible barricade for myself, we had moved the Habitat pine table long ways, parallel to the wall; I sat on the bench between the wall and table in a kind of protective space, away from the kitchen hurly-burly.

In a small alcove in the wall, just above my head, were two shelves of books. Anthony was kneeling on the blue-flowered bench beside me, removing books and building a tower on the table. Richard was about four months old at the time. Standing the half finished bottle, on the table, I said, 'Come on, little Richard. How about some wind?' Lifting him onto my shoulder, I patted his back, and as I looked at him, he gave me a sleepy grin. I kissed the top of his head just as I heard Anneliese call, 'Susan, the bottle.'

I turned to see Anthony lifting the bottle of formula by the teat, twirling it round above the table, throwing a defiant little grin when he saw me watching. My heart pounding, I felt a blaze of heat rising from my neck to my hairline. I leapt up, and bursting with fury, the baby still in my arms, I thrust myself towards Anthony and knocked him off the bench.

He lay on the floor, screaming.

Anneliese had seen it all; shocked, abandoning Vanessa, she ran to lift Anthony and comfort him.

Horrified by what I had done, I pushed the table away and grabbed him from her arms. 'Anthony, Anthony, I'm so sorry.'

The children were crying, and so was I. He's only two years three months, I kept telling myself as I hugged him. Quite normal behaviour for a two-year-old, coupled with his boisterous temperament. Who would have thought that, years later, he'd say, 'You smacked me a lot when I was little.'

I, who always believed in gentle reasoning, had completely forgotten ever smacking him whereas this kitchen incident has stayed burnished forever in my memory.

Some days after this horrible event, we went again to the Skin Hospital.

'None of the creams seem to work, and I just don't know what to do,' I told the consultant.

Sitting back in her chair, her hands resting in her lap, she said, 'Could you tell me something about the atmosphere in your house?'

'I'm not sure I understand.' Shifting uneasily, I frowned.

'You have a handicapped child, a boy aged two and this little one.' She indicated Richard with a quick smile. 'Quite a handful. How do you manage?'

I had been reticent during our early visits, careful to contain my emotions in case they affected the baby, but now it all poured out. How I had worked with Vanessa, but finally had to give up when we saw so little progress. That she continued to be jealous of Richard, growling when she was near him, angry with me. How I overreacted to Anthony, always cross with him because he seemed such a handful.

'But I know he's only a two-year-old.'

And the broken nights, the constant exhaustion.

'Do you have any help?'

'A wonderful German au pair girl.'

She made a few notes, looked at me gravely. 'It's time you considered some alternative arrangement for your handicapped child. You *must* do it.' She threw a quick glance at Richard. 'He will not recover until the environment is calm. Eczema children are very sensitive and this is often a protest against conditions they find intolerable.'

I stared at her in horror. Clutching Richard to me, I took a ragged breath. What was she telling me? That one child would suffer because of the other, and that I would have to choose between them? A selection. It was unbearable. My heart was cracking in two.

Later, driving past the maternity hospital, I had a sudden flash of memory of the conversation I'd had two years before with Mary, the psychiatric social worker. We had both been hugely pregnant when she told me what the doctor had repeated today. I almost closed my eyes as I drove, so torn by the image that came to me of Vanessa broken with crying as I left her in some shadowy far off place, and walked away.

The winter months were particularly difficult, getting up every morning at four o'clock to give Vanessa a drink, at six because Anthony was an early riser and he would stand banging his fists on the cot calling, 'Orange, Mummy.' Richard slept later, thank goodness, a reprieve of sorts, but bone weary, I had to get through each day. Only Anneliese and her cheerful presence kept me going.

'I'm so happy here, and so lucky to be with you,' she said, one dark day in January. 'Thank you.'

I was making the various lunches: fish fingers, oven chips and peas for Anthony, liquidised fish and vegetables for Vanessa and for Richard, now six months old, semi-solids. Anneliese was squeezing out two buckets of nappies that were soaking in Napisan, before loading them into the washing machine.

'It's wonderful you're happy with us but you don't need to thank me.' I threw a grateful glance at her. 'We must thank you. The children love you, especially Vanessa. But how do you mean, *lucky?*'

There was a pause; leaving the nappies, she came over. 'When I saw you were Jewish … they told me at the Labour Exchange… I was so eager to come so I could do something, anything to help…' Her voice faltered. 'But I was also apprehensive. How would you think of me, a German?'

A little shocked, I murmured, 'It's more than twenty-five years since the end of the war and I would never have sought a German au pair girl if I felt…'

She smiled. 'People can't help their deepest feelings, sometimes they seep out without us realising…'

'Anneliese, have we ever been antagonistic towards you?'

'You've always treated me like a friend.'

'And so you are.' I breathed a sigh of relief. 'Heavens, you had me wondering for a moment.'

'I had better finish the nappies,' she said, a little embarrassed, and perhaps wondering if she had said something untoward. 'I can see the lunch is almost ready.'

We fell silent, both uncomfortable, pretending to be intent on our tasks. Then softly, I spoke. 'For some time, I've been feeling you wanted to talk about the war.'

'How did you know?' Her gaze was uncertain.

'You think deeply. Also, I've noticed your expression when there's something about it on television – your look unhappy.'

'I do want to talk about it, but I don't know if it would upset you.'

'I was a little girl at the time, and only remember a few things,' I smiled at her, 'but some things I do recall vividly.'

Acknowledging my smile, she said, 'I'd love to hear about them. The most important thing for me is to know the bigger picture. About the Jewish people, their history, their lives.'

Richard was banging the high chair tray with his spoon, Anthony was shouting, 'Dinner, dinner,' and Vanessa was joining in, crying.

'Let's give them their lunch, and talk after,' I said, and sat down in front of Richard. 'Here's your dinner, hungry boy. You'll love that.'

Smiling as she put Anthony's plate on the table, Anneliese fixed the pelican bib around his neck. 'Your favourite: fish fingers and chips, sir.'

Then she sat to feed Vanessa.

Later that day, I picked up where we'd left off. 'I guess that my upbringing, the socialist, internationalist beliefs of my parents had a huge influence on me. You know my father, well one of his sayings –'

She smiled. 'He has many interesting sayings.'

'This one, probably garbled, is what I grew up hearing all the time: *The world is my country, to do good my religion.* Thomas Paine, the English philosopher said this, I think. They both believed it was their duty to make the world a better place.'

'If only everyone was like that.' Anneliese shook her head. I could guess what she was thinking.

I told her about the pen friends I'd had when I was sixteen: French, Spanish, German. Then I related something which might open up our conversation about the war: that with a German friend, Marlyss, I had been to the student cinema one evening in Aix-en Provence.

'I was twenty, like you. It was almost the summer. We sat outside on wooden benches to see a film called *Orfeu Negro,* or *Black Orpheus,* a huge success the previous year. Based on the story of Orpheus, and set in a slum, a *favela,* during the Carnival, in Rio de Janeiro. Marlyss and I were thrilled and we sat waiting impatiently.

'But another short film opened the evening. It showed a concentration camp the day it was liberated – the people in their terrible striped rags, their filth, their skeletal bodies. With the rest of the student audience, we watched it in horror. I had seen photos before, but not in this stark reality. Glued to the screen, I heard someone cry out. It was Marlyss, she had flung herself forward, her hands almost touching the floor, sobbing dreadfully. Glancing around, I saw others were crying, their heads in their hands.

Anneliese fell silent. Finally, she asked, 'Did you stay to see the main film?'

'We did. I persuaded her to stay. Marlyss calmed a little when I said we could discuss the other film afterwards. *Orfeu Negro* was brilliant, a tragedy of course, and somehow blending well with our feelings after the first film. This happened in 1960, only fifteen years after the war. Marlyss told me they knew very little about the Holocaust, what Jewish people call the *Shoah*, only the outline of what the Nazis had done. But I'm sure you know a lot more.'

'We've learned in school, in almost every class. But though we heard it again and again, and it was horrible, I wanted to know what Jewish people really felt and thought. Three years ago, I saw pictures of our Chancellor Willi Brandt, in Warsaw, as he knelt in front of a memorial for the victims of the Nazis. He was an opponent of Hitler, one of the Resistance, he wasn't even in Germany. It so moved me, I knew I had to do something. At least I could help you.'

'It wasn't you,' I said. 'But what about your father? Can I ask what he did in the war?'

'He was a soldier, captured in Russia. He never spoke of it.'

She wanted to learn, and I told her all I knew about Jewish history, the blood libel, expulsions, forced conversions, how my grandparents escaped Tsarist Russia, fleeing pogroms, the deadly attacks by local people, the anti-semitism instigated by the Church. The need for a land where Jewish people could live, about my months on a kibbutz in Galilee. About a friend whose family had lived in Jerusalem for six generations.

There were happier moments. Anneliese's dedication shone out in the half a dozen photos we had of her. Her exceptional skill with Vanessa glowed in one of them: Vanessa sits in the wooden chair which she normally disliked, while Anneliese supports her head with one hand while giving her a drink. Vanessa is laughing, and so is Anneliese.

In another Anneliese holds Vanessa, who has on her winter coat, red tights and dark blue trousers, while she shows her some seaside treasure, a stone or a shell. Anthony sits straddled over a low wooden balustrade beside her, his legs straight and sturdy and wearing his red wellington boots. A further photo shows Anneliese sitting with them both together, on her knee.

Life should have been easier.

But at the beginning of March, I developed severe back pain, a slipped disc according to Doctor Griffiths. I would just have to put up with it since everyone had this at some time in their lives, he said. A physiotherapist he recommended, whose rooms were opposite the surgery, examined me. 'I can't touch it.' She shook her head slowly. 'Too much inflammation. You need to spend three weeks on your back for it to settle. Then I can do something.'

'Three weeks?' I groaned as I levered myself off the examination bed with slow, agonised movement. 'I have three tiny children to look after.'

Desperate for something, anything to help, I consulted a local osteopath who told me this happened frequently after women gave birth. 'The sacroiliac joint is pushed out of place with childbirth. All women should have manipulation at this time,' he stated. 'I can probably help you but I should warn you, it will hurt.'

Knowing that Anneliese would be leaving in four weeks, I resigned myself to the pain and had several sessions of treatment. I have to get onto my feet again, I told myself when he kneaded and pressed and yanked my limbs. The morning I was going to collect Vanessa from Pictor House School and drive with her to St Anne's, where we were staying in a holiday flat with Sid's parents, I thought, 'Bugger this. I'm absolutely fed up with the whole thing. I shall ignore it.'

And mopped the floor.

Whether it was the dour osteopath and his manipulation that day or whether the pain was subsiding naturally, I drove to St Anne's with Vanessa safely strapped in the car seat beside me, and without a twinge.

It was hard to say goodbye to Anneliese when she returned to Germany, in April 1974, to celebrate Easter with her family, and resume her studies. I knew I would miss her cheerful presence, her lively intelligence, her willingness to learn and her strong arms, which surely carried me as well as the children. My eyes full of tears, I held each of them up at the window to wave goodbye, before Sid took Anneliese to the airport. It was something of a surprise that in 1984, she would write to say that she was married, and that she and her new husband had joined a church that supported Israel.

'Because of all I learned from you about the long history of the Jewish people, this was one positive thing we could do.' The blue airmail letter was flimsy but her handwriting was strong and well-defined, just like Anneliese herself.

Chapter 23

Anneliese had gone, it was the Easter holidays, and I was alone with the children.

Vanessa sat slumped in her chair, her head barely skimming the tray, her eyes sullen, her body a heavy mass of unhappiness. When I went to coax her from this bitter mood, for I couldn't bear seeing her like that, Anthony would tug at my jeans, demanding attention. Only Richard sat silent in the pram, sucking his thumb and absorbing everything. A little sponge making no demands on me.

I became more and more weary, plodding through the days, my back often sore, and my limbs as leaden as if I had run a marathon. Sometimes I would even shout at Vanessa: 'Why can't you sit properly in a chair? It would be easier.'

She would remain hunched, unresponsive. I no longer had the heart, the strength, to look for another au pair girl. I was weary of sharing our lives with someone else, and so was Vanessa. For a few weeks a lively chain-smoking sixteen-year-old girl from Rochdale came to help; she liked the children but she chose not to stay, telling me her mother was ill and she needed to go home.

Richard's eczema was still as raw and red as ever. He was forever scratching any patch on his arms and legs that wasn't covered. Little Moonman we called him, thanks to his enormous blue eyes and oval face, even when he acquired a mass of tight little curls. Given the opportunity, he would cling to my arm as I carried on my hip, my little crab, full of sweet affection.

A dark, unbearable thought began to flit through my mind like a bird of evil portent. Those words of the consultant at the Skin Hospital when she'd said, 'You must make alternative arrangements for your handicapped child or this little one will not recover.'

I tried to ignore it, but it circled ever closer.

In May, when Vanessa was seven, Anthony two years and nine months and Richard ten months, I made two decisions to help me manage. Taking advantage of night care facilities available during term-time at Pictor House School, I arranged for Vanessa to stay all week, coming home on Friday afternoon. Knowing she loved the night-care sister lightened my heart, although on Saturday, she would lie on the floor in the kitchen crying hour after hour. On Sunday, she realised where she was and sometimes, she smiled.

To give me a brief respite from Anthony's terrible twos, I found a local playgroup and forced myself to believe that being away from me one morning would be good for him. But sobbing at the door of the playgroup, he would cling to me, shouting, 'No. I don't want to stay here, Mummy. Let me go home with you.'

Hardening my heart, I entrusted him to the care of the playgroup organiser, promising to come for him at twelve o'clock exactly. But organisation was not what he needed. It was an uncomplicated person to person relationship that I could never give him, held as I was by my awareness of Vanessa. Playgroup was of little value to him. He wanted me.

Even my one respite, the French evening classes were becoming a pressure. Without Anneliese's capable, calming presence, we just managed the change over with Sid returning from work around half past six and me dashing out as he walked through the door, racing through Cheadle to arrive before the students at a quarter to seven.

Despite being submerged by domesticity and the all prevailing fatigue, I suggested to Sid we invite our old friends for coffee. Norma had been in St Mary's with me, even buying *The Power of Positive Thinking*, (how long ago that seemed now) and her husband Harry had played bass in Sid's band even before I had met him.

Harry was playing every evening except Monday, so we settled for that. Monday came, and I was worn out. We'd had a particularly exhausting weekend – both boys full of colds, miserable and cranky, Vanessa crying the entire Saturday and Sunday, only ceasing when Sid took her on his knee.

Having carried Vanessa to the waiting taxi that particular Monday morning, I kissed her. 'Have a lovely time at school, and we'll see you on Friday.'

Back in the kitchen, I persuaded Anthony to wear Vanessa's red plastic overall to play with funnels and bowls at the sink, and while he was occupied, I tried to create some order, putting away the toys, bits of bricks, pencils, torn paper, socks and bibs scattered all over the floor. Then I cleared and wiped the kitchen worktops, and gave the lavatory a desultory clean.

My head was so heavy, I wondered if I was getting the boys' cold. With slower and slower steps, I mopped the floors and hoovered the lounge. By the time I was back in the kitchen, Anthony had disappeared, leaving pools of water on the floor. I swabbed them with an old tea towel. Creaking floorboards on the stairs told me had gone to his room. Should I call him?

An immense weariness weighed me down and I sank onto a chair. My elbows resting on the table, letting my head fall into my hands, I closed my eyes. Tears started to stream through my fingers. I began to sob, huge hoarse sobs coming from deep within me.

I can't see Norma and Harry tonight. I can't make cheerful conversation. I can't go on.

For long moments, I cried, but then, barely able to stand, my eyes almost blinded by tears, I made my slow way through the kitchen to the telephone in the hall. Still weeping, I leant against the wall and dialled Jessica's number.

She answered and I tried to speak. 'Jessica, it's me.' But I sobbed down the phone.

'Sue, what's the matter?' Her voice was sharp, anxious.

'It's Vanessa...' Trying to calm myself, I inhaled deeply. 'It's ... I can't go on. *I can't go on.*' The words seemed to echo in the silence of the hall.

For a long moment she was silent. Now I heard her saying, 'I'm coming round. Where are you?'

The question flummoxed me. Lifting my head, I saw the stairs, the door to the front room. Turning, I saw the kitchen behind me. 'In the hall.' I sank down on a small stool by the window. I waited.

When she arrived, her gaze was concerned. Giving me a quick hug, she steered me into the kitchen. 'How about some tea?'

I sat at the table that in the early days had seen so much of my work with Vanessa, then Anthony building bricks beside me, followed by that terrible unforgiveable event when I had knocked him to the floor in anger. Now, in my desperation, I was unable to utter a word. All I could do was to wipe away the tears which continued to fall on my hot, swollen face.

Jessica sat on the opposite side and handed me the tea. Leaning forward, she said softly, 'What's happened? Can you tell me?'

'I can't bear what I'm thinking.' I broke down again.

She tore off a couple of sheets of kitchen roll and handed them to me. I blew my nose. Slowly, little by little, I told her the story: how it had got harder over the months, how Anthony was wild, often naughty and demanding; that Richard's eczema was so severe. She nodded encouragingly. Then I related what the consultant had said about sending Vanessa away, barely bringing myself to utter the words. And how permanently exhausted I was. She made no comment, but her eyes were full of compassion.

And today? I couldn't understand why this had happened today. For once the house was clean, but I couldn't face these old friends tonight, even though we liked them so much. 'I can't go on,' I whispered. 'But how can I send Vanessa away? I can't bear it.'

I sat hunched, my head in my hands.

She got up, touched my arm. 'I think we should call your doctor. Is that all right?'

'Don't know. I suppose so.'

'It's Doctor Griffiths isn't it? What's his number?'

In minutes it seemed to me, he arrived, and I heard his deep Welsh tones as Jessica opened the front door. 'Where is she? In bed?'

'No, Doctor Griffiths. She's down here.'

Still overwhelmed by my feelings, I stayed with my head dipped, my eyes closed. Only when he had placed his bag on the table did I look up.

'What's the problem, Mrs Stern?'

Halting, wiping my eyes every few minutes, I managed to explain.

'As it happens,' he said, 'we've decided to appoint a social worker to the practice for the first time. An experiment. She's young, enthusiastic. I'll send her to see you.'

I thanked him without really taking in what he'd said. Opening his bag, he asked, 'Need any medication?' This was directed as much to Jessica as to me, but I answered, 'I'll manage, thank you.'

'All part of the service.'

Jessica saw him to the door; there was a low exchange of words. She returned, just as I sprang up, 'Richard. He's been asleep all morning. I must go to him. Something's wrong.'

'Don't panic. He knows what's happening, and he's waiting until you're ready.'

Anthony must have sensed something, too. For once, he was playing alone in his bedroom, unusual for him. Now he bumped down the stairs on his bottom, flinging himself against my legs, his arms tightly entwined, calling, 'Mummy! Mummy! Mummy!'

I hugged him tightly, whispering into his hair, 'My lovely boy.'

He wriggled away, sliding along the hall carpet, 'You're squashing me, Mummy.'

'Sorry, sorry, Anthony.'

He wandered into the kitchen while I hastened upstairs to find Richard standing in his night clothes, rattling the end of the cot. Seeing me, he lifted his arms, 'Mum, Mum.'

'Such a good boy,' I said, wanting to break down again. 'You must be wet and hungry. Let's go into the bathroom first and then you can have breakfast.'

In the afternoon when I was calm, Jessica went home.

Over the next few weeks, hiding his true feelings I knew, Sid tried to reassure me, but I couldn't stop the thought – I have killed my daughter... I have killed my daughter. The words never left me.

There were days when I would plead with her, 'Please try and sit upright, try not to fall, to slide down in the chair and then I could feed you. Then maybe I can keep you here.'

She would stare at me, her eyes like stones.

I would hide away in the downstairs toilet and cry.

Added to this, Anthony was often the recipient of my anger as he reacted to my miserable feelings. Rejected before he was born because of my devotion to Vanessa, now he was over-chastised for his increasing naughtiness, his only means of expression in a situation he couldn't possibly understand.

Such an atmosphere of bleakness, so bad for them all.

To some extent, Jessica helped me rationalise my feelings. 'You believe this is wrong but I tell you, it's the best for all of you. Especially Anthony and Richard. All children separate from their mothers when they're seven. You must talk to Vanessa, prepare her. Explain why, and tell her what will happen. Help her grow up.'

'You think so?'

'I've seen this with my girls. At seven, children move away from their mothers and go into the wider world. You must also reassure Anthony that he's not going to be sent away like Vanessa.'

'I never thought of that.' I looked at her in surprise.

'He will certainly wonder about that, when she goes, so you must tell him now that he'll stay at home with you. Sue, you're perfectly capable of doing it – just let go of your guilt.'

'Put positive energy into all you do.'

'That's right.' She shook her finger at me. 'Guilt is totally negative.'

Following her advice based on common sense, I stopped weeping inside. Over the next few weeks, I talked to Vanessa. 'My sweetheart, we all love you very much but you're a big girl now. I can't look after you properly any more. Soon you'll be going away, and other people will look after you. Not Pictor School. Somewhere else, with someone very nice.' I talked to the person behind the crooked, helpless body and I believed that she understood.

Her teacher called me one evening to say that Vanessa was unhappy at school. 'She's crying all the time, jealous if anyone else receives attention and constantly wanting to be picked up. Is there some problem at home?'

I told her what was happening.

'We'll spend more time with her now. And she's always happy with the night-care sister.'

'Thank you. It's such a relief to know she's all right when she sleeps over. If only Pictor School was residential or had a residential facility, it would be the most wonderful solution for us.'

'It would be,' said her teacher. 'That's what they want to do, but it's money. Always down to money, isn't it? Anyway, I'm glad you told me about what's happening. It explains a lot.'

The social worker from the group practice came, very young, very enthusiastic, making her first visit.

'Somewhere small, homelike, not an institution,' I insisted. 'That's what I want for her.'

'I'm sure we can find something like that.'

I made enquiries as well: I wrote to the Rudolf Steiner schools hoping they had changed their policy. The reply was unsurprising: they couldn't take children needing nursing care. Learning about Brookvale in North Manchester, a facility for Jewish children and adults with a mental handicap, I drove over to see it. A large settlement spread out in the countryside in Prestwich, where I saw many young adults with Down's syndrome or with various learning disabilities but no one in a wheelchair, none like our daughter, and their answer to my query was identical to that of the Steiner schools: they couldn't take a child that needed nursing care. Then I tried *Buckets and Spades,* a small foundation on the south coast, another home for young disabled children. But Vanessa was too handicapped.

At my request, the Spastics Society social worker made an exceptional visit.

'Did you know you can have her assessed by the Spastics Society doctor?' she asked, crunching a digestive biscuit.

'Really? How do we do that?'

'Leave it with me. I have all her details. I'll put in a request for you.' Placing her mug on the table, she opened her briefcase.

'Do you think that will help?' Now I was excited, even hopeful.

Busy writing in her notebook, she looked up. 'That's the normal procedure if you want your child assessed for one of our residential schools.'

'Residential schools? I had no idea they existed.' A little light of hope began to burn in my heart. 'Where are they? What are they like?'

'There's Meldreth Manor in Hertfordshire, Craig y Parc near Cardiff and Ingfield Manor School in Sussex. All a long way from here, though. To tell the truth, I don't know of anything local. Hopefully, the social worker from your surgery will find something.' Suddenly, she dropped her gaze. The little light began to fade.

'But if your schools are suitable, maybe that would be the best thing for her?'

'The thing is, Mrs Stern, I can't promise anything.' She drained her mug of coffee, gave me an uneasy look. 'Actually, she may not be suitable.'

So that was it: *she might not be suitable.*

'How do you mean?' I persisted.

'Depends on how the doctor finds her. What he thinks.'

She had offered me sustenance, and then whipped it away.

'We would like an assessment,' I said firmly. 'How long would we wait for it?'

She stood up then, slung her bag over her arm, and smiled. On safe ground now. 'I'm sorry to say, it's at least six months and probably not until early next year.'

'Next year? Could you possibly hurry it up?'

'I'll do my best. Well, I'd better be off. Lovely coffee, Mrs Stern.'

Somehow we got through the weeks. We even held a first birthday party for Richard. Supported by all the grandparents, we were all there to blow out the candle and sing Happy Birthday. Then came the summer holidays. Now Anthony was three and Richard could partly feed himself, I just about managed them all.

Weeks passed: Richard became a toddler, with a wonderful head of tight brown curls, following his brother everywhere, still not talking but absorbing everything Anthony did. Anthony spoke for him, 'Richard needs a drink. He's hungry, Mummy.'

Our boisterous older son had begun to change, slipping into the role of big brother, guiding, pushing, and fighting with Richard in due course. He was three years old in August, and we had decided some months before that he should start nursery. Although I believed so strongly in preschool education, I found nothing suitable, nothing that met my expectations. A Montessori Nursery would have been my first choice but there were none locally. Nor did I think he needed to go every day but we came to a compromise decision.

Yeshurun Synagogue, where we were members but which we attended rarely, had opened its own nursery, supervised by a lively, enthusiastic American woman, aided by qualified nursery nurses and volunteers. Further along our road a denominational state primary school had just opened. Clearly, the boys would attend this school, so near to our house, receiving a secular and Jewish education. We'd had long discussions about schools offering a religious education; while not really upholding the idea, this one was modern, not coercive and we both felt it would add to their Jewish religious awareness, something we couldn't give them. Sid also reasoned that if Anthony attended the synagogue nursery, he would make a group of friends who would continue to primary school. In this way, his life would have some kind of 'normality.'

Now it was November.

Six months after she had begun her search, the social worker called to say she had something to tell us. When she entered, her uneasy gaze told me it was not good news.

'I've searched all over the country,' she said, giving me a sombre look. 'I'm so sorry, the sort of provision you were seeking doesn't seem to exist.'

'That's impossible.' My heart began to thrum in my chest. 'There must be some small homely place where Vanessa could go.'

'I wish there were.' She looked away, as though wanting to avoid my gaze. 'I'm afraid there's only a subnormality hospital in Cheshire.'

'You mean Cranage Hall Hospital?' I shot her a look of consternation.

'You've heard of it?' Her eyes lit up. 'Have you visited Cranage?'

'We haven't, but I've heard of it all right. Terrible things.'

She moved uneasily in her seat. 'Could you tell me what kind of things?'

'Our friend's autistic daughter was chained to the wall when she was there. The staff said it was to stop her hurting herself but our friends were horrified. Lucky for them, they found a place in a Steiner school near Aberdeen. We went there with them, when Vanessa was two. Their daughter's making progress now.'

She flushed red. 'I visited the hospital two weeks ago. I saw nothing like that.'

'It's the very last place I wanted for her,' I blurted out, then stared at the floor. My heart had shrunk to a tight black knot inside me.

'I believe there's a school,' she murmured.

'A school?' This made me look up. 'Can you find out about it?'

'Of course. I've brought Doctor Griffiths up to date with my enquiries and he suggests you take Vanessa for a trial stay. See how she gets on.'

When my parents came as usual the Sunday after this conversation, I told them the outcome of the social worker's search, and my father rose from his chair. 'No, you can't send her away. I'll pay for someone to look after her here.'

I knew they had little money and my father had old-fashioned ideas about the cost of things. Besides, we had made this decision, awful though it was, and I couldn't go back on it. I shook my head.

'It's very kind of you, Dad, but we've made up our minds. I can't cope any longer. We have to take her there, at least for a few weeks.'

Chapter 24

The social worker phoned a few days later saying she'd written to Cranage Hall Hospital but had received no information about the school. Then it was the first week in December, and as I hadn't heard from her, I called the surgery.

'I can't tell you,' the receptionist said. 'She has her notes with her. Besides, she's off sick and won't be back until the New Year.'

With no heartening information about the hospital school, I was even more apprehensive when a buff-coloured official looking envelope arrived in the post. With icy, shaking hands, I tore it open and drew out a badly typed letter headed: *Hazel Villa, Cranage Hall Hospital*. For a second, I envisaged a cosy, homely little cottage but I shook the image away, knowing that the hospital had more than six hundred patients in various wards. Hanging on to a kitchen chair for support, I read the letter: a bed would be available for two or three weeks over the holiday period, and should we wish to take up the place, we were requested to contact Hazel Villa directly by telephone.

Such a rush of shame and guilt flooded through me, it was as though my insides were dissolving. I stood rigidly beside the table. The rest of the day I was sleepwalking. Despite putting the central heating to 'high,' cold shivers ran up and down my back, I kept rubbing my arms, I put on layers of cardigans, but nothing could dispel the freezing sensations that gripped my entire body.

When Sid came home, I passed him the letter. Something sparked off inside me. 'I can't take her that day.' I was defiant, almost shouting.

He read the letter, slipped it back in the torn envelope, and looked at me. For once his gaze was impenetrable. 'What do you propose to do?'

'Take her after Christmas.'

He frowned. 'Why do you want to do that?'

'Because my mother is expecting us on Christmas Day. The only day we're all together. I don't want to disappoint her. I want Vanessa to be there, too.'

Many Jewish people took advantage of the Bank Holiday to hold a family get-together but for Mother it had extra resonance. After her own mother's death when she was a few weeks old, she was fostered by a Christian woman, a member of the Socialist Women's Guild. She and an older sister were sent to Sunday school, brought up as Christians despite being Jewish. Barbara, her family and mine, were all my mother had, and she treasured this day, all of us together.

I knew in my heart that this year, I was the one who needed my family's support. With Sid's agreement, I phoned Hazel Villa to ask if we could bring Vanessa after Christmas. They told us the twenty-eighth of December would be fine.

It was a subdued Christmas day we spent together. As we left, Barbara enveloped Vanessa in her warm embrace, holding her for a long moment, and then did the same for me. My mother didn't linger as usual by the front door, waving to the children in the car, but stayed in the hall where she whispered to me, 'Don't worry, we'll be there early on Saturday morning. You know Anthony and Richard will be fine.'

Two days left. Vanessa lay on the bed Sid had made for her while I packed a few clothes in a bag. 'Vanessa, my darling,' I said, as I took her trousers and tights from the little white chest of drawers, 'on Saturday, Daddy and I are taking you to a place called Hazel Villa, to see if you'd like to stay there.' But my voice cracked, I couldn't go on. I had to take her downstairs to lie on the floor near Anthony and Richard, who were playing with bricks.

Saturday the twenty-eighth of December, dark, dank, forbidding.

My parents arrived early as they'd promised, and we wedged Vanessa into the car seat so she wouldn't slide down. Bravely, I held up her arm to wave goodbye to Grandpa and Grandma.

And we set off.

Along the M56 then the side road past Tatton Park, through Knutsford and into the flat Cheshire countryside. Along ever more narrow, winding roads until on the left, we saw the hospital sign and my heart quivered. Around there was the entrance to Cranage Hall Hospital, with its collection of buildings set far back from the road as if to hide them from people's gaze. We drove between manicured lawns dotted with evergreen shrubs and trees until we saw that classic hospital sign, the tall chimney.

We arrived at Hazel Villa. In silence, we carried Vanessa to the door and Sid rang the bell. We soon heard the sound of hurrying feet, bolts being drawn, keys being turned, and the door was opened by a middle-aged woman in a blue crossover apron, faded and worn.

She smiled. 'Mr and Mrs Stern? Are you bringing Vanessa to stay with us?' Glancing at Vanessa, she smiled again.

'Yes.'

'Please come in.' She held the door, then locked and bolted it behind us. 'I'm Mrs Caldwell. Been here for years, for my sins.'

We were in a small entrance hall. Again, Mrs Caldwell unlocked a door and we followed her into an enormous room where one wall, on the far side, consisted of huge windows from floor to ceiling. Heat, the hospital smell of disinfectant, and something else, something rank, oozed over us. There was a cacophony of noise: Christmas carols blasted out through some kind of loudspeaker system, a television fixed high on the far wall was playing a Christmas comedy at full volume, and from dozens of children in wheelchairs and curled up on mats came the sounds of high repetitive cries and grunts and moans.

I stared in horror. I saw angular faces, scrawny limbs. Some laughing silently to themselves, others rocking, still others banging their heads on the wheelchair tray. They dribbled down overalls; the small bibs round their necks were sodden with moisture. Oblivious to the television, to the streamers criss-crossing the ceiling, to Father Christmas large on a wall, to the whole festive Christmas atmosphere, they had retreated into repetitive movement which spoke of their desperate need for stimulation and attention. Clutching Vanessa closer to me, I turned my anguished gaze to Sid but he shook his head. 'Let's just see.'

Mrs Caldwell had started ahead. Aware that we weren't following, she turned and seeing my horrified expression, twisted her apron between her hands. 'I know it looks bad but there's only three of us to look after thirty children.'

I took a deep breath. 'I understand.'

'You want to see the ward where they sleep?'

I nodded.

Making our way between wheelchairs and mats, with Vanessa held fiercely in my arms, I followed her through swing doors at the end. A vast open ward met our eyes; some kind of L shaped room, with row upon row of beds but without any dividing screens or curtains to offer privacy. There was a simple nurses' station with a desk, telephone and a couple of chairs. Behind this was a low wooden partition, separating the desk from two rows of beds but allowing anyone sitting there a complete view of the area, up to the wall and window, which overlooked the driveway. I could just make out someone lying covered with a blanket on the furthest bed, but no face was visible.

As we gazed around, a stockily built man in his late forties ambled over. Half a dozen pens in his top pocket caught my eye, making me think he was a clerk or an overseer, not a nurse or carer at all.

'Hello, I'm the charge nurse here, I look after this ward.'

By now I was so affected by the children in the day room and the appearance of this ward, all I could hear was my heart drumming in my ears and didn't catch his name.

'Is this Vanessa? That's where she'll sleep.' He pointed to a grey tubular cot just beyond the nurses' station.

We followed him round.

'Her bed?' A cot more suitable for a two-year-old, but I told myself she might be able to fit in, since she was so small.

With a kind of smirk he said, 'We like to have them close when they first arrive. Keep an eye on them.'

'We get to know their little ways.' Mrs Caldwell was hovering behind him. 'Well, I better get back to the day room. I haven't finished yet.'

He didn't reply. Instead, he turned to me. 'You'd better put her in the cot and leave her to settle down.'

I held Vanessa in my arms and drew on my courage. 'We've got her clothes, so where shall we put them? I have also got a drink of Bournvita in warm milk. I would like to give her some before we leave.'

He shrugged. I removed Vanessa's coat, draping it over the chair, and proceeded to give her the drink. Sid followed him to the nurses' station and returned a few minutes later, saying we should put her clothes in the small cupboard by the cot, leaving the rest in the suitcase underneath. In a low voice, he added, 'Hadn't you better say something about her feeding?'

'You're right. I'll do so when she's finished.'

A few minutes later, I went round to the charge nurse. 'Excuse me, I wonder do you have any information about our daughter?'

'Only what your doctor wrote us.'

I frowned. 'I had better explain about her feeding. My husband suggested I speak to you.' Possibly the sort of man who disparaged women but if I mentioned my husband, he'd take notice. 'She has a tongue thrust. She can't help pushing food out of her mouth, and you have to scrape it up and give it to her again. And she can only suck. She has cerebral palsy.' I searched his face but was sure he hadn't a clue about what I was saying.

For a long moment, he stared. Pushing back his chair, he said offhandedly, 'We've had all kinds of handicaps here. The ladies, that's Mrs Caldwell and Mrs Booth – you haven't met her yet, are very experienced.' I wanted him to offer me a moment's reassurance, but there was nothing. Instead, he said, 'Best thing is to put her in her cot and let her settle.'

The time had come.

Lifting Vanessa over the cot bars, I whispered softly, 'I'll be back tomorrow to see you. Bye-bye, my darling.' I kissed her and dragged myself away, as she began to cry.

As we reached the swing doors, the charge nurse called, 'Telephone, if you like.'

'I will,' I answered hotly.

We drove home in silence. I had curled into the deepest, darkest part of my being. I couldn't think. But the moment we got back, I telephoned; they told me she was doing nicely, whatever that meant.

Sid persuaded me not to visit her the following day. 'You'll upset her. You'll upset yourself. Just give her a week to settle down. We'll go next weekend.'

Her little white face as we left and those poor children in the day room continued to haunt me hour after hour, day after day. I was so desperate for her, so ashamed and full of guilt that I'd made such a dreadful decision, I stopped feeling altogether. For days I was sleepwalking. I did phone the hospital every day and received the same message: *She's doing nicely.* I kept hugging Anthony and Richard as though to remind myself why we'd done such an awful thing.

And then came the long-awaited letter from the Spastics Society; dated early December, it must have been lost in the Christmas post. With a frisson of apprehension, I read that we should take Vanessa to Pendlebury Children's Hospital for an appointment in three days' time. Eight months after my discussion with the social worker.

We decided not to visit Vanessa over the weekend but collect her on Monday for the assessment. Again, we left Anthony and Richard with my mother, making the forty-minute journey to Cranage Hospital where we found Mrs Caldwell sitting beside the cot, giving Vanessa a drink.

'She gave me a lovely smile just now,' Mrs Caldwell said, as Vanessa shouted and wriggled when she saw us. The ice in my heart began to melt, tears filled my eyes but I swiped them away, I didn't want Vanessa to see me crying.

But pulling on her clean tights for the interview, I found large bruises on her legs which must have come from banging them against the cot sides. I decided to say nothing to Mrs Caldwell, cherishing the hope that after today's assessment, Vanessa would be going to a Spastics Society school, and we would never set foot in this place again.

The cross-country journey to the Pendlebury Children's Hospital took more than an hour; it was almost midday when we arrived. Another grand Victorian building where over the next hour, we were directed to various departments. A nurse took Vanessa's medical history; she was seen by an optician, a physiotherapist, and finally we went to the psychology department where the assessment would take place. Between these consultations, I had given Vanessa drinks, but now I asked the receptionist if we had time to give her some lunch. Checking a list, she said, 'We're running late as usual. But that gives you about half an hour.' Showing her the ready-prepared jar of toddler food I asked if I could warm it up.

'Of course. I'll get someone to do it for you.'

I was struck by her kindness and thanked her. A few minutes later, I had enveloped Vanessa in her red overall and was stuffing layers of kitchen roll around her neck. She was starving, and swallowed the food avidly while two little boys, presumably also waiting to see the psychologist, came to watch. I had just wiped her face when a nurse called us and we followed her until we saw *Psychologist* on a consulting room door. She knocked and a voice called, 'Enter'.

A woman rose from behind the desk. Her hair was coiled in a black chignon and she wore a smart black trouser suit. She gave us a piercing look, and I saw that her green eyes were accentuated with eyeliner and turquoise eye shadow, carefully applied. What drew my attention, and Vanessa's, who couldn't stop staring, were her enormous red spectacles arching to a point at each corner. Tiny inlaid gems glittered as the psychologist turned her head. Holding out her hand across the desk, she said, 'Good afternoon, Mr and Mrs Stern. I regret that you have waited so long. Please sit down.' With her right hand she indicated two chairs nearby. I stopped to take in the consulting room. She repeated, 'Please sit down.'

I recognised the long vowels and careful enunciation of an educated Frenchwoman but something about her made me uneasy. Without knowing why, I disliked her, and so did Vanessa, for turning her eyes to me, she made a lip.

The woman was owl-like, imposing and struck me as someone with formidable intellect. There was nothing gentle or caressing about her. A mind in action, and I wondered if her whole demeanour was devised to intimidate the children she interviewed. But I took the chair, holding Vanessa on my knee as upright as I could while tucking her head beneath my chin. This way, she would face the psychologist and I wouldn't keep shifting her up with my shoulder, or manoeuvring her back into a sitting position when she fell sideways. I knew the psychologist was observing us even as Sid drew up a chair and sat down beside me.

'You have come here today,' she said, staring at each one of us in turn, 'because some months ago, you requested an assessment from the Spastics Society.'

'Yes,' I murmured. Sid inclined his head.

'My intention is to discover what Vanessa can do, what she understands, in order to create a portrait of her mental and psychological development. My findings will be collated with the other investigations that have already taken place.' She managed a faint smile but her green eyes remained watchful.

I felt Vanessa grow rigid in my arms.

'We'll start, Mr and Mrs Stern, with something called the Wechsler Preschool Primary test. We use it to ascertain intellectual functioning in verbal and performance cognitive domains, as well as providing a score that represents a child's general ability. We do this for every child who comes here.'

While she was selecting whatever material she needed, I glanced quickly at her desk. Facing us, on the left-hand side, were three rows of coloured bricks, in perfect lines. On the other side, were a series of brightly coloured boxes, which I imagined held the toys she needed for the assessment. In front of her on the desk, was a mimeographed sheet; reading it upside down, I could just make out Vanessa's name and a series of questions, a small box beside each one. The space between the questions was presumably where the psychologist added her comments.

And so it began. First were bricks with a zigzag line which Vanessa had to match with corresponding bricks the psychologist gave to her. My breath caught in my throat as I felt Vanessa's hands quiver and she raised her head once more. I kept my eyes fixed on a window behind the psychologist's chair; I knew this was beyond Vanessa's ability. I longed to direct her hands and arms, helping her select the right ones. After a long moment, when no one stirred, the psychologist removed the picture and replaced the bricks in a box.

There was another silence. Her face devoid of expression, she uncapped a black fountain pen and wrote something on the sheet. She selected an assortment of coloured bricks from the line nearest to her. Addressing Vanessa once more, she said, 'I want you to make three things with these bricks. First, a bridge.' I lifted Vanessa closer to the table, willing her to pick up just a single brick, even if it was many months since we'd done anything like this. Sid shifted in his chair. Of course Vanessa stayed with her head bent and didn't move.

I had to say something. Taking a quick breath, I ventured: 'Some years ago she was able to lift up bricks or small objects because of the work we were doing with her. But lately, it hasn't been possible, so I don't know whether she can do it now.'

The psychologist gave me a level look but continued with the test. She asked Vanessa to make a gate, then a flight of steps, indicating the different sizes of bricks on the table. Our daughter continued to sit with her head down. The psychologist carefully returned most of the bricks to their place, setting several aside. She marked the assessment sheet.

'Now a game with colours. Can you do that? I want you to show me the red one.' She spaced bricks out in a straight line, close to where Vanessa's head was almost resting on the desk. 'Show me the red one,' she repeated, her voice commanding.

Slowly our daughter lifted her head and focused intently on the red brick.

'Good. Which is the yellow?'

Vanessa repeated the movement, eye-pointing towards the yellow brick.

The psychologist went through the primary colours, all of which Vanessa knew and which didn't surprise me at all. The test completed, the psychologist removed the bricks, placing them in their box.

'Now,' she said, 'I want to see if you can draw a shape.' She slid a sheet of paper towards us, together with a thick red crayon.

Didn't she remember what I had just said? But she was determined to follow the sequence on the list. Light from the window caught the frame of her glasses, making the tiny gems glitter, and Vanessa sat transfixed again.

But heedless of the mesmerising effect of her spectacles, the psychologist pointed to the crayon. 'I want you to draw a cross on the paper.'

Vanessa fell sideways on my knee and I straightened her with my shoulder. I could bear it no longer. 'I don't think she can pick up the crayon or make a cross. She hasn't any fine movements in her hands, any sensation at all.'

'I see. Thank you, Mrs Stern.'

A series of pictures followed: a cat, a baby, a boy painting, a girl reading. Sid and I exchanged relieved smiles. Out of the dozen or so images, Vanessa eye-pointed correctly to nine of them. Things were looking up.

Then more complex tests, which I knew would be out of the question. Shooting us a baleful look through those fierce red spectacles, the woman put the material away. Sitting back, resting her arms on the desk, the psychologist demanded, 'What exactly *can* she do?' She folded her arms.

This woman was incapable of assessing any child, let alone one who had complex disabilities.

'Sid,' I said, 'could you take Vanessa for a moment?'

Launching into a description of our work in the first four years with the physiotherapists and with Doctor Wilson, I explained about the wooden table, how I had worked with Vanessa to teach her the basic skills of a young child. I added that the speech therapists at Pictor House School were astonished at her command of words, saying she had the understanding of a two-year-old child.

Expressionless, the woman wrote something on the sheet. Rising from her chair, she extended her hand. 'Thank you for bringing Vanessa today. The assessment is finished. All my findings will be conveyed to the doctor who will call you shortly with his verdict.'

So that was it.

I couldn't imagine what she'd discovered. Watching Vanessa 'failing' these simple tests, I couldn't accept these were suitable for a handicapped child. I stood, my heart pounding so loud I could hear it. I said, 'You asked us at the beginning if we had any questions, and I said no, not then. But I do have one now: aren't these tests more suitable for children who aren't handicapped?'

Her eyebrows shot up above her glasses, if that were possible, and she gave me such a dismissive look with those cold green eyes. She must have felt challenged, as though I'd attacked her judgment, because she replied sharply, 'Mrs Stern,' and her French accent became more pronounced, 'Mrs Stern, we are obliged to have some sort of baseline. We use these fundamental tests for all children, handicapped or not, or how would we ascertain their skills, their developmental age?'

Back in the waiting room, which was crowded with young children and parents, we sat down again.

'Vanessa didn't like her, did she?' Sid said, giving me an uneasy glance.

'Not surprised. Neither did I. Analytical and cerebral, the worst kind of French intellectual.'

'Sue, you amaze me. I thought you liked people like that.'

'Not in these circumstances. She lacked all empathy. With a different sort of person, perhaps Vanessa might have responded better.' I was so angry, so upset, I continued, '*Vixen*, that's what she was.' But then, I sighed. 'What on earth will she tell the doctor? It doesn't bode well.'

Then came the verdict. The doctor was tall, thin, his hair cut close, giving me the impression of some kind of military person, perhaps he'd been a doctor during the war. Whatever it was, he spoke with a clipped, upper-class accent. At first, when we entered his consulting room and sat down, there was a certain kindness in his voice. Settling his thin-rimmed spectacles on his nose, he re-read a document on the desk before speaking to us.

I sat, leaning forward, anxious to hear every word. In my mind I was preparing to ask him about the Spastics Society's schools, re-jigging the questions as he spoke.

He cleared his throat. Looking from Sid to me, he said, 'Mr and Mrs Stern, I'm afraid you have a very seriously handicapped child.' His gaze fell upon Vanessa who was sitting on my knee, but he lifted his eyes, which were grave, serious, before going on, 'Her mental age is below that of a child of twelve months and she is now eight. When she's sixteen, her mental age will be that of a two-year-old.'

I gave an involuntary grasp, and gripped Vanessa tightly.

'I strongly advise you to arrange for residential care in the hospital where she is now.' Looking away for a moment, as though to avoid our shocked faces, he began again. 'You have put great energy into the care of this child but the output doesn't warrant the input.' Now he directed his gaze at me. 'You will wreak great damage on the rest of your family and on yourselves, if you continue to live as you've done. You know this already. I shall write to the medical superintendent of Cranage Hall Hospital strongly recommending that Vanessa remains there.'

I threw Sid a glance of consternation but he was staring at the floor. With one last desperate breath, I whispered, 'Your social worker mentioned the Spastics Society schools, and I was hoping she might attend one of them.'

'She is ineducable, Mrs Stern.' He shook his head. 'You must understand that what I recommend will be the best for her and for all of you in the long run.'

It was brutal. But at the depths of our being, we recognised the truth. And I sensed that he had spoken in this way to force me to consider the other children, and face our situation. We could not bring her home. Instead, we drove back to Cranage Hall Hospital for the Severely Subnormal where we left her in the cot at Hazel Villa.

Chapter 25

Over the next few weeks I felt as though someone had clawed away part of my heart.

I drove through the streets, tears streaming down my cheeks, repeating, 'I have lost Vanessa.' This happened even when the boys were in their car seats behind me; I would glance through the driving mirror to check if they were affected by my grief. I'm sure they were aware of it, although Anthony, always ready with a question or interesting comment, said nothing, and I managed a teary smile when I unstrapped them.

The place Vanessa had filled physically in our lives, emotionally in my psyche, sleeping or waking, was now a void. I would pause, looking for her in her wheelchair, or upstairs I'd see her empty bed and would imagine her lying there. I would talk to her, telling her things, asking her how she was, seeing her so far away in the hospital, talking, always talking. It would take me a year to get used to her absence.

I didn't know that Jewish ritual had three stages of mourning – after the death came the *Shivah,* the seven days of mourning, the most intense and specific period; followed by the *Shloshim,* the thirty days, which allowed the mourner to return gradually to everyday life, and finally, there was the year, when it was believed the soul would progress from the grave to eternity.

I mourned her for the year, even though she was alive.

Sid was a man of deep feeling but fortunately, he remained calm, non-reactive, which was best for us all. Our families said little, knowing how we felt, but brought toys and sweets for the boys as though to make up for the loss of their sister. A reminder for me of where my focus should now be. Accustomed to her being away all week, Anthony, aged three and a half, talked about her occasionally but was not as far as we could see, affected by her absence. Richard, eighteen months, watching and absorbing everything but still only making short sentences, was too young to be affected, or so we hoped. But over time, the eczema which had troubled him so profoundly seemed to diminish. One blessing, at least.

And from what we could tell, Vanessa had accepted her move to Cranage with the minimum of distress. Of course, we visited her often, sometimes as a family and frequently, on Saturday when Sid worked all day, I would take the boys on my own so that he could have the day off on Sunday. At first Anthony and Richard were delighted to play with the toys in the day room while I sat with Vanessa by her bed, giving her drinks and food, all the while talking to her. She was so excited to see us, although she'd cry when we left. But if I phoned later, the staff told me she had stopped the moment I was out of sight.

So much troubled me about Vanessa's life in Cranage Hall Hospital. As soon as she was resident in Hazel Villa, I didn't hesitate to ask the charge nurse about the bruising on her legs caused by the metal cot, so unsuitable to her needs.

'Can I tell you about something that's worrying us?' I said carefully. 'I wonder if you've noticed the marks, bruises I think, on Vanessa's legs.'

'It's the ladies who look after her. They dress and undress her. Maybe you should ask them.' He turned away.

'I know it's not obvious but would you mind coming to see? Because I think we have a solution to this.' Somewhat reluctantly he followed me to where Vanessa was tangled up in the bars and I had to extricate her. I rolled up the bottom of her trousers to show him. 'This happened at home when she was small,' I went on, 'and my husband solved the problem by making her a special bed.' I described it to him. 'It will stop her bruising her arms and legs on the bars. It's so broad that she can lie on her tummy and push herself up. Then she can see everything. More stimulation.' I smiled at him. 'We would love to bring it over for her. Would that be okay?'

'It would,' he said, 'or I could ask the carpenters to make one, but that could take weeks.'

'My husband's off work next Sunday; we'll bring it then.'

One concern crossed off the list. But I was so troubled that Vanessa was spending almost all her time on the bed. I rarely saw her in the wheelchair and nobody explained why. Perhaps they treated her as a baby, and with so much work with the older children, it was easier to leave her there. With the primitive extension reflex she had never grown out of, pushing her backwards when her head touched anything solid, her body was becoming ever more twisted, more deformed.

For long periods, she was left without stimulation. I imagined someone passing might say a few words, but how overworked they were. Three people to care for thirty doubly-incontinent children and teenagers. Such dedication they demonstrated, especially Mrs Caldwell and Mrs Booth, a cheerful dark-haired woman who seemed greatly devoted to all the patients. With what little reward.

By chance, shortly after Vanessa's admission, I learned from Mrs Booth that a teacher came to the ward, working with a small group who didn't attend the hospital school. My heart leaped. This was the first reference to any sort of education since my conversation with the social worker almost a year before.

'Why can't they all go?' I asked.

'Because we've more than a hundred children in the villas and the school's very small.'

'I do want Vanessa to have some education. She's been going to the Spastics Society School for five years. She misses it so much. Could you possibly say something to the teacher? Please, Mrs Booth.'

'I could ask her,' she said doubtfully, 'but it's really up to her.'

Thinking fast, I said, 'When is she next on the ward?'

'Wednesday, I think.'

The following Wednesday, leaving Richard with Grandma Stern, I charged along the motorway and caught the teacher about to leave. Begging her to include Vanessa in her group on the ward, I elaborated on the work we'd done, the activities she enjoyed at Pictor School. She listened, finally promising to try.

'But I can't do it at once. Maybe in a few weeks' time.'

Careful not to push it too much, I felt my first glimmer of happiness. Success! Two weeks later, I heard they had room for her and she'd be included in the group.

So long as I could do something to improve Vanessa's situation, I was buoyant, but away from her, I battled with guilt and grief. She had been at Hazel Villa for about three months, when just before the Easter holidays, a dark cloud of sadness dulled my mind and I was desperate to talk to someone who would understand. Dropping Anthony at nursery, I drove to Pictor House School and walked in unannounced. Carrying Richard, now twenty-one months, I avoided the classroom where Vanessa would have been and made my way to the matron's office.

I knocked, and went in. Luckily, she was alone, and seeing my face, asked me to sit. Always compassionate and encouraging, she listened as I talked. Often wiping tears away, holding Richard so close in my arms, I couldn't stop. But I had finally shared my guilt and troubled feelings with someone who knew our daughter.

'It's easier,' she said, 'for some people to have a handicapped child than others.' I frowned. What did she mean? 'I'm thinking,' she continued, 'of someone whose life is centred on her home. This kind of woman can be happy to have a baby with her for always.'

'Yes,' I said, a sudden memory of Gorton coming to me. 'I do understand what you mean. When Vanessa was a year old, I was wheeling the pram down Gorton Cross Street, and a customer came to look at her. You'll have a baby all your life, she said. She said it as though it was something wonderful.'

'Exactly,' she smiled. 'It also depends on what expectations you have of your children.'

I gave her a puzzled look. 'I'm not sure about expectations. I love her and still I sent her away to such a dreadful place.' Tears blurred my eyes.

She shook her head. 'Don't feel guilty. You've done what you thought best for all your children.' Darting a little smile at Richard, still sitting on my knee, she handed him a nest of Russian dolls on her desk that he'd been eyeing. He unpacked them, lined them up, arranged them into a family of five and finally, put them together again. Gravely, he handed them back to her. Meanwhile, she looked at me sadly. 'They'll all end up in a subnormality hospital.'

Following her gaze, I turned towards the classrooms behind us. 'Those children?'

'All of them. When their parents are ill or old or for a hundred reasons, they can't look after them anymore, they'll all go to a subnormality hospital.' She sighed, her eyes dark with sadness. 'The tragedy is there's nowhere else.'

For a moment we were silent. Then I stood up and lifted Richard from the floor. 'Thank you, Matron, for listening to me. You've helped me see things differently. You've lightened my heart.'

One Saturday afternoon in the summer, after Vanessa had been there for six months, I left the boys playing in the day room, surrounded by the children in their wheelchairs, when Anthony, nearly four, pushed open the swing door with a jolt followed by Richard toddling behind him. I was sitting by the bed, chatting to Vanessa whose happy gaze was on my face when they charged towards me.

'I don't like it in there, Mummy,' Anthony shouted. 'I want to stay here with you and Vanessa.'

'Don't like there, Mummy,' Richard repeated.

'What's the matter?' Their worried little faces surprised me.

'Those funny people in the wheelchairs.' Anthony clutched at my knees. 'I don't like them.'

With Vanessa in my arms, the two boys clinging to me, I went round to speak to Mrs Caldwell who was seated at the nurses' desk. 'Is there somewhere we could go in the afternoon? Somewhere I could take Vanessa and her brothers?'

'There's a nice garden centre down the road, with a lovely cafe. Other parents go there sometimes.'

This became our treat.

From then on, we went to the cafe and while I gave Vanessa mashed up scrambled eggs, beans, bread and butter, the boys chose cakes, a biscuit, sweets, and it was like a treat for everyone, Vanessa especially. We'd take her back to the ward and I'd drive home, often reminding the boys that they would never have to go away like Vanessa but would stay with me. 'Because Vanessa is special.'

'Like those funny people in the day room?'

'A bit like them. So she needs special people to look after her.' Through the rear view mirror I could see Anthony considering this. 'But you know how Vanessa smiles a lot?'

'Smiles,' piped up Richard.

'Yes, and everyone smiles back at her?'

There was silence. I could see Anthony pulling out his mouth with both hands to make an enormous Vanessa type grin, and Richard copying him. My eyes filled with bittersweet tears, I recognised how cheerful, how accepting of Vanessa our boys were, and once again, I had to recognise that now, they must be my centre.

I continued to worry about her. My constant fear was that her limbs would seize up, she would lose muscle tone, her legs would be more twisted, her body too. And she would become withdrawn and ever more handicapped without the attention she'd always received. As one friend had said, 'You talk to Vanessa all the time, even when I'm speaking.' I had to do something: I began to pester the staff and the ward teacher, begging them to let Vanessa go to school, even though I hadn't yet seen it.

I pleaded, I nagged, I cajoled until one morning in October, ten months after her admission, the charge nurse phoned: 'We've found her a place in the school. Only mornings, mind. She can start in a couple of weeks.'

I smiled to myself – my persistence had won after all. Vanessa had been especially lethargic and unresponsive although I didn't mention this to him. I'm sure he'd take it as a criticism of their care. Instead, I began to thank him, but he cut in: 'We'll see how she goes on. Goodbye, Mrs Stern.'

Collecting Anthony from nursery later that morning, I said, 'Vanessa's starting school, just like you'll be, in January.'

'Both of us going to school,' he observed solemnly, munching a piece of apple. 'Will it be like mine?'

'I don't know. We're going to see your school soon. Won't that be exciting?'

'I don't know,' he echoed, 'I haven't seen it yet'

But Richard remarked: 'Nessa's going to school' He grinned, glad to be taking part in the conversation.

Few people visited our daughter. Friends went once but never again. One Sunday, Jessica came, and gazing at all the children rocking, head banging, and shoving their hands down their throat while they sat in their wheelchairs, she remarked, 'There's so much energy here. How different they would be if they'd had the attention you gave to Vanessa.'

My parents went on another occasion, but said they would prefer to see her at home; Rachel made one visit, my father-in-law would never go. And some months after Vanessa had settled we began bringing her home for the day. Convinced we must continue as a family, we brought her back often. A routine developed: I would fetch her from Cranage and Sid would take her back in the evening when I found it difficult to drive along the unlit country roads. In addition, she always came home for birthdays and parties.

The staff told us Vanessa seemed livelier when she returned from school at the end of the morning. But I waited until she'd been there some weeks before I paid the school a visit. It had been a cinema, its low redbrick buildings reminding me of my primary school. The difference here was that all the doors were locked.

The little classrooms were decorated with mobiles and pictures, the windows also used as a display area, especially at Christmas. At my first visit I was delighted to see there were only six or seven children in Vanessa's class. A summary of each child's characteristics was pinned on a notice board together with a photograph showing how each one should be carried. There was a chart of activities to encourage, with notes underscored in red ink about unacceptable behaviour.

'Look,' said her teacher, 'I've noted here that we must ignore Vanessa's temper tantrums if she doesn't get all the attention she wants, the second she wants.'

I grinned. 'I'm glad you've done that.'

They would soon discover that her tremendous spasm, the throwing back of her head and arms was something she could control voluntarily and they ignored it.

'Nobody removes her from her chair until she's stopped crying.' Her teacher laughed. 'I must tell you, I was scared of hurting her mouth when I first fed her, she seemed so fragile. But she isn't, at all.'

'She loves rough-and-tumble play, and being tickled and rolled,' I said. 'Whatever you do like that must be good for her.'

I didn't stay long, I drove home elated. This was the moment when I began to let go of my deep sense of guilt.

Christmas at Hazel Villa was something to be seen.

The day room was transformed: long tables were set out in rows filling the room. Decorated with paper tablecloths, streamers, paper hats and crackers, a traditional English high tea was laid out for parents and children to enjoy. Sausage rolls, mushroom patties, sandwiches, jellies and trifle, Christmas cake, mince pies crammed every space, and we were invited to sit down by the staff all wearing their Father Christmas red hats and carrying round trays of sherry and wine for the adults, or handing out sweets to the children.

It was our first meeting with many of the parents, who told me they had travelled long distances to be with their children. They were older than us, and I understood why they made such infrequent visits. Having a child so strange in appearance, so difficult to handle was a great burden. At the Christmas party, Anthony and Richard looked at me with fear in their eyes. People were smoking, the air seemed hazy, and there was so much noise, so many strange faces. It was utterly alien to them, and for several years afterwards I would go on my own until they were old enough to come, taking advantage of the boxes of

Quality Street chocolates which they'd stuff into their pockets while I was intent on Vanessa.

She had settled into this new, unchanging life in Cranage Hall Hospital and I had accepted it in my heart.

Chapter 26

On that terrible day in May 1974, when I made the anguished call to my friend, saying I could no longer look after Vanessa, she had replied, 'She is seven years old. All children begin to separate themselves from their mother at this age, it's the seven-year cycle of growth and maturation. Surely you don't want to stop her developing?'

The words stayed with me, but I couldn't believe them. I felt that I had thrown Vanessa out of the house, that I had rejected her. That I had killed her.

Two years later, I began to see there was truth in what Jessica had said. Extraordinary as it might seem, Vanessa was making a journey. A journey of independence. How could that be? How could a child who could barely lift her head, sit or hold a cup in her hands do such a thing?

It started soon after she went to Hazel Villa and she became one of the thirty children on the ward. No longer could she demand attention and get it. She would smile at the care attendants, they'd smile at her. That was her attention. There was three or four busy, frequently harried nursing staff that would dress, wash and feed her. Paid staff who might have been resentful or miserable as they ruminated over their own issues while they gave her food. At Pictor she'd been fed by loving volunteers, while at home in the evening, it was I who gave her meals, or perhaps Anneliese, where food meant love. But she came to accept being fed by people who did this as part of their work.

Vanessa's world consisted of the ward, what little she could see of it, and her mornings in school. Of course, there were our visits, and her times at home, all of which she loved. A doorway near her bed opened onto the sluices with their smell of bleach and industrial disinfectant that could never mask their true purpose, and later, whenever I caught a whiff in some other institution, I would be back in Hazel Villa. The care staff's work was heavy and grinding. Most of the children were teenagers, doubly incontinent, unaware of the nurses' work, cleaning them up, changing their nappies, lifting them in and out of wheelchairs.

Vanessa was certainly aware of the others, especially once she'd started school. But while she lay on her bed in the early months, she couldn't have seen the three bed-bound people further along the row, and whom I began to notice every visit. There were two young boys, brothers who had Hunter's disease, a degenerative condition which Mrs Booth told me meant they would die in their teens. And at the end of the row, in a corner beneath the window, was someone rolled in a blanket or sheet, their head turned towards the wall. A woman would visit this person, we began to talk and I learned that he was her son. One day, I caught sight of him and had to stifle a gasp. His face was a dark, oval shape with hollows for his eyes and an outline for the nose, only his mouth was visible. But his mother, coming with such devotion, was always smiling. I was so thankful of Vanessa's ability to express her feelings, to engage with people.

But there were occasions when she needed me to speak for her. One of these was eighteen months after she had gone to Cranage Hospital.

A heat wave began in May, followed by the hottest summer on record. Lately, she'd been listless, lacklustre, and I was worried. I arrived one afternoon and was shocked – her face had a greyish tinge, her eyes were half closed. There was no wriggle, no shout of recognition. I lifted her up and her mouth turned into an angry grimace. She was a rigid doll in my arms, fragile and light. Had something happened? Was she ill? Or was it hunger?

I walked over to the nurse's table where Mrs Caldwell was dozing in the heat. We exchanged the usual platitudes about the weather and I asked her how Vanessa had been since I was last there.

'She hasn't had much to say for herself.'

I hesitated but conscious of how frail my daughter felt in my arms, I decided to take the plunge, even if it suggested they weren't looking after her properly, 'Do you think she's lost a little weight?'

Mrs Caldwell bristled, 'She's exactly the same as when I weighed her two weeks ago.'

'I just wondered.'

I had brought some stewed fruit and cereal for Vanessa, a little treat, and she couldn't get enough of it. Devouring every spoonful, her eyes fixed on the plate. She was starving. That evening, I waited until the boys were in bed before I told Sid.

'What will you do?'

Suddenly, I was angry with him. Why was it always me who had to solve the children's problems?

'I have no idea,' I retorted. 'You suggest something.'

'What about her school?' He gave me a baleful look. 'Find out what they think.'

I frowned. 'Wouldn't that go behind the back of the nursing staff?'

'Don't see why. Aren't they supposed to work together as a team?'

Once again he'd made a practical suggestion and I accepted it. 'You're right. I'll go and talk to her teachers tomorrow.'

Next morning, with Richard stowed in the car seat, I sped back to Cranage and marched directly to the school. I rang the outer doorbell and the headmaster ushered us in. When I explained the reason for my unexpected visit, he nodded soberly, 'Why don't we go to her classroom? Have a word with her teacher.'

Through the classroom door I could see Vanessa lying on her tummy across a beanbag. The headmaster spoke to her teacher, and Richard ran in. Crouching beside Vanessa, he patted her on the shoulder. 'Hello, Nessa.'

She ignored him. My heart plummeted. With a worried little frown, he grabbed my hand as the teacher was saying, 'So nice to see you, Mrs Stern. I understand there's a problem.'

Telling her my fears, I ended, 'I'm sure she's lost weight. And she's so unresponsive.'

'I'm afraid we agree with you.' Her gaze was serious. 'She's hungry when she arrives at school so we've been giving her *Complan*. You know, the protein food you make up with water or liquid? A mug full when she comes. Another before she goes back to the ward.'

'Complan?' My voice rose. 'But what are they giving her to eat?'

'Bowls of cereal and jars of baby dinners, only sufficient for a nine-month-old child.'

I let out a muffled cry, but conscious of Richard close to me, and eager not to increase his anxiety, I folded my lips. 'That's ridiculous.' I felt heat rising in my face, my heart booming with anger. 'What can I do?'

'If I were you, I'd make a complaint to Doctor Kanjilal, the medical superintendent.' Her face softened. 'He's a lovely man. His only concern is for his patients. Make an appointment to see him.'

I felt the anger disperse now that I had a course of action. 'Thank you so much. I'll phone the moment we get home.' I caught her hand. 'I knew you'd help us.'

I phoned the superintendent's secretary, and to my relief and astonishment, she asked me to come in the following morning. This would be my third trip along the motorway. I found the office block and was directed to the medical superintendent's room, where he saw me at once.

A very gentle man in his late forties, Doctor Kanjilal was tall, slightly stooped, and with fine features. 'What can I do for you, Mrs Stern?' he asked, indicating a chair in front of his desk.

I told him my story and he took notes, finally sitting back and nodding. 'We'll attend to this right away. I'll have a word with the dietician but meanwhile I'll ask the staff at Hazel Villa to give her more frequent feeds.'

'That's wonderful. Thank you.'

He gave me a weary smile. 'I'm sure you realise how hard it is on the children's wards with constantly changing staff, plus the system of alternating shifts that operates in this hospital, all of which disturb those who need special feeding.' He paused, brightened a little. 'Maybe giving her protein reinforcements will build her up again?'

'I used to add Farlene to her drinks. Perhaps you can do this too?'

'Farlene, did you say?' He jotted it down. 'So, is there anything else you wish to discuss with me?'

'I don't think so. Thank you for seeing me so quickly. I had no idea it could be possible in a hospital of this size, or in any hospital.'

'It's best to solve problems as soon as they arrive, don't you think?' He smiled.

Vanessa began to regain her weight and her sense of well-being, thanks to Doctor Kanjilal taking me seriously.

When Vanessa was small, I learned to be bold, pestering doctors or physiotherapists for things she needed until I got them. Now, like my daughter, I had to be patient, to negotiate, but then made a happy discovery: we had allies in the teaching staff. Not only did they understand the work we'd been doing, but as qualified special teachers, they had similar goals. Mysteriously, Vanessa always identified with them rather than with the children in her class. She insisted on having her drinks at the teachers' table while the others had theirs sitting in their wheelchairs.

I did wonder if this was a remnant of the close, responsive relationship we'd had in the early years – or was that some far-fetched idea of mine. Whatever the reason, she communicated with her teachers, they worked with her, and she received attention, stimulation, praise and rewards. Going to school all day, in the second year of her life there, she took huge psychological steps as she strove to learn and she blossomed.

This was another stage in her journey of independence, I felt sure, and I was glad about it.

We received school reports, just like any child in an ordinary school. Wonderful reports detailing educational programmes tailored specifically for her. From the start, her teachers recognised that she adored being the centre of attention, smiling and laughing, whereas by frowning and crying, even pouting if she disliked someone, she showed displeasure. We'd known this already but now it had a social significance.

Her teachers discovered things we didn't know: that she could *bite*, albeit with a sucking motion, provided they supported her chin and helped her seal her lips. This was a first step towards speech. That she could raise her arms towards an adult if she expected to be picked up, and that she loved it if an adult tripped up or sneezed. We were thrilled that she had such insightful teachers.

In Vanessa's second report of December 1978 they explained how they had capitalised on her love of being with adults and her sociability by giving her little tasks. She helped to wash the cups, put them away, tidy the table, all enabled by an assistant or helper. A programme which encouraged her to use her hands, for she had to grasp the handle of a cup, as she sat in her wheelchair and then be taken to the sink, where she'd be encouraged to hold a dish mop in one hand, a cup in the other.

All those weeks, months and years we'd spent trying to teach her to pick up bricks, bang drums, put wooden spoons inside bowls, following Doctor Wilson's programme and I had failed. I always believed that her hands lacked feeling. Not at all. It had failed because she wasn't the least bit interested.

The staff also focussed on her obvious communication skills:

We've been working with Vanessa, her new teacher, Mrs Lunt wrote*: to establish a means of communication by eye pointing. A chocolate button and a drink are held at eye level and by looking at one she is able to demonstrate her choice. She is able to discriminate and choose when the same objects are represented by pictures on cards.*

Their ultimate goal was to encourage Vanessa to recognise two cards representing *yes* or *no*, so that she could answer simple *yes/no* to questions such as, 'Do you want a drink?' Tears of joy filled my eyes as I read the report.

Vanessa liked all the staff in the hospital school and adored Pauline Lunt. Dark-haired, slim, wearing glasses, she was warm and intuitive. I liked her and greatly respected her empathy and insight towards the children she taught.

In the 1978 report, she wrote: *Vanessa tries very hard to do what is asked of her, and can show great determination and sustained effort. She likes to please and in return enjoys being praised.*

Thank goodness for enthusiastic, loving teachers like Pauline Lunt.

Such a contrast with that fateful diagnosis of the Spastics Society doctor who'd told us Vanessa was ineducable, and I wanted to laugh in his face. To hold the reports up to his nose and cry, 'You were wrong!' Her teachers were finding alternative ways to help her progress, and were succeeding. And what about that supercilious psychologist? I was positive that the tests she used were appropriate for children without disabilities, and here was my justification. If only she'd shown the slightest bit of empathy, but she hadn't.

For some years the school reports were headed *Cranage Hall Hospital School* but in June 1980, I was thrilled to see it had become *Woodlands School*, more intimate, more accessible, and I wondered, was this an indication of changing attitudes towards disabled children? I was sure the idea had come from the staff.

Nevertheless, I had been anxiously noting how Vanessa's body, particularly her legs, were becoming more distorted from lying on the bed for hours, but I could do nothing about it.

Then, good news: a physiotherapist was appointed. Such a great relief and something I had wanted for years. She showed the teaching staff how to pattern Vanessa, which they did four times a day. Not as we'd done years before, when I was teaching her to crawl but to straighten her limbs, to invigorate her. Our daughter loved this activity just as she loved any kind of physical movement, swinging or bouncing up and down, although this was discouraged as it increased her spasm, but stretching up her arms when she was sitting on the floor was fine, making her laugh.

It was seen that our daughter showed her dislike of different members of the nursing or teaching staff very clearly. It became a joke to say, 'Don't let whoever it was feed her today or she'll be in a bad mood all morning.' She began to indicate her needs to her teachers by crying when she was wet, licking her lips when she was thirsty, and chewing and staring at the cupboard when it was biscuit time, and they responded.

And how she benefited from this regular existence where she didn't have to compete with the boys for my attention, and become angry and frustrated with emotions she could never express. Her life was calm; she attended school for six hours a day with people she liked. Returning to the ward at about three o'clock, she'd spend the rest of the day on the bed but she'd had time away, enjoyed stimulation, laughter, challenges, and rewards. A satisfying life, more secure than that of many children in the wider world.

One afternoon our eyes were opened to something amazing: the unexpected but wonderful influence she exerted on hospital life, simply by being herself.

We were going *en famille* to visit her. Picnics in a field close to the motorway had become a family treat, especially when Sid came too.

Arriving early at Hazel Villa, we went through the day room, Anthony marching ahead, and Richard throwing an apprehensive look at the children in wheelchairs, and rushing back to grab my hand. Leading the way through the swing door, Anthony stopped, and shot me a look of surprise. Someone was sitting by Vanessa's bed. Small and round, nodding and smiling. With black hair cut in pudding basin style, and rosy red cheeks, the little woman wore a longish skirt covered by an apron.

'Who's that, Mummy?' He pointed at her.

I caught hold of his hand. 'Mustn't point, Anthony.'

'But *who* is it?'

Hearing our voices, Vanessa gave a great shout, and wriggled and moved about on the bed while the woman grinned at her.

'Hello,' I smiled. As I approached, realisation dawned. She had Down syndrome and was a patient in the hospital.

'Hello, Mrs Stern.' A voice from behind me and Mrs Booth stopped on her way to the sluice. 'Have you met Polly? She's Vanessa's friend.'

'Her friend? How lovely.' Leaving the boys, who were solemnly watching, I went over to the bed. 'Vanessa, I didn't know you had a friend, and she's called Polly.'

Vanessa grinned away. The boys stared. I turned to them and took their hands.

'Come and say hello.' But they hung back. Turning to Polly, I said, 'How nice to meet you, Polly. These are Vanessa's brothers, Anthony and Richard.'

Anthony eyed Polly warily but Richard told her, 'I've got a friend called Avi.'

They continued to stare with narrowed eyes, but she rose from the chair and with a surprisingly deep voice, announced, 'Going now. Going Vanessa. Bye-bye.' She leant over the bed, aiming a kiss, but missed. Unperturbed, she passed in front of us, disappearing into the day room.

Sid walked through. He gazed at the boys still focused on Polly's departure. 'What's the matter? You two are very quiet.'

'Vanessa's got a friend,' Anthony said, his forehead furrowed. 'I didn't know she had one.'

'She's called Polly,' Richard added. 'Vanessa and Polly. Polly and Vanessa.' He shot a solemn look at his dad.

'You have friends and I'm very glad Vanessa has a friend in Cranage Hospital. Someone who likes being with her.'

'And does Vanessa like being with her?' said Anthony.

'Don't you like being with your friends?'

They both nodded. Reassured, they grinned, then hanging over Vanessa's bed together, they asked if she wanted to come and play in the field.

With Vanessa on my knee and the boys strapped in their car seats, we made our short journey to the field. Sitting in the front seat of the car, I would give Vanessa her meal while the boys ate their sandwiches and chocolate biscuits. Then they would play hide and seek or football and Vanessa insisted on joining them. With my hands beneath her arms, I would carry her with her legs dangling, helping her kick the ball to the boys, even to Daddy. She adored this, screaming and laughing with excitement.

Back in Hazel Villa, we saw Mrs Booth talking with a group of people standing beside Vanessa's empty bed. 'There you are,' she called. 'The trainee nurses have been waiting to see your daughter.'

I shot her a look of surprise. An older woman emerged from the group. 'I hope you don't mind if we visit Vanessa. We wouldn't like to spoil your afternoon.'

'Just bringing her back,' I said uncertainly.

'I had better explain. I always bring the student mental health nurses at Cranage Nursing School to visit patients. Normally we'd come on a weekday, but I'm on leave from tomorrow, and I did want them to meet your daughter.'

I exchanged a half smile with Sid. Now he stepped forward. 'Perhaps I should take the boys to the car, while you talk?'

'It's Vanessa they want to see.' And she was straining to look at them while in my arms. 'Sorry, I must put her on the bed. She's getting really heavy.'

Vanessa shouted and this broke the tension. The students, three women and two men, watched as I laid her down carefully.

'I always bring the students,' said the supervisor, 'because Vanessa has had so much stimulation that despite her considerable disability, she has great communication skills. Using her eyes, even though she has no language.'

Approaching the bed, everyone smiled at Vanessa who obliged them with her usual enormous beam. All our work wasn't in vain after all, I thought, as I watched. She's actually teaching the teachers!

As we drove back, Anthony piped up: 'Why were those people looking at Vanessa?'

I reminded them of how she smiled, how others responded to her. 'Those people are learning to be special nurses who'll look after children like Vanessa.' I added, 'Because we all talked and played and showed Vanessa different things, she understands what people say. She shows what she wants by staring at it. She knows a lot.'

'And she has a friend,' he added thoughtfully. 'She knows loads of people. Everyone knows Vanessa.'

I made another surprising discovery – I was making a journey, too.

It was Rachel who pinpointed the physical change in me. Like my parents, the Sterns had supported us in every possible way. Now they could enjoy their grandsons while still being devoted to Vanessa. Most Saturday afternoons, when I didn't go to Cranage, we'd take the boys to visit them. Always so hospitable, it was Rachel's pleasure to spoil us with food, in true Jewish grandmother fashion. That day, almost a year after Vanessa had gone away, Rachel lifted her cup of tea but setting it back on the saucer, she threw me a serious look, and I wondered what was coming next.

'What a change in you,' she said, laying her hand on my arm. 'You were half a person when Vanessa was at home. Exhausted by two o'clock in the afternoon. White faced in the evening. Look at you now, alive again.'

'I didn't realise that,' I said, 'but I do feel better.'

'Good job,' she concluded. Giving me a satisfied nod, she proceeded to drink her tea.

Chapter 26

My mother might have recognised more profound aspects to the changes in me but I knew she would never mention anything unless I brought up the subject. She might have seen that by letting Vanessa go away, I was loosening the extreme bonds of attachment we had – bonds of love it was true, but which were intense, even obsessive. It was healthier for us all when I let her go, relinquishing most of the responsibility, entrusting her to others.

Clearly, in the first few months, I couldn't have intervened in her life at Hazel Villa even if I had wanted to. Exhausted, full of grief, I didn't realise it might also encompass a grief for that special relationship we'd had from the beginning. I was grieving for myself. Now I was able to turn towards Sid and the boys and embrace their world.

Chapter 27

I often wondered if I'd have chosen a different spiritual path if we'd lived somewhere else. During one of our holidays we camped near Fréjus in the south of France and Sid was so taken with the place, he told me he wouldn't go back to Manchester, and since I would earn more money teaching English than he did as a pharmacist, we could live on that. Just supposing this had happened, I might have renewed my fascination with Catholicism; or if we had gone to live in one of the outer Scottish islands, another location that appealed to Sid, I might have been drawn to a different spiritual process, not paganism exactly but something similar. I'm sure we are influenced by so many things: where we live, whom we meet, what inspires us. But from the moment I found myself whispering, 'Awake, awake, Dvora!' to our baby when she was three days old, I was being led along a path to discover my religious heritage with Vanessa as my teacher.

Was it by chance that Ros and Alan, and Tina and Ralph, two couples on a spiritual journey something like my own, had come to live nearby, and become significant in our lives? Of course my husband wasn't in the running for spiritual enlightenment but he and Alan had a love of music in common, Ros and Tina were teachers, and Ralph was a larger-than-life character who engaged with everyone he met. What is more, especially in the case of Ralph and Tina, we were socialists.

They took me along to lectures and discussions on the practise of Judaism; they lent me books, and introduced us to others who had come to live near the synagogue in order to respect the Sabbath. I began to attend more frequently which made me feel part of the local community and of the wider community of the Jewish people, while their ancient history and cultural background fascinated me. This growing sense of a Jewish self offered me the roots I had always wanted.

Then there was Transcendental Meditation, taken up by the Beatles in 1967. I discovered it in 1975 when I was still overcome with guilt and grief at sending Vanessa into residential care. Several months after she went away I joined the course. By chance, the teacher told me that it often helped parents of handicapped children. When I asked her if it would help parents who'd sent their child into residential care, she naturally looked confused. To cover her feelings she said, 'Of course. I do recommend you try it.'

There was a charge which was unusual for a spiritual practice and I paid what would now be the equivalent of sixty pounds; I followed the course, and was given my mantra, which I repeated for twenty minutes morning and evening. I would go into Vanessa's room, rest my hands upwards on my knees, (as instructed) count the two minutes' preparation time, and recite the mantra. There were days when I lost awareness of my body, becoming only conscious of the small space in the centre of my forehead. I would have to remind myself to end the meditation but I would come out of it with my mind clear and centred.

By 1978, Vanessa had been living in Hazel Villa for three years. Her arrival in my life had been complex and challenging but had given me direction and purpose. Then came the boys, who occupied my days entirely while they were small. Evenings and weekends were taken up with the family's needs; I had left my job in the local adult centre and found two days a week teaching in a private school for little girls.

I had time to myself at last. Meditation and learning about Jewish life almost like a convert helped me tremendously but I needed something practical and fulfilling during the day. The answer came like a bolt from the blue. For several years we had been motor caravanning with the boys, though sadly without Vanessa, the original purpose of the van. Wherever we went – to Dordogne, Brittany, Paris – we'd meet up with Elisabeth and André, once even with Béatrice and her brood of little boys, we would also visit Michèle and her husband André, in the tiny village where they lived near Blois. The Easter we had arrived in Gatley in 1969, they had been the first visitors to our new house.

This particular holiday in August 1978, we were eating supper in the beautiful kitchen Michèle's husband had built, when we heard the sound of footsteps marching along outside. Then a harsh woman's voice: 'Keep walking. Do not stop.'

'Who are they?' I asked Michèle, a spark of apprehension making my heart beat faster.

'They're from the Insane Institution at the far side of the village.'

'I would like to see. Excuse me, Michèle, I'll be only a couple of minutes.'

I skirted the house and walked to the tall wooden gate which gave directly onto the road, and peered through the slats. Young people, dressed in *blousons*, the routine blue overalls worn by all children in French schools, filed along the rough reddish-hued road. Opening the gate gingerly, I came face to face with a young Down syndrome boy, a narrow rope wound around his waist attaching him to the girl behind. Her angular vacant face spoke of a learning disability. Then I saw they were all tied together in a chain. Leading them, pushing a wheelchair, was a grey-haired heavyset man. In the wheelchair was a scrawny boy of about fifteen, his eyes rolling up into his head. Bringing up the rear was the hatchet faced teacher or supervisor, whose voice I must have heard from the kitchen. She wore a *kepi,* a kind of flat hat, and a *chatelaine*, a chain of keys, knives, and scissors which jangled at her waist. Those children were tied together like animals.

That night in the camper van, while the boys slept, I whispered heatedly to Sid, 'I have to do something about it. I just *have* to.'

Sid said. 'You can't run around the world telling people there's nothing wrong with disabled children, that they shouldn't be tied together, even if it seems criminal to us.'

'I'll do something.'

As we boarded the ferry, I thought about these children, hidden away, feared and rejected. But they were *people*, loving and wanting to be loved. As though my subconscious had finally prepared me, watching the dark blue and grey of the waves unfurling and slipping away as we approached Newhaven, an idea leapt into my mind. 'I shall *write* about her,' I declared to Sid standing beside me.

'About whom?' he said.

'Who do you think?' I was glowing with certainty. 'That way I can show the world the truth about having a handicapped child.'

I decided to write an account of our lives with her up till that time. It would eventually become the blueprint for this memoir. I went on to write short fiction and even attempted a play. Eventually I wrote a story about the Batmitzvah of a disabled child exactly like our daughter. A Batmitzvah ceremony that could never happen for it highlighted the mother's mental state and her painful recognition of reality. I continued to rewrite it until it was published in a small magazine some years later. Published at last!

Around this time I met playwright Deborah Freeman, who encouraged me in my writing. Through her, as an antithesis to my spiritual search, I rediscovered feminism, and we pored over the magazine, *Spare Rib*. Several years younger than I, Debbie was already a feminist while I had grown up in the fifties, with the mind map of the era when girls were expected to become wives and mothers, only occasionally to have careers. Nevertheless, Women's Lib appealed to another part of my personality. Perhaps because my mother and grandmother had been radical women – my Russian grandmother Sophia, an anarchist, my mother, an active socialist who had marched with my father against Mosley and his fascists in the East End of London.

In the magazine I read fiction by distinguished writers like Micheline Wander and Jane Rogers, articles describing demands for women's aid services and changes in abortion laws. Even though it conflicted with Orthodox Judaism where women had carefully defined roles, I loved poring over it. A little bit of defiance. When they put out a call for poems, I sent a short piece, not about Vanessa but about marriage. It was rejected, saying the poem didn't quite work but they understood the sentiment. I wouldn't let this one rejection stop me writing. I became determined to carry on.

The following year, 1979, something extraordinary happened. One morning in early January I answered the telephone and was surprised to hear that a woman called Sharon Gould, a TV researcher who worked with David Elstein, director and producer at Thames Television, wanted to speak to me. They were making a television programme on the subject of Primodos. Would I like to be involved?

The background to the story is this: in 1966 there were no pregnancy tests as such, only the age-old wait for twelve weeks before you could be certain. If you believed you were pregnant, you told nobody in case you miscarried before that time. Pregnancy was still a 'woman's domain' and we wore voluminous smocks and pregnancy dresses as though there was something shameful about it. There were no urine tests and the idea of an instant pregnancy test carried out in your bathroom was the stuff of science fiction. But then Primodos appeared on the scene.

A vivid image came to my mind when I heard the word: Primodos. I saw myself crossing the road to Doctor Burt's surgery, where almost blushing, I'd asked him how I could be sure if I was pregnant. He'd held up a small white box containing two pills and saying. 'Why don't you give them a try?

From then on, we thought no more about it. Only once, I remember, had I mentioned it to a woman waiting with me at the local clinic. She had also taken these tablets but clearly, there was nothing wrong with her little boy bouncing around the waiting room.

Lately, I had begun to read about the *Association for Children Damaged by Hormonal Pregnancy Tests*, in the *Manchester Evening News,* the local evening paper. This claimed that the hormonal pregnancy test tablets, Primodos, had caused birth defects to hundreds of babies and children.

Puzzled, I read an article by Doctor Isabel Gal, a paediatrician doing research, who had noted various disabilities among her patients after mothers had taken Primodos. She had warned the authorities, but her warning was ignored. In April 1978, with the encouragement of the MP Jack Ashley, the Association was set up and many parents joined in order to demand compensation from Scherings, the pharmaceutical company, who had manufactured the pills. London Weekend Television immediately made *Primodos,* a programme researched by the journalist, Greg Dyke.

But I didn't feel or think like the members of the Association. I had such a different understanding of our daughter's disability, I don't know why I got involved. Yet spurred on by my newfound delight in writing, I offered to write to the press if this would help.

Coming out of the blue, the telephone call was so unexpected that I didn't know how to reply. I thought about the other parents, their anger, their desire for compensation and finally I told her that my view of our daughter was worlds apart from theirs.

'I believe she was destined to come to us.' Would she think I was a little mad?

'That's exactly why we'd like to talk to you.'

Her voice was so warm and friendly, I lost my reserve. 'Could you tell me about it?'

'Mrs Stern – or can I call you Susan?'

'Of course you can.' Using someone's first name is everywhere nowadays but unusual at that time.

'This is the thing: we're investigative journalists interested in a story which has moral and maybe political implications. The programme will cover the period from when Doctor Gal finished her research up to the present day.' I listened but didn't say anything. 'David is the director. He's asked me to contact you. I could pop up to Manchester for an initial chat and if you felt comfortable, David will interview you, and we'd do a short filming.'

'Would I need to go to London?'

'No, we'd interview you at home. Perhaps meet your daughter if that's possible.'

'I'm not sure. Can I think about it?'

'Absolutely. I'll call you at the end of the week. Don't feel any pressure to be involved if you don't want to.'

First thoughts – there was something flattering, exciting, about being in a television programme. Then I asked myself whether it was right for me to take part. Surely my complex view of Vanessa might undermine the thrust of the programme? I didn't know the others or what they thought, but I had read how angry they were, how they compared their situation with that of children affected by thalidomide.

'What shall I do?' I asked Sid that evening. 'Would I be deluded to say yes?'

'I don't know. Do it, if you think it would help.'

For days, I vacillated. By joining the association out of sympathy with the other parents, I had drifted into a situation that made me feel conflicted. How illogical that was, considering my views, fearful of saying what I believed to the world – that Vanessa was destined to come to us. What people would call 'loony.' Worse, this had called up my guilt and grief at sending her into residential care when the other parents still had their children at home.

I couldn't do it. When Sharon Gould telephoned, I would say I wouldn't take part.

But then two things happened.

On Thursday evening I went to a religious talk at a friend's house. The rabbi told us that in the Torah, the religious teachings, were references to reincarnation, to the transmigration of souls, which he called *gilgul*. Translated as, 'the turning wheel'. If you failed to learn something essential to your soul in this life, you were bound to return.

I shivered. Here was an authoritative Jewish belief which echoed my own.

If this were not enough, the following day I did a long meditation, asking myself whether I should take part in the programme. In the clarity of my mind came the thought that if I could help one person with my way of thinking, being in the programme would be worthwhile. They might be able to let go of their bitterness. I finished the meditation feeling strong, with a sense of freedom, and valuable in a way I hadn't done for ages.

When Sharon phoned that evening I told her that *yes*, I wanted to be part of the programme. But she had to understand it was nothing to do with claiming compensation.

She came, and I liked her tremendously. Fair haired, intelligent, engaging, and very easy to talk to, she sat at the kitchen table with a reporter's pad in front of her, taking notes as I explained where, when, what we did with Vanessa. She was very interested in the work I had done in the early years, continuing to ask many questions. When I told her how we'd had to send our daughter into residential care, tears filled my eyes, and I couldn't carry on.

'I didn't mean to upset you. I'm so sorry. But I have enough already.'

So we drank coffee, chatted, and eventually she left to interview another parent in Birmingham. At the door she said, 'It's been especially fascinating to hear how you worked with Vanessa. I'm certain David will want to meet you.'

'I've just finished writing a short account of our life with her. Would you like to read it?'

Her eyes lit up. 'That would be fantastic.'

Because I had written in long hand I'd had it typed up professionally and I gave her the top copy. Then we called a cab and as she got in, she waved and smiled as though we were old friends. How positive she is, I thought as I closed the door.

When David Elstein arrived, charming, smiling, to interview me, I drove him to a local Indian restaurant where we sat in one of those intimate alcoves with the red plush imitation tapestry walls found in such places. Secure in our privacy, I told him about Vanessa, her birth, our work with Doctor Wilson, the arrival of the boys and the trauma of sending her away.

His eyes intent, he listened closely as I talked. A little younger than me, I guessed, extraordinarily intelligent I could tell, he was as warm and engaging as his researcher.

When I finished, he leaned towards me, his gaze serious. 'What is your opinion of the pregnancy test tablets?'

It threw me for a moment. Dipping my head, I avoided his gaze until I could reply. 'From what we've read,' I said at last, 'I understand the other children have mainly heart defects. That's why they're making claims against the pharmaceutical company. Only a few have cerebral palsy like Vanessa.' Biting my lip, I turned my gaze to the tiny dishes of hors d'oeuvres and a half-eaten plate of golden rice, while I felt the pounding in my heart. 'We've virtually never thought about the tablets since she was born.' I threw him a sombre look. 'I suppose it's possible. But so terrible if this were the only cause.' I inhaled quickly, clasping my hands together to banish such a crippling thought. I hesitated. 'I see her so differently.'

'What does your husband think?'

'About Primodos?' I frowned. 'He says we can't know.'

'Tell me how you view Vanessa.'

With gathering certainty, I told him my beliefs in the plurality of lives and about reincarnation, which interested him enormously. 'But how can I be in the programme?' I demanded. 'My views are so far from those of the other parents. Won't mine be an apology for the pharmaceutical company?'

'Hardly. I'm eager to represent everyone's understanding. I would be so glad if you could share your views. Would you?'

Gripping the table with my hands, I looked at him directly; his eyes were kind, encouraging. I smiled. A little frightened, a little uneasy, I agreed to do it.

The television crew set up in our front room the following day, and filmed the interview. Afterwards David appeared to be very pleased, thanking me, smiling, shaking hands with Sid who was looking after the boys, telling us they would let us know when it came out. They left, but for months afterwards, there was only silence.

Then a letter from Sharon Gould with startling news: the film had been banned, not allowed to be shown. Too many political and material complications. In court, the pharmaceutical firm claimed it would cause problems to the reputation of the contraceptive pill they also produced. The contest between Thames Television and the pharmaceutical manufacturers went to the House of Lords, two out of three of whom were favourable to the firm's arguments. Only Lord Denning spoke on behalf of David Elstein and his programme. Somewhere in whatever format Thames Television became, the film would remain filed away, seen only by the television crew, one or two members of the association representing the parents, three members of the House of Lords.

I was relieved. I had come to such a different understanding of our daughter from the others, while identifying with their grief. Especially now that all was progressing so well for Vanessa in her life in Cranage Hall Hospital.

Around this time, Sid was becoming restless with the house, seeking to move somewhere different. The kind of house we wanted locally was beyond our budget and we chose to remodel ours, dividing the long kitchen into two, extending the dining room which would become a lovely light room with French windows, opening onto the garden. The boys had abandoned the kitchen/playroom long before, spending all their time in the front room, watching television, with Anthony playing on his new Spectrum computer. It seemed better to create new spaces that suited us. We'd make a small room overlooking the front of the house, becoming sometimes a music room, sometimes a tiny sitting room. It was all change.

It would have a purpose that we could never have envisaged.

Chapter 28

The United Nations had declared 1981 to be *The Year of Disabled Persons.*

In March, a reporter from a local Jewish newspaper called, asking if I would like to be interviewed. Delighted to tell our story, I agreed but when I read her article the following Friday, I was furious: she had described some horribly disabled child, a non-person. Not Vanessa. Perhaps if the reporter had seen the charismatic little person behind the twisted body, her piece would have been closer to the truth.

I was so angry I wrote my own article in response. It was published in the rival Jewish newspaper and apparently read so well, friends asked why I didn't send it to a national paper. Recalling the adage in *The Power of Positive Thinking*: 'Be bold and mighty forces will come to your aid.' I sent it to *The Guardian*, and they liked it.

In August, *Afternoon Tea with Vanessa* appeared on the *Guardian Women's* page. I was paid one hundred pounds for it, a truly extraordinary sum. It was my first glorious taste of being published in such a prestigious newspaper. Here's an extract from it:

…We reach the little cafe where we always have afternoon tea. It's full of cyclists in bright gear and families out for a Sunday ride. Good, there's room in the corner. Someone closes the door behind us, people nod and smile; we are regulars.

'Scrambled eggs, baked beans and a slice of bread. A pot of tea, and may we use the feeder cup please?' I say to the smiling woman who's come to take our order. Now I prop Vanessa up on my knee. If she sits with her back to me facing the room, I can support her with my body. I tuck her head under my chin, another anchor for her heavy head. But she's restless. Her body taut with anticipation, her eyes wide and directed towards the kitchen, she twists her head away and gazes at me beseechingly. She's licking her lips once more.

'I know you don't want to wait for your tea, but you must. Just like everyone else.'

Damn, I think, I've forgotten to borrow a nappy to use as a bib. I'll have to exhaust the tumbler full of paper napkins on the table.

Juggling the teapot, feeder cup and Vanessa, I manage to pour a cup of tea for each one of us. She drinks noisily, so much of it dribbling down her chin. When I investigate later, I find a large brown stain on her vest where half the liquid has come to rest.

Still holding her with my left arm, bottom on my knee, legs dangling over it, I mash up eggs, beans and bread to a pulp, and with a handful of tissues forming a pad under her chin I begin to feed her. She has a tongue thrust. As soon as food reaches her tongue, this pushes the food out. But there's a knack, once learned, which makes feeding effective. Twenty minutes later, she stops to stare at a group of cyclists who joke and chat as they go to the door. 'Would you like an orange for the little boy?'

'Well, she's a girl actually, and thank you, but she can't eat it.'

More smiles from the cyclists. Vanessa strains to watch them go. She likes men. I believe she really prefers the male nurses. When someone asks me how old she is and I say that she's *fourteen, the person tells me she looks three or four years old. Then, if they ask me how it happened, Vanessa reacts violently, frowning and stiffening in my arms. She stops eating and makes her noise for no. She certainly understands and I must tell this person quickly that it's a very long story. And I say nothing of the early days – the difficult pregnancy, the complex delivery or the realisation at five months that she would be a very handicapped child.*

My daughter would sit with me forever. But we must go.

We manage door, car door, car seat and belt and drive slowly back to the hospital. As much as I enjoy the visit to my daughter, the return always grieves me. For I must leave her and go back to the everyday world and all it entails. Vanessa has already had seven years of family life, four of which were hers entirely, night and day....

'Here we are,' I say brightly when we reach the hospital, and I sit with her on my knee beside her bed. I can't go yet. For thirty minutes I let her suck at a small bar of white chocolate. Then I place her on the bed, her eyes fill with tears and she makes a lip. She's going to cry. I kiss her and the charge nurse picks her up, and she laughs.

I slip away. In the dark I make the return journey down the motorway, my thoughts ticking over with the miles. She's happy there. She is much loved and she returns it. Life at home would be less pleasant for her than it is now.

But if only she didn't live in a hospital. If only there were smaller units near to towns. If she could live in some homely family unit where she would have more visitors, then more of us would benefit. I dream of many small homes being built for all those children now living in the hospital. Their lives would be so much brighter.

I wasn't the only one who believed it was socially and morally wrong for people to be hidden away in such places. There were murmurs from the teaching staff that many of the children, including Vanessa, might be relocated into the community. Someone even mentioned a small house in Cheadle Hume, barely a fifteen minute drive from us – but they warned me to keep it to ourselves. Vanessa might live nearby? I hardly dared believe it would happen. It was too good to be true.

In September, the time of the Jewish New Year, I saw that Stockport Spastics Society was seeking a head teacher for a small local school. I was longing for something new and this seemed such a great opportunity. With all my experience with Vanessa, knowing other hospital children, my teaching work with people of all ages, surely I stood a chance? I phoned, and was delighted when they asked me to an interview on Saturday the third of October. A confirmatory letter followed and I agreed to go along.

Then, coincidentally I heard a rabbi talking of the traditional Jewish belief in the Good and Evil inclinations that it is believed we all had. There was the *Yetzer ha Tov*, the little spirit of good inclination sitting on the right shoulder, who would say, 'Don't do this. It's not good for your soul,' while the *Yetzer Hara*, the bad inclination, would argue, 'Why don't you do it? It's not such a terrible thing, and you'd love to do whatever it was.'

I would immediately experience the terrible power of these duelling spirits, urging me in opposite directions, when, glancing again at the interview letter, my heart began to race. Horrible realisation dawned. Saturday 3rd of October was one of the most important Sabbaths of the Jewish year, if not *the* most important. Called *Shabbat Shuvah*, the Sabbath of return, it came between Rosh Hashanah and Yom Kippur, the acme of the period for examination of one's misdeeds, shortcomings, and sins.

I read and re-read the letter. The interview was two days away. On Friday, feeling my heart curl up inside me, I knew I should not attend the interview. Considering all I was absorbing about Jewish practice, it would be crazy, and I would regret it. Decision made, I phoned the Spastics Society – but there was no answer. What could I do now since the interview was the following day? I would just have to go.

Saturday morning – Sid was at work, the boys watching television. I lay down on the bed, anxiety fuelling my indecision. I argued with myself, first one way, then the other, with something like a surge of black smoke of anxiety filling my eyes, my mind, my thoughts while my heartbeat raced and raced.

I lay there, my eyes half closed, my stomach taut, over breathing, and then something happened.

I had a vision of Vanessa.

She was there, in front of me, as though walking towards me through the air. A dark shawl over her head like the one we'd draped round her head and shoulders against the hot sun. But now she was a tiny skeleton with dark eye sockets. Smiling and smiling as she came nearer and nearer. I felt myself grow rigid, my heart almost leaping into my mouth. I sensed she was coming for a reason. I shut my eyes, and when I opened them, she was there no longer.

My heart told me this was a message. She was telling me she would die very soon. I knew in the depths of me this was so. The soft September light beamed through the windows, my hands were ice-cold. I trembled, and all thoughts of the interview fled.

I told nobody.

In the end I went, but so shaken I behaved like an imbecile, barely able to speak, and naturally, I didn't get the post.

And so 1981 passed, my vision always lingering in my mind. Yet strangely, this was the most beautiful year for Vanessa. Her school report was the longest and most complex we had ever received. It was glowing and her teachers were delighted with all of her achievements.

We read about how they were teaching her to communicate the word *yes*. Any sound she made was acceptable. She was awarded a star and whoever worked with her would repeat, *Vanessa says yes* whenever appropriate. She was learning that closing her eyes meant *No, I don't want it*. She was responding to their verbal requests: *Give me your hand. Put your tongue in. Smile good morning.*

They had even created a special seating module where she could sit with the others at the table, taking part in all their activities. She could move her arms a little, and now she did hand painting and modelling with clay, relishing her every achievement. Most remarkable was the head support they had devised, attached to her seating module. It formed part of the contact switch which Vanessa was learning to operate by touching the side of the support with a metal button sewn on her hat. The intention was to teach her how to operate battery toys and a tape recorder. It was truly amazing, and Vanessa was blossoming with health, enormously happy at school, on the ward and even when we brought her home.

It was truly her wonderful year.

Sid and I were delighted, thrilled, to read of the progress they'd achieved.

'We'll have to go and see her use this battery thing after the holidays,' I said to him. 'I can't believe it.' I was so moved I had to disappear into the hall to wipe the tears from my face.

From that moment, all memory of the little skeleton disappeared. Our precious Vanessa was making such wonderful progress. We were unbelievably grateful to the school, the teaching staff, and the devoted assistants on Hazel Villa.

But then on New Year's Eve, I dreamed I was travelling over snowbound mountains, on and on, trying to reach Vanessa, but as I neared where I thought she was, the path turned towards more mountains. The dream changed, repeated itself. I searched and searched, but I could never find her.

Chapter 29

Afterwards, afterwards, I would wonder why every heightened second of that week wasn't etched forever in my heart. But it wasn't like that. Not for any of us. What we remembered was dark, hazy. Occasional scenes, things people said to us. There was no continuity. Nothing was clear.

The phone call at half past five, I remember that, and the words of one of the staff at Hazel Villa when I picked up the receiver. I think I was making shepherd's pie, our usual Monday evening meal. I hadn't seen Vanessa for three weeks; the weather had been so severe, roads and schools in Cheshire had to be closed, but now there was a thaw, and I was planning to go the following weekend.

Richard had come in, saying he was starving, 'And when's dinner ready?'

'Twenty minutes. Surely you can wait?' I was mashing the potato for the topping before putting the dish in the oven. He disappeared just as the phone rang.

I snatched up the receiver, 'Yes, it's Vanessa's mother here.'

Then I heard Mrs Caldwell's anxious voice. 'A temperature of 105 degrees.'

'What did you say? 105 degrees?' I began to shake.

She told me that Vanessa's temperature had risen all afternoon. She thought it was probably the flu; most of the staff had gone down with it. 'We don't want to take her to the medical unit. You know how she nearly died there last time. But what should we do, Mrs Stern?'

I gathered myself together. 'Have you sponged her?'

'Sponged her?' She sounded confused. 'What do you mean?'

'I do this with the boys when they have a fever. You need a bowl of tepid water – not too cold, and a flannel. Several flannels. Dip them in the water, squeeze them out and place them on Vanessa's face and neck. The flannels should absorb the heat. I think that'll help.'

'All right, I'll try that.'

'We'll come as soon as we can. My husband gets home just before seven.'

I forgot about the shepherd's pie. I tried again and again to get through to Sid but the number was always engaged. He was probably phoning the order to the wholesalers for the next day. I was very worried because I knew 105 degrees was dangerously high. This stayed in my mind.

The potatoes had congealed in the saucepan, the mincemeat gone cold in the Pyrex dish. The boys had fish fingers and baked beans for their tea.

I also remember sitting on the windowsill, the curtains drawn back as I waited for Sid to appear round the corner, willing him to come. When he opened the front door, my face told him everything.

'What is it?' He closed the door behind him.

'They phoned from Cranage about an hour ago. Vanessa has a very high temperature. I think we should go.'

'Okay, but I need to eat something.'

'I'll make you a sandwich and a coffee.'

He took off his coat, hung it in the hall. 'What about you? Aren't you eating?'

'I can't. I'll just have a cup of tea.'

'And the boys? Have you got someone to stay with them?'

'Julia from round the corner, she's old enough now. She's fourteen.'

We travelled in silence, the snow finally melted although the car headlights beamed up greying mounds beneath the hedges, drifts of blackened sludge in the fields. The overhanging trees cast threatening shadows as we passed beneath them.

Cranage Hall Hospital again.

Vanessa lay with her eyes closed, her nostrils flared, breathing harshly. I saw dry crusts on her lips, her skin strangely mottled with red patches. Mrs Caldwell said the sponging hadn't helped and when I touched Vanessa's forehead, it was burning. Beside her bed was the bowl of water, a flannel draped over the rim.

'Have you called the doctor?' Sid asked Mrs Caldwell, who was hovering, her eyes anxious. She shook her head. 'I think you should. '

It was well after nine when the doctor arrived. She barely examined Vanessa but asked to use the phone. Through the screen between the nurses' table and Vanessa's bed, I could hear her saying *pneumonia* but then I heard, 'I think toxaemia has set in. I want her admitted at once.'

What did it mean? I turned my shocked gaze to Sid but she came round to speak to us. 'Your daughter is very ill, I'm afraid, and she needs to be hospitalised. I have found a bed for her at Leighton General Hospital. Do you know it?' Sid shook his head, and she explained where it was. Turning to me, she said, 'An ambulance is on its way. Will you go with her, Mrs Stern?'

How could she have asked such a thing? I would have gone to the ends of the earth for Vanessa. 'But can you tell us what it is?' I said.

'Pneumonia, I think. With complications. We'll know for sure with the blood tests. But the symptoms are pretty clear.' She sighed. 'I'm sorry I can't stay to see her into the ambulance. I have another urgent call.'

When she'd gone, Sid told me he'd follow in the car.

A nightmarish journey through the dark, empty country lanes, the ambulance blaring its way, lights flashing. The men had attached an oxygen mask to Vanessa's mouth, so I could barely see her face. As we arrived, I had the impression of a brick building with large windows, built in the sixties, more like extended prefabs than a hospital.

They carried her in on a stretcher but asked me to wait until she'd been admitted. Sid found me, sitting on a chair in the corridor, and after half an hour, we were allowed to go into the ward. Open plan, lights dimmed for sleeping children although I remember none of them. Only our child in a bed, with an empty one either side of her. Already, they'd attached a drip, but she was the same, her breathing harsh, her face oddly flushed.

A little nurse told us they were giving her antibiotics and something to reduce her temperature. Like all children nursed in hospital, they'd removed her nightdress so she wore only a nappy. We sat beside her until it was time to get back for our babysitter.

When I woke next morning, something had changed in me. I was forty-three and believed that I was going through an early menopause like my mother. Whether what I experienced that Tuesday morning was physical, that I was premenstrual, or a psychological response to the shock of Vanessa's illness, I would never know.

Numb, detached, outside of myself, that's how I was. I must have made telephone calls: to the hospital to see how she was, to the school where I worked, saying I wouldn't come in that day, to ask someone to collect the boys after school. But now I have no memory of doing so.

Instead I made this new journey through Cheshire, oddly untroubled, as though it was a normal visit to Cranage Hospital, and not to see my very sick daughter. That feeling of being too calm stayed with me. When I reached Leighton General Hospital, the sister told me that indeed, Vanessa had pneumonia with complications, and they would know better when the labs had analysed the blood tests.

'But she had a comfortable night, and with the antibiotics and the treatment we're giving her, I am glad to say the temperature is falling.'

When I walked round to Vanessa's bed, I saw her eyes open. She made a lip as though to say that she didn't like being there.

'Hello, my darling. I'm so pleased to see you're a little better.'

All Tuesday and Wednesday I sat with her, smiling, talking a little. Sometimes going to the cafeteria for a cup of tea, an occasional sandwich. All the while, I knew I was too calm, that I wasn't recognising the gravity of her situation. I even asked myself if I was indifferent. No, not that, only that I was unnaturally detached. I sat beside her as she struggled, waiting for the infection or whatever it was to diminish, knowing I had lost that precious connection we'd always had. I couldn't sense what she was feeling. All those years of intuitive awareness, of closeness, had dispersed and I didn't know why, or how. I couldn't understand myself. I felt frozen.

And something else horrifies me when I look back – I can't remember giving her food. Did someone feed her? Was she fed only through the drip? Or was she, unbearable thought, deliberately left to starve? And then I remind myself of all they were doing to defeat the pneumonia, the toxaemia. But it wracks me. How can I have forgotten that, of all things?

On Thursday, when I arrived in the ward, she wasn't there. The bed was empty, the sheets and blanket neatly tucked in. Where was she? I ran to the Sister's office where she was checking and refilling the medicine trolley. 'Where's my daughter? Where's Vanessa?'

'Oh, I'm sorry. Has no one told you?'

'No. What's happened?' I felt my body shake.

'She's in the high dependency unit. There was a sudden deterioration in the early hours. We thought it best do everything to support her. Would you like me to take you there?'

It was more like a box than a room; I think there were windows on each side, yet there was also a door. It seemed to be in the centre of the ward, a little way from where she had been.

A high bed where Vanessa lay, shining machines with tubes attached to her nose, her arm. Buzzing, whirring machines, measuring and recording. She was pale now, her eyes closed. I wanted to rush to her, hold her in my arms.

'Should I phone my husband?' I asked anxiously.

The sister's gaze was compassionate, serious. 'That would be a good idea.'

There were public telephones near the entrance. I got through, and told him. I heard the tiny gasp, a sharp intake of breath. 'I'll close the shop. I don't really know the way but I'll find it.'

'How long will you be?'

'Don't know. Probably about two hours.' Of all that happened over these five days, this was Sid's clearest memory, his two-hour cross-country journey from Rochdale to Leighton General Hospital. Not knowing whether...

All day, we took it in turns to sit with her. Her eyes remained closed; we wondered if she was in pain and hoped that the medication filtering through the drip would help. Every so often, a nurse would come in, look at her, then at the machines, and then note something on her folder clipped to the end of the bed.

Once Sid got up and read them.

'What does it say?'

'Only what they've already told us. But the antibiotic is new.'

That gave us a little hope. With Sid being there, my feelings returned, flooding through me, myself again. I would lean over the bed where she was lying, her skin translucent, her face still beautiful, and take her hand, stroking or kissing it, and whisper, 'You'll get better, Vanessa. You can do it. You've done it before.'

Talking her in, as Rachel would have said.

Late on Thursday evening, we forced ourselves to leave. I wanted to stay but there were no facilities for parents to sleep overnight in this hospital.

When we got home, I said, 'We should tell the boys.'

They didn't say much, and I was glad they didn't ask the ultimate question. I knew it was time to tell the family. We hadn't told them yet, hoping that Vanessa would improve. I telephoned my mother and Barbara, my sister, while Sid spoke to his brother, Michael, who knew about Vanessa already because Sid hadn't been at work for two days. Rachel and Abe were on holiday in Tenerife, and Michael said he would contact them.

Then it was Friday.

It was probably Sid's idea to tell the Gabbies how ill Vanessa was. We called Paula, and then took the boys to school, telling them someone would take them to the Gabbies at the end of the day. When we told Paula what was happening, asking if the boys could stay overnight, she was very upset we hadn't said anything before. Afterwards she told us she couldn't work. She cried most of the day.

We returned to Leighton Hospital.

Back in the tiny room, we could see there was no change, no improvement. Vanessa continued to lie without moving, her eyes closed, while the machines whirred and shone and bleeped. And then, towards lunchtime, a doctor came in, shutting the door behind him.

Shooting a serious glance at us both, he said, 'I need to discuss something with you. I'm afraid her kidneys are losing function.

I would like to send her to a renal unit in Liverpool. Would you agree?'

My response stayed with me forever – I didn't want her to go. She was in pain, so ill, so frail that I couldn't bear to increase her suffering. The thought of an ambulance bumping at speed along country roads, round the motorway to Liverpool, with Vanessa bounced and jolted as they drove appalled me. But I didn't say anything, and in the end, it wasn't our decision. An hour later, the doctor returned. 'I'm afraid the consultant at the renal unit will not accept her.'

From that moment, and for the rest of the day, I knelt or sat beside her, holding her hand, urging, imploring her, just as I had done when she was three days old, 'Come on, my darling Vanessa. You can do it. You can get better. Come on, my darling.'

She would make a little grimace, a tiny moan.

Very late on Friday evening, the doctor on the night shift told us to go home, get some rest. We stood up.

'What's going to happen?' I asked him, unable to utter the words.

'We don't know.' His eyes were sombre but he smiled. 'She can still rally.'

Saturday, the thirtieth of January.

It was a quarter to nine – we were just leaving, when the phone rang.

I answered it, such a tumult of noise in my ears, my heart pounding.

'I'm so sorry, Mrs Stern. Vanessa died during the early hours.'

'Yes,' I whispered. I threw an agonised look at Sid, and shook my head. He was standing beside me, his hand on the front door. His face was stricken. 'We're coming.'

She was still in the room when we arrived but the machines were silent.

For some moments, we gazed at her and then Sid covered his eyes with his hand, but I couldn't grasp what I saw – I walked round and round the bed trying to understand, trying to perceive what had happened. Her face, so familiar, so beloved, was unchanged. She seemed to be sleeping, the corners of her mouth upturned. Almost, a smile.

I touched her head, which was cool, moved back the sheet and saw that her limbs were straight, without spasm, perfect. Her body was warm, only her eyes were swollen, a mottled bruise marking her right cheek where the ventilator had been. Her tongue was pressed up against her top lip, as if she slept.

I couldn't believe she had gone.

My darling, my dear one, where are you now?

Sid was sitting on one of the chairs, his handkerchief over his eye; I could see his shoulders were heaving. I sank down in the other, and began to sob.

Time passed.

Someone knocked on the door, the registrar came in. 'Mr and Mrs Stern, I know Jewish funerals should take place within twenty-four hours. Would you like me to contact the registrar?'

'Thank you,' Sid said.

The doctor hesitated. 'I need to ask you something else.' He paused. 'We would like to move her. Two other children have died on the ward this week. It's harrowing for the nurses if we leave them here.'

We agreed.

I kissed her then, trying to drink her in with my eyes, knowing this would be the very last time.

And we left.

The deputy registrar kindly opened the office in Crewe, made out the death certificate, and we drove home.

Chapter 29

We stood very close together leaning against the radiator in the kitchen, needing the comfort of its warmth. We cried for a long time.

Chapter 30

None of us remember when we told the boys. Probably Phil brought them back, and I believe we told them quietly at home. They were very calm, very serious, but because she had lived away for seven years while they were growing up, I hoped it would not affect them too deeply. Michael had contacted Rachel and Abe, who despaired when they could not get an earlier flight. I telephoned my parents and sister.

That evening Doctor Alan Unterman, the new minister at Yeshurun Synagogue, came to see us. He was gentle, approachable. He told us that Phil had come to him early that morning, telling him how ill Vanessa was, and he'd made a special prayer for her in the synagogue. 'But I wondered if it was too late already.'

While we sat together on the sofa, exhausted, he told us what would happen – that Vanessa would be taken to the Jewish Hospital where *the tahara*, the ritual washing, would take place. It would be done by a group of women who anonymously undertook this work. Vanessa would be dressed in a simple white garment, and the funeral directors would bring her to Agecroft Cemetery as soon the time of burial had been verified.

'When will we know?' Sid asked.

'In the morning, I hope. I'm sorry I won't be there since I have a wedding. But Rabbi Rabinowitz will officiate. We'll arrange for evening prayers to be in your house.' Doctor Unterman turned to Sid. 'It's probably preferable if you come to synagogue in the morning but there will be enough men to make up a quorum at night. If you're happy about it, we'll have prayers here. It's a *mitzvah,* a good deed, for people to come to you. To the place where your daughter lived.'

Early Sunday morning, someone telephoned – the funeral would be at three o'clock that afternoon. Doctor Unterman came to do the *keria*, the tearing of the garment. We gave him my old cardigan, Sid's little-used jumper. He made a small cut on the left-hand side; we completed the tear with our fingers. It lay above our hearts. We wore this for the whole week of the Shivah.

Everything followed with its own momentum. There was nothing for us to do except to let our family and close friends know the time of the funeral. But many knew already. People had contacted others, and through the network, everyone in the community and further afield was alerted. It was our friend Ralph who went, with another member of the *Chevra Kaddishah*, to collect Vanessa. We wouldn't have known had he not told us. He said that when they covered her, and he lifted her up, he couldn't believe how light she was. They both wept as they drove her to the Jewish Hospital.

Three years before, my brother-in-law Michael had married Val, a lovely warm woman, a primary school teacher. She came to our house and covered the mirrors in the ritual way so that you shouldn't see yourself looking well and healthy at this time. She also brought a memorial candle which would burn for seven days in the room where the prayers took place. Then she stayed for the rest of the day with the boys.

Sid and I discussed whether to take Anthony and Richard to the funeral and decided against it. Something I would question later, but at the time, we felt we couldn't support their grief and perhaps their fear, because it was hard enough to contain our own.

It was time.

Just after two o'clock, Ros and Alan drove us to the cemetery in North Manchester, where already many cars had gathered. As we walked to the doors of the *ohel*, the small building representing the synagogue, the hearse with its blackened windows arrived.

I shuddered and thought I would faint.

My parents were standing with Barbara and David beside me. Barbara grasped me firmly, her arm around my shoulders. I took a shuddering breath. We watched as the men opened the rear of the hearse and lifted out the tiny beechwood coffin. It was pale, almost white. No decoration, nothing. We watched them place it on a low black trolley and push it into the centre of the *ohel*. People made way for us to go in.

It was a dingy, shadowy building without windows, empty but for a few chairs against the wall on the women's side. Sid and I separated, the women going to the left, where I walked to the front, while Sid went with Michael to the right, accompanied by the men.

Her coffin stood in the centre.

Still shaky but controlled, I stared at the box, pale in the darkness, and couldn't believe that my lovely Vanessa was inside it.

Mother stood close to me, her eyes full of sadness but she didn't weep. Barbara was sobbing now, a handkerchief pressed to her mouth. Thin black prayer books for the funeral service were handed out. Behind me, densely packed together and silent, were the young women we knew, together with older women from the community, many relations and friends. It was the same for the men who stood opposite us. When the doors were closed, many more waited outside. I watched Sid, anxious for him now. He was standing with his head bowed but I knew that even though his parents hadn't returned, his brother Michael would support him.

The service began.

Rabbi Rabinowitz stood facing us. Beside him was the *chazan*, the cantor, who had a beautiful tenor voice. He began the service. Reading the Hebrew prayers was beyond me. I kept glancing at the coffin. I couldn't understand that my darling, my dearest child was lying in that white box. At the end, the cantor sang: *El Maleh Rachamim, God full of mercy*, an ancient, haunting prayer for the dead whose melody always broke my heart.

With an effort I listened while the rabbi spoke; all that remains in my memory are his words, 'No one can explain why such a thing has happened to Sid and Susan, but we hope they will be comforted by our support.'

The doors opened; men carried the coffin along a stony path, stopping several times as we walked while the chazan chanted a psalm, the men following behind. I knew that women, even modern Orthodox women, didn't go to the graveside, remaining behind until it was over.

'I shall go,' I said fiercely to Barbara.

I walked to the grave and stood beside Sid. All the women followed. Again the cantor sang the prayer for the dead and I took a shuddering breath, pressing my closed hands against my breast. Sid and his brother, together with the men, began to fill the grave with earth. I stepped forward, knowing that I had to do this for my daughter and for myself – I had to know she had gone. I shovelled in a spade full of earth, and heard the dull thud as it fell on the coffin. Stepping away, I began to fall but my sister caught me and held me close.

Then Sid chanted the Kaddish, the mourner's prayer, tears choking his voice, and we returned to the dark of the *ohel*. Men and women made two lines and we walked between them. The first steps in our new life without her. Then we sat at one side while people came to say a few words, embrace us, clasp our hands, and wish us *long life*.

Everyone finally washed their hands in the ritual way before leaving the cemetery.

We were driven home.

Val had stayed with the children. She had prepared the special meal of hard-boiled eggs with round bagels, to represent the turning of the wheel of life. I was shocked to find I was actually hungry, but then I had hardly eaten all week.

From then on, from Sunday afternoon until Friday morning, we didn't leave the house while friends and neighbours came to see us, to support us. At night, they came for the prayers. Every day, our friend Ros, nine months pregnant, arrived at lunchtime with a large meal which she served us in the kitchen. On Monday evening, when Doctor Unterman came to lead the prayers, he handed me a book: *The Jewish Way of Death and Mourning*. 'You might find this helpful to read. It answers many questions people have at this time.'

I read it throughout the week, sometimes quoting things to Sid until I saw that all he wanted to do was to get through each day.

But then, that Monday night, the day after the funeral, something remarkable happened.

For two nights I had taken a small dose of Valium to help me sleep. On Monday night I decided to face my grief. The following day would have been Vanessa's fifteenth birthday. Sid was asleep and I lay on my side thinking about her and our life together since her birth. I turned onto my back, my eyes open, gazing out at the darkened room.

A hazy white column of light appeared before my eyes. I knew it was Vanessa.

I heard a voice saying, 'You looked after me, Mummy, now I shall look after you.'

She spoke to me so beautifully, and for the very first time.

The white light grew smaller, and faded into the darkness.

I heard myself sigh – a great sigh of relief and delight. I turned over and fell deeply asleep. The next morning, I hardly knew where I was.

But although this had been indescribable, profound, it didn't connect with how I continued to feel for the rest of the *Shivah* although I wondered about this, trying to understand why.

All week, when Doctor Unterman wasn't present, Ralph led the prayers. At eight o'clock, in the empty, newly-extended dining room with its bare floorboards, the men said the evening prayers and occasionally, I joined them. Traditionally, women stayed in another room but this was changing. As days passed, I would take a prayer book and standing at the back, I tried to decipher the words. Several women joined me.

There must have been forty to fifty people every night. We were rarely alone. So many people, so many foil containers of food, of cakes, of fish balls, that the freezer was bursting. We were ever surrounded by loving hearts. Most evenings my parents would be there, to be joined by Rachel and Abe on Wednesday. A man of restraint, my father-in-law was deeply upset when they came, his face suffused with emotion. 'I felt worse than when my parents died. All Sunday I walked backwards and forwards, beside myself.'

Later on Wednesday, Doctor Unterman came to tell the boys they could go back to school.

'We'll stay with Mum and Dad,' they said in unison.

Their expression of loyalty lightened my heart and I smiled. So they stayed, quietly, coming to listen when people visited in the afternoon, watching, observing. In sweaters and jeans, on their heads the blue and gold kippot they wore for school. At night, standing beside Sid, they would join the men saying the prayers and someone would point out the place in the prayer book. I watched them with absolute sadness.

There were days when I cried, sometimes talking to other women, often when a man conveyed such sympathy in his eyes – someone I hardly knew – and I would find myself sobbing. Then Paula or Debbie would come and put their arms around me, drawing me back into the room, telling me not to cry.

I remember saying, 'But I have to. I need to.'

It wasn't all sadness – that wasn't the point. People could talk about Vanessa or they could talk about something to lighten the atmosphere. Whatever helped. One afternoon, one of the women made me laugh, telling me about the intricate arrangements for her daughter's Batmitzvah along with several other girls. The arguments and resistances. Another afternoon, I broke down when someone said, 'She's dancing with all the children in heaven.'

On Thursday evening, I opened the front door to find Pauline Lunt and Vanessa's head teacher outside, and I told them how delighted I was they had come. Pauline said she had visited Vanessa in hospital after I left, the previous Wednesday, and again, Vanessa had made a lip as though to say she didn't like being there. I held back my tears when she told me this, knowing how Vanessa loved her, how dedicated and caring were all the staff in Woodland School.

But the week of prayers was informal, comfortable – men would arrive in their clothes straight from work, women in skirts or trousers. Before they left, everyone would take our hands and wish us long life.

On Friday Doctor Unterman came to tell us we could get up, that is, getting up from 'sitting Shivah.'

'Did you find the book helpful, Susan?'

'I did. I began to understand some of the spiritual purpose behind the ritual.'

'The Shivah week demonstrates that you can live through one week after your loss. That's what it's for, or at least one part of it.' He smiled. 'See you in *shul* tomorrow.'

Going to the synagogue next morning wasn't an ordeal, as I had expected. When people came up after the service saying, 'I wish you long life,' I could smile and thank them.

On Monday we went back to normal, to work and to school.

During break, in the staff room, when someone made a joke, I laughed. One of the teachers looked at me in surprise. 'Susan, how on earth can you laugh?'

People raised their heads, a little awkward, as I looked round at them. 'I've been carried,' I said to them, 'the Shivah has burnt it out of me.' I wasn't sure what I meant by that, but at lunchtime, talking to a member of staff whose husband was a Church of England minister, I explained about the Shivah, where I was surrounded by love, carried through the days, which meant that I could start this week lighter, untrammelled by the grief. She said what a wonderful practice this was; she couldn't understand how the Church had abandoned it. 'People don't know what to do,' she continued. 'If they see someone who's suffered bereavement, they cross to the other side of the road. They don't know what to say.'

I had to recognise that not everyone felt the same, very private people often found it an ordeal. I knew Sid was happy to get back to work.

Later came the letters, innumerable letters from people who might have felt more distant but still wanted to send condolences – from Sharon Gould, the TV researcher, saying I mustn't feel guilty about anything I believed I should have done, a common reaction she had experienced after losing someone; from David Elstein sharing that now he had a child he was beginning to understand what a parent could feel.

And then a wonderful letter from Hetty, my ultra orthodox friend who had taken me to the Mikveh in 1970, twelve years before. Her letter was luminous – she wrote, *Vanessa has completed her task.* An allusion to *gilgul*, the turning wheel, the transmigration of souls. It thrilled me to believe that Vanessa had done something so significant for herself.

But grief did not entirely fly away during the seven days of Shivah.

In my diary of 1982, on the fourteenth of April, I wrote simply, *I weep for her.* I wrote this many times over the months. Once, a few weeks after we'd lost her, I wrote with horror that I imagined her little face putrefying, her body becoming a skeleton, and vowed never to think that again. I added: *I don't believe she's there. She must be somewhere else. She must be.*

Once I dreamt that I was at Hazel Villa, feeding her with scrambled eggs, I telephoned my mother to tell her – in the dream – and my mother said, 'That's impossible, Sue. We've buried her.'

One morning at the end of April, three months later, it was very still, very early, with birdsong, I heard a voice, clear and cheerful: 'Vanessa is with God.' It made me feel better, I could accept this.

So many times, I wrote that I couldn't believe I would never again hold her in my arms. Never see her dear beautiful face, those amazing blue eyes, her tiny perfect nose, her all-embracing smile.

These thoughts continued for six months until June, when I became harshly aware that I wasn't with her when she died. It broke my heart. Wracked with guilt, I felt that I had abandoned her. Debbie Freeman was with me, and with her to give me courage, I telephoned Leighton General Hospital, and asked to speak to the ward. Barely able to speak, I asked the sister what had actually happened on that day. She told me Vanessa had fallen into a coma around three o'clock in the morning, very peacefully, without suffering.

It was enough.

And those two visions I had of Vanessa? Perhaps Doctor Unterman could enlighten me. I made an appointment to see him in his house near the synagogue. We sat in his tiny office crowded with laden bookshelves, papers, his desk, and while he filled his pipe, tamping it down and lit it, I ventured to ask about my visions. What did he think? Was there something wrong with me?

Seemingly unconcerned that I had broken Shabbat Shuvah, that most significant Shabbat in October, he said, 'You wouldn't believe how many people have such experiences but never share them with anyone. Fearing, like you, they'd be considered a little weird. Not at all, it's very common.'

'How do they happen?'

'Often when someone is extremely worried.'

'I was conflicted,' I admitted. 'I knew it was such a holy day, while wanting so much to go to the interview.'

'You might have asked them to make it another day,' he suggested. 'But in any case, Vanessa wanted to tell you something.'

'Yes, and deep down, I knew, but during her last week, I had completely forgotten the vision. Her death, when it happened, was a great shock. I even told a friend that I hadn't realised... which is even more of a mystery.' I paused, and a thought flashed through my mind: 'Is it because what you learn in your spirit or psyche isn't present to your conscious mind? Different ways of perceiving, of receiving things?'

'I believe so.'

I continued to grieve for Vanessa but it became easier, although when Pauline Lunt telephoned in July to see if I would become the first parent governor of Woodlands School, I couldn't do it. I wasn't ready to go there even though I felt it was a great honour to be chosen. That same month, it was time to decide about the 'stone setting' choosing the stone and the day we planned to erect it. We knew many people waited a year before setting the stone. 'Because the soul has a journey of ascent until it's bound to the bond of eternity,' Doctor Unterman had said. 'Traditionally believed to take a year, although most wait eleven months, others place the stone whenever it's suitable for the family.'

'We thought the twenty-third of October, before the winter comes. Would you be free that day, Doctor Unterman?'

He checked his diary and told me it would be fine.

Then he explained what should be written on the stone – there should be a sentiment in English, another in Hebrew. Vanessa's Hebrew names were Devorah Esther, the names of strong and beautiful women. Devorah the wise woman, the leader, her story written before the writers of the Scriptures were forced to focus on men alone. And beautiful Esther, the young girl who had saved the Jewish people many generations later, in Persia. This gladdened my heart.

Sid and I talked over what we wanted to say about Vanessa in the English inscription. It was harder to find something in Hebrew, but after reading the book of Esther, I glowed with certainty. Here was a wonderful description of Esther and of our daughter completely. I visited the stonemason, not a pleasant man, and gave him what Doctor Unterman had outlined.

Nine months after the funeral we returned for the first time to Agecroft Cemetery. There was such a different feeling as we gathered in the ohel. There were fewer people but a crowd all the same.

Addressing us, Doctor Unterman said, 'This is not supposed to be a sad occasion. Rather, a kind of completion.'

There was a short service when the chazan sang psalms, and *El Moleh Rachamim*, the heart-breaking prayer for the dead and I felt my eyes well up and my heart begin to race. Leaving the *ohel,* we walked together to the grave. There was no problem with women being present at a stone-setting. Someone had already come to visit her, leaving the traditional tiny stones around the grave, an ancient custom going back to the beginning of time. The white sheet covering the headstone was lifted, people stepped back to allow us to read it first. We gazed, hardly recognising the words we'd planned so carefully as we sat at the kitchen table three months before.

I barely registered the Star of David carved at the top, my eyes travelling down to the words in Hebrew:

The child Devorah Esther, who died on Shabbat, 6 Shevat.

Then there were single Hebrew letters which stood for: *Here is buried… May her soul be bound up in the bond of eternal life.*

The English we'd chosen: *In loving memory of Debra Vanessa Stern, who died on 30 January, 1982, aged 14 years.*

Sadly missed by her devoted parents, brothers, grandparents, aunts, uncles, teachers and friends.

And then my words: *Handicapped but she spoke with her eyes, and her smile was all-embracing.*

Pulling my handkerchief from my bag, I pressed it to my eyes. Even though I had devised this, worked it out and rearranged the words to get everything in the space, still my heart groaned.

I spelt out the Hebrew words: *And Esther obtained grace in the sight of all those that looked upon her. Esther 2. 15*

She did, I thought to myself with a deep breath. Our beautiful girl with the all-embracing smile and the shining blue eyes, she did find grace in everyone's sight.

The End

Acknowledgements

The thing about a memoir is that there are so many people to thank, those who helped us live through the experience, as well as those who helped me write it.

I will never be able to fully express my love and appreciation for my husband Sid, whose devotion to Vanessa, clear-sighted, unflappable approach to problems, and a certain sense of humour (which I didn't, and often still don't get...) carried us through many difficult times.

When they were small, our sons Anthony and Richard constantly demonstrated their acceptance and love of their sister: Richard would ask me to bring her home from Cranage while Anthony found ways to entertain her and make her laugh when she was here. Anthony and his wife, Jane, now have a beautiful little daughter, whom they have chosen to call Maia Vanessa – such a great tribute.

Very sadly, our daughter's grandparents, Efra and Hymie Merrill and Rachel and Abe Stern, are no longer with us. We owe them a great debt of gratitude for all they did for her and for us. My mother Efra deserves special thanks for the weeks and days she looked after Vanessa in her home, telling her stories and singing songs. Our parents were ever generous with emotional and physical support, as were my sister Barbara and her husband

David Gordon, together with Sid's brother Michael and his wife Val Stern.

And then to our friends: Phil and Paula Gabbie, who played a significant part in Vanessa's life; to Jessica who helped me at the darkest times, I owe enduring thanks for her wisdom and humour; Judith Stone for the welcoming flowers, Brenda Freedland, who said that Vanessa had 'a light behind her'; Debbie and Jeff Freeman, Ralph and Tina Barnett, Ros and Alan Burland; to my life-long friend Gwen Venor whose phone calls enveloped me in loving-kindness, Michèle Viau and her family, Marie-France Boizou, and the many others who remember our daughter and her all-embracing smile. Thank you.

My deepest thanks to Doctor Epstein and Miss Burgess at the Duchess of York Children's hospital; to nursing assistants, physiotherapists and teachers at Rodney House, Pictor House and Woodlands School – especially Pauline Lunt – and those generous souls who cared for the severely disabled children at Cranage Hospital. The wonderful Doctor Warrell, whose team saved me during the hot summer of 1973, rightly has a special unit named after him at St Mary's Hospital, Manchester. And finally, my gratitude to our lovely au pair girls who became our friends: Anne, Beatrice, Elizabeth, Connie, and Anneliese.

When, in 2013, Cath Staincliffe invited me to rejoin the Manchester Novel Writers Group, I felt hugely honoured. Cath, Mary Sharratt, Anjum Malik and Olivia Piekarski, experienced novelists and writers for television, gave me rich, insightful feedback over the year and nine months it took to write the first draft. Their gentle critiques on the page, and at the sweet scented Buddhist Centre, our meeting place, were invaluable to me; I learned so much from being with them.

Acknowledgements

Sincere thanks to my writer friends, Deborah Freeman, Marnie Riches and Sophie Claire for reading early drafts, sharing ideas for TV dramas/novel series/setting up writing workshops together and for pulling me out of the slough of despond when it all became too much! As always, Martin de Mello and Peter Kalu at Commonword offered encouragement and wise counsel.

I am grateful to Russell Phillips who was quick to respond to phone and email queries, and proofread the final draft of this memoir with uttermost care and precision. www.authorhelp.uk/

Short bibliography

ANON. *The Plurality of Lives.* Germany 1958

FINNIE, N R. *Handling the Young Cerebral Palsied Child at Home.* SBN 43310380 9 London: Heinemann Medical Books 1968

SPOCK, BENJAMIN. *Baby and Childcare.* ISBN 0-370-00 271-7 London: Bodley Head, 1968

Both books continue to be sold extensively, revised and updated to include the latest developments in child care and the care of children with cerebral palsy.

About the author

Sue studied modern languages at the universities of Leeds, the Sorbonne and Aix-Marseille and taught French and English as a Foreign Language. In 1984, feeling she had not 'completed her task,' she worked with a voluntary organisation, supporting people with learning disabilities and mental health issues. In 1991, returning to Manchester University to study comparative religion, she also taught courses in the Extra-Mural Department on the life and lifestyle of Jewish women.

She has always written – diaries, stories, plays in French for the children she taught. In the nineties, she discovered Commonword, the wonderful Manchester writing agency, and began to write seriously. She has an MA in writing the adult novel/children's fiction, 2006 (MMU). Deeply affected by her radical upbringing – grandparents, Russian Jewish anarchists, parents, committed socialists and sometime fellow travellers – Sue often explores themes of alienation in her work, drawn to writing about people who are 'different.'

Babyday, a novel for adults, is the 'silent twin' of this memoir. It is the story of a woman who 'has' seven babies on her fiftieth birthday. Who they are and why they have come to her is what she must discover. Shortlisted in the first *Myslexia* novel competition, 2012, it will be published in 2019.

Rafi Brown and the Candy Floss Kid, a middle-grade novel about a dyslexic boy who is a brilliant cartoonist and his friend, a child carer, who bunk off school, was highly commended in the Frances Lincoln Diversity competition. (2010). Sue published this in 2013, and was thrilled when the Royal National Institute of the Blind produced a large print version for their children's library.

Inspired by the life of Sophia, her Russian anarchist grandmother, *How I Broke Mama's Commandments*, is the story of a girl who falls in love with an anarchist while crossing the Baltic Ocean from Petersburg to London. Its first chapter appeared in *Migration Stories*; (Crocus).

One of her poems was shortlisted for the Bridport Prize, then published in Poetry from the Cheshire Prize for Literature 2016; A Woman in Black, about meeting a woman wearing a nikab while walking to Cheadle, came second in the Yorkshire Evening Post's peace poetry competition, and highly commended in Lilith Magazine's international poetry competition, in New York. Other poems have appeared in Stand Magazine, The Jewish Quarterly, Jewish Renaissance; The Best of Manchester Poets, 2013, 2014, and many others.

A collection of her poems: *Too High for Pigeons and Other Poems,* will be published in spring, 2019

www.suestern-writer.co.uk